Leading and Managing Early Childhood Settings

Inspiring people, places and practices

Leading and Managing Early Childhood Settings: Inspiring people, places and practices examines what it means to be a leader, manager and administrator across the early childhood education field.

The first section of the book introduces readers to a number of core concepts, including self-understanding through professional reflection and consideration of people's beliefs and values. These chapters explore the challenges of working within various early childhood settings and the importance of connecting and communicating with families and the broader community. The second section considers four key roles that early childhood professionals often undertake – team stakeholder, policy designer, pedagogy creator and rights advocate.

This book challenges readers to make links across research, theories and everyday practices by thinking, reflecting, sharing with others and writing stories. The storytelling approach guides readers through the chapters and explores the themes of embodiment and sustainability. Written in an engaging and dynamic style, *Leading and Managing Early Childhood Settings* is an invaluable resource for pre- and in-service educators alike.

Additional resources for instructors are available online at www.cambridge.edu.au/leadingandmanaging.

Nadine Louise McCrea is Associate Professor of Early Childhood Teacher Education in the School of Education at the University of New England, Armidale, New South Wales.

Leading and Managing Early Childhood Settings

Inspiring people, places and practices

Nadine Louise McCrea

CAMBRIDGE UNIVERSITY PRESS

CAMBRIDGE
UNIVERSITY PRESS

University Printing House, Cambridge CB2 8BS, United Kingdom

One Liberty Plaza, 20th Floor, New York, NY 10006, USA

477 Williamstown Road, Port Melbourne, VIC 3207, Australia

314–321, 3rd Floor, Plot 3, Splendor Forum, Jasola District Centre, New Delhi – 110025, India

79 Anson Road, #06–04/06, Singapore 079906

Cambridge University Press is part of the University of Cambridge.

It furthers the University's mission by disseminating knowledge in the pursuit of education, learning and research at the highest international levels of excellence.

www.cambridge.org
Information on this title: www.cambridge.org/9781107669185

© Cambridge University Press 2015

This publication is copyright. Subject to statutory exception and to the provisions of relevant collective licensing agreements, no reproduction of any part may take place without the written permission of Cambridge University Press.

First published 2015 (version 3, May 2018)

Cover designed by Tanya de Silva-McKay
Typeset by Integra Software Services Pvt. Ltd
Printed in Australia by Ligare Pty Ltd, April 2018

A catalogue record for this publication is available from the British Library

A Cataloguing-in-Publication entry is available from the catalogue of the National Library of Australia at www.nla.gov.au

ISBN 978-1-107-66918-5 Paperback

Additional resources for this publication at www.cambridge.edu.au/academic/leadingandmanaging

Reproduction and communication for educational purposes
The Australian *Copyright Act 1968* (the Act) allows a maximum of one chapter or 10% of the pages of this work, whichever is the greater, to be reproduced and/or communicated by any educational institution for its educational purposes provided that the educational institution (or the body that administers it) has given a remuneration notice to Copyright Agency Limited (CAL) under the Act.

For details of the CAL licence for educational institutions contact:

Copyright Agency Limited
Level 15, 233 Castlereagh Street
Sydney NSW 2000
Telephone: (02) 9394 7600
Facsimile: (02) 9394 7601
E-mail: info@copyright.com.au

Cambridge University Press has no responsibility for the persistence or accuracy of URLs for external or third-party internet websites referred to in this publication and does not guarantee that any content on such websites is, or will remain, accurate or appropriate.

Please be aware that this publication may contain several variations of Aboriginal and Torres Strait Islander terms and spellings; no disrespect is intended. Please note that the terms 'Indigenous Australians' and 'Aboriginal and Torres Strait Islander peoples' may be used interchangeably in this publication.

Image sources: Compass icon © shutterstock.com/Filip Dokladal; journal icon © shutterstock.com/lineartestpilot. **Text permission:** Gandhi quote on p. 146 from GANDHI ON NON-VIOLENCE by Thomas Merton, copyright © 1964, 1965 by New Directions Publishing Corp. Reprinted by permission of New Directions Publishing Corp.

To Doug and Mister

Foreword

Like the author I am approaching retirement, so I have also been reflecting deeply on my own professional journey and how the field of early childhood education has changed since I landed my first teaching position in 1968. In my teaching and writing, I use the overarching term 'early childhood administrator' to describe both the leadership and management functions of directors of center-based programs. I was delighted to see how Nadine has embraced the unifying role descriptor *leader-manager* throughout this book. In my thinking, *leadership* functions relate to the broad view of helping an organization clarify and affirm values, set goals, articulate a vision, and chart a course of action to achieve that vision. *Management* functions relate to the actual orchestration of tasks and the setting up of systems to carry out the organizational mission (Bloom, 2014; Talan & Bloom 2011). In the day-to-day world of early childhood administrators, leadership and management functions are really two sides of the same coin.

How appropriate then that this book begins with an opportunity for the reader to dive deep into an exploration of core values and to gain an understanding of how background and dispositions impact one's effectiveness as a leader-manager. The capacity to reflect and engage in candid introspection is at the heart of achieving self-awareness. Having a better understanding of oneself is the first step to having a better relationship with others, because self-awareness provides a window to expand our understanding about other points of view and perspectives. The goal of this kind of reflection is not merely to see who we are and better understand ourselves today, but to envision what we might become tomorrow (Bloom, 2007). As one who is stepping down the ladder and nearing retirement, I can attest that it is a lifelong process – a journey of self-discovery, meaning making, and identity shaping.

Reviewing this book was also a gift because I have always been intrigued by the cross-cultural nuances of early childhood program administration. Despite contextual differences in licensing and regulations, the actual job of leading-managing a program in Australia, New Zealand, the United Kingdom and the United States is remarkably similar. The leader-manager's role is multifaceted and complex. They are the gatekeepers to quality. Teachers may impact children's experiences directly, but leader-managers impact children's developmental outcomes by structuring the conditions that support teacher effectiveness. There is no getting around it – virtually everything leader-managers do directly or indirectly

Foreword

influences the reputation and success of a program (Bloom, Hentschel & Bella, 2013). My guess is if you are the leader-manager of an early childhood program you'll identify with these different aspects of your role:

- As **pedagogical leader** you ask the deep philosophical questions that get to the heart of your center's mission. What is the purpose of education? What traits do you want children to have as a result of their experiences in your program?

- As **vision builder** you work with staff to translate your center's core values into a clear roadmap for reflective and ethical practice. Creating a vision is really about shaping expectations, both individual and collective.

- As **talent developer** you make sure everyone has the time and resources for, and access to, professional development opportunities.

- As **data manager** you collect and organize information for accountability. More than ever before, programs need to document the outcomes of their work to funders, regulators, parents, and community partners.

- As **knowledge broker** you structure opportunities for people to share their experience and expertise with one another. This means being intentional about providing the time and the emotional climate that encourage teachers to become active partners in each other's learning.

- As **systems engineer** you implement the policies and procedures needed for continuous quality improvement. Keeping track of scheduled meetings, assessment data, professional development opportunities, and resources to support learning requires big-picture thinking and well-thought-out systems to ensure smooth operations.

- As **idea igniter** you stimulate and encourage teachers to look at their classroom and organizational practices in new and creative ways. By regularly asking 'What if...' and creating the spaces and places for ideas to flourish, you can rev up your center's creativity quotient.

- As **cheerleader** you work to maintain a positive energy that encourages efforts and celebrates accomplishments.

- As **change agent** you monitor carefully how much 'new stuff' people can absorb at any one time. This means being mindful of workload and the changes in relationships people experience as new ideas are implemented.

Foreword

- As **CEO (Chief Example to Others)** you serve as an inspiring role model of lifelong learning and professional renewal. This means willingly acknowledging areas of your own practice that need to be strengthened, actively participating in your own professional development, and eagerly sharing what you have learned with others.

I am confident that the Travel Guide template provided in this book will help you to achieve a deeper understanding of the importance of your leader-manager role and your unique gifts which can make that role a vibrant force for achieving program excellence.

Paula Jorde Bloom, PhD,
the Michael W. Louis Endowed Chair
McCormick Center for Early Childhood Leadership
National Louis University
Wheeling, Illinois, USA

Contents

Foreword by Paula Jorde Bloom		*page* vii
About the author and contributors		xiii
Acknowledgements		xv
INTRODUCTION		1
Opening ideas		2
Taking a journey		3
Closing ideas		6
Part 1	**THINKING ABOUT PEOPLE AND PLACES**	7
CHAPTER 1	**UNDERSTANDING SELF**	9
	Broad concepts	9
	Step 1: Is 'knowing oneself' relevant?	10
	Step 2: Who am I personally?	11
	Step 3: Who am I professionally?	17
	Step 4: What is leading with managing?	24
	Conclusion	28
CHAPTER 2	**EXPLORING COMMUNICATION**	30
	Broad concepts	30
	Step 1: Why is communicating with others essential?	31
	Step 2: How and why are our words so powerful?	34
	Step 3: What does professional communication encompass?	41
	Conclusion	54
CHAPTER 3	**CONTEMPLATING WORKPLACES**	56
	Broad concepts	56
	Step 1: How diverse are early childhood settings?	57
	Step 2: What are some beyond-the-fence contexts surrounding early childhood settings?	68
	Step 3: What constitutes an organisation?	75
	Conclusion	79

Contents

Part 2	**THINKING ABOUT PRACTICES AS ROLES**	81
CHAPTER 4	A PROFESSIONAL ROLE – A TEAM STAKEHOLDER	83
	Broad concepts	83
	Step 1: What are the leading and managing facets of a team stakeholder role?	84
	Step 2: Which staffing responsibilities are key?	92
	Step 3: Where do rights and rules fit into staff sharing and workplace give-and-take?	97
	Conclusion	100
CHAPTER 5	A PROFESSIONAL ROLE – A POLICY DESIGNER	102
	Broad concepts	102
	Step 1: What are the leading and managing facets of a policy designer role?	103
	Step 2: What policies are needed and why?	108
	Step 3: How are policies created and cared for?	115
	Conclusion	117
CHAPTER 6	A PROFESSIONAL ROLE – A PEDAGOGY CREATOR	120
	Broad concepts	120
	Step 1: What are the leading and managing facets of a pedagogy creator role?	121
	Step 2: Which responsibilities help frame children's learning?	134
	Step 3: Who is involved in children's learning?	140
	Conclusion	144
CHAPTER 7	A PROFESSIONAL ROLE – A RIGHTS ADVOCATE	146
	Broad concepts	146
	Step 1: What are the leading and managing facets of a rights advocate role?	147
	Step 2: Which responsibilities link with professional vision and moral higher ground?	152
	Conclusion	161
References		163
Index		189

About the author and contributors

The author

Nadine Louise McCrea has worked within the early childhood education field for many years. ECE leadership and management and children's food learning are her focal interests. Nadine is Associate Professor of Early Childhood Teacher Education at the University of New England, Armidale, New South Wales, Australia.

The contributors

Diane Nailon has spent more than 25 years in universities teaching, researching and delivering workshops in early childhood leadership and management. In her work as a consultant to early childhood organisations she focuses on strategic and educational leadership, team building, performance management, coaching and mentoring, and leading in times of change. Di and Nadine worked together in Queensland.

(See 'Dear Nadine' letters)

Jan Carr has worked in the Australian early childhood education field for a number of years. She is a director of a preschool in the rural, regional town of Inverell, NSW. In 2014, the preschool was awarded a National Quality Standard rating of 'Excellent'. Aspects of Jan's childhood and professional life appear in each chapter.

(See 'Feature professional reflection: Jan's story')

Lavinia Tausere-Tiko is a PhD candidate and part-time lecturer at the University of New England. At the time of writing this book, she was on special study leave from an ECE lecturing role at the University of the South Pacific, Suva, Fiji.

(See 'Professional reflection: Lavinia's story' in Chapters 5, 6 and 7)

Lisa Sonter has recently completed her PhD studies at the University of New England. Lisa teaches kindergarten children at Mitchelton Pre-Schooling Centre in Brisbane and is co-partner of Consultants at Play, a play-based-curriculum consultancy. (And thanks to *Alice Sonter*, Lisa's daughter, for the 'blue figure-8 knot' in the photograph in Chapter 2.)

(See 'Professional reflection: Lisa's story' in Chapters 2 and 6)

Leo Prendergast is a Director-teacher who has worked in community-based children's services since 1980. He lives on the north coast of NSW and is an active participant in the broader Early Childhood Education sector and profession.

(See 'Professional reflection: Leo's story' in Chapter 4)

About the author and contributors

Dianne O'Malley is a longstanding early childhood educator. Her early childhood career began as a volunteer in a rural remote preschool, where her eldest child was enrolled. Dianne has worked in numerous roles and diverse communities. She has continually upgraded her qualifications, including a BEd(EC) from the University of New England.

(See 'Professional reflection: Dianne's story' in Chapter 7)

Ivan Thornton is the Graphic Designer within the University of New England's Learning Innovations Hub. He has a diverse role. He willingly created two figures for this book, working from rough scratching on bits of paper!

(See Introduction, Figure 0.1, and Chapter 1, Figure 1.1)

Acknowledgements

There are many people to acknowledge as a writing project like this reaches the final stages. Thus, I want to offer my thanks to the following people who have supported and guided my author's journey.

Doug Hume has been a 'rock' and shared my personal and professional life for about 40 years. Our background informed my undertaking this task. Doug encouraged me to write the book from the beginning and later read drafts and cross-checked all the references. Thank you, Love. Thanks also to Isabella Mead at Cambridge University Press, for her guidance, editing and patience.

Several other people have been directly involved in the creation of this book and each one appears as a contributor on the two previous pages. My deep thanks to Diane Nailon and Jan Carr, who wrote passionately for each of the seven chapters. A big thank you to the cameo writers for their professional stories: Lavinia, Lisa, Leo and Dianne. Thanks also to Ivan Thornton for preparing Figures 0.1 and 1.1. Finally, a special expression of gratitude to Paula Jorde Bloom for agreeing to write the foreword, which is a challenging and time consuming task. All these contributors helped create inspiring ECE stories and ideas about people, places and practices, for which I am grateful.

Nadine Louise McCrea
University of New England, Armidale,
New South Wales, Australia

Introduction

There are many things we can trust people to do, but speaking the truth is one of the most important. Think of all the things you know about the world around you, about the past, about distant lands, and about how other people feel and think. Now think about how much of that knowledge depends on trusting what other people have told you ...

Katherine Hawley (2012, p. 7)

Introduction

Opening ideas

This book is about *people*. It focuses on being a leader, manager and administrator within a diverse range of early childhood settings. It will also touch on being a member of a management committee or board of directors and similar positions. Additionally, this book is about the *places* where early childhood education professionals do their work, and the professional *practices* (or roles and responsibilities) in those settings. These roles encompass interactions, everyday tasks and advocacy. In this book, the notion of leader can represent positional roles (an established or ongoing job) as well as situational or distributed roles (an intermittent or changeable job). Leadership is firmly linked with management, which is why you will encounter the double-word terms *leader-manager* and *leading-managing* throughout this book.

The fundamental philosophy underpinning this book is that you should be encouraged to be actively engaged with making connections between the contents and your own lived experiences, rather than being a passive or distant reader of the pages. This approach is about starting from where you are now and actively developing yourself from there. A key aim is to help you flourish as a thinker so that you become a more capable leader-manager of early childhood settings. Figure 0.1

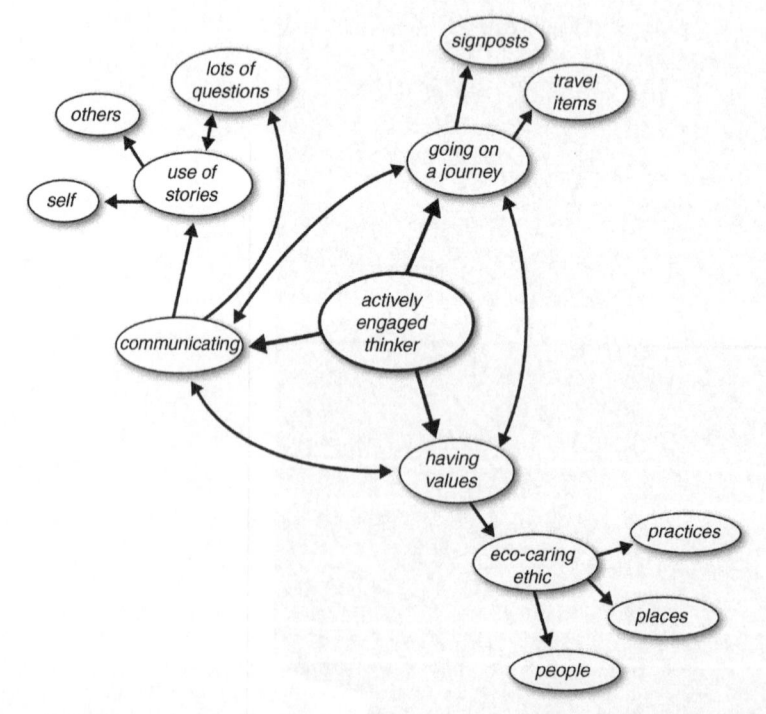

Figure 0.1 *Philosophical positioning of readers with key ideas that underpin this book*

Introduction

represents the essence of being such a thinker. This aim also means that big ideas and issues are paramount for authentic leading-managing. While everyday 'bits and pieces' and ordinary 'how to' practices are essential, they are not sufficient for creating a holistic and ethical framework for early childhood settings or leading-managing them. As such, a number of 'Steps' frame your engagement with this book. These are noted early in each chapter as a list of questions. Pedagogical features, or signposts, support these steps; they include:

- Lots of questions for you to think about and write about
- Various inspiring stories for you to contemplate and relate to
- An overarching ethic of eco-care for you to reflect on and aspire to
- Recurring engagement tasks that support your self-study
- Professional challenges to guide your story documentation of personal–professional thoughts, feelings, inspirations, aspirations and forward plans
- The metaphor of you being a traveller on a journey stepping along a particular professional path.

Taking a journey

Engaging with this book is like taking a leader's journey, and this introduction serves as a map that broadly charts your way. Your starting point and various destinations along the way can be checked against this map. Leading-managing ideas might represent a traveller's nourishment or sustenance, with these broadly grouped as *people*, *places* and *practices*. Taking this whole leading-managing journey involves readers in moving conceptually back and forth from *people* (self and others) to *places* (early childhood settings and beyond) and to relational *practices* (roles and responsibilities). When making professional choices and decisions about each of these contributors to leading-managing, it will be necessary for you to move beyond today and also consider the future. Our thinking and decision-making now, may have either joyful or regrettable influences (Arnold, 2005, pp. 121–2) on our lives tomorrow. This idea is implied in Robert Frost's (1920) poem 'The Road Not Taken'. For these travels, a few provisions can help set the scene for your explorations and interactions. As this professional journey unfolds, you decide when and where to re-visit and re-explore the travel guide below. Overall, this literary and metaphorical engagement of travellers who are going on a leader-manager journey encompasses two key travel items or provisions:

- A professional path with signposts
- A travel guide.

Introduction

A quick Travel Guide for a leader's journey

These icons support travellers on a journey along a professional path for leading-managing various early childhood settings. The 'journal' appears most often in the margins of chapters to highlight links between the text and your thinking and writing. The 'compass' as a guiding concept and tool also appears in places.

The compass represents one's 'ethic of eco-caring'. Consulting and watching the needle will help you to check your position and stay on track. It helps guide a traveller's philosophical orientation or direction. In this book, this broad ethic encompasses two main orientations: embodiment and sustainability. Embodiment encompasses people's bodies, attributes and other human features, with gender being a key consideration. Embracing sustainability means taking a holistic view of every aspect of the Earth and also committing to act in eco-responsible ways. Both embodiment and sustainability appear across the following chapters; they are also considered fully in an e-resource included in the companion website (available at: www.cambridge.edu.au/academic/leadingandmanaging). The compass can guide decisions about 'near and far' influences – people, places and practices. It can help readers to clarify and enlarge near ideas as they encounter them, with 'near ideas' usually representing micro and meso layers of society. The compass can signify the self and considering issues which are more personal or close to home; yet, it may also signify others beyond self and the act of looking outwards. Big ideas and the 'big picture' are usually represented in the exo and macro layers of society. Whole settings and beyond-the-fence people and places are encompassed within such bigger views. Another aspect of 'looking beyond' means looking beyond people to the more-than-human aspects of the world (Martusewicz, Edmundson & Khan, 2012, p. 54).

A professional journal provides the space for you as traveller to record and document your leader-manager's journey along the way. This is also a space for noting the passage of time, which relates to Bronfenbrenner's (2005) chronosystem. Your considerations and reflections are written here, as well as your musings and self-questions for later consideration. Let's call this: 'My professional leading-managing journal'. It is where you think about various questions and the chapter Steps, as well as personally extend the stories and storytelling throughout the book to your current perspective and background. We will discuss storytelling and story writing further, both below and in Chapter 2.

Telling stories

Autobiographical storytelling and professional communicating further support your leader-manager journey, as early childhood education leaders revisit and reflect on their own professional paths and career journeys. Across the chapters, these people reflect on and share their life influences and their professional journeys. These stories will prompt you as reader to share your own stories as you regularly stop along the professional path to write or draw in your journal. You are also encouraged to record your stories with a broader awareness of world ecology (Kaza, 2008; Wielkiewicz & Stelzner, 2005). For example, Lindholdt (1999) encouraged university students to go

Introduction

outdoors for 'writing from a sense of place'. Such communications, interactions and storytelling are explored further in Chapter 2.

Walking a pathway

The professional path laid out here chapter by chapter is dotted with leading-managing 'Steps', presented as questions. The Steps relate to leading-managing early childhood settings in terms of *people*, *places* and *practices*. People and settings are the focus of Part 1: 'Thinking about people and places', while the meanings of professionals' everyday interactions and their work responsibilities are the focus of Part 2: 'Thinking about practices as roles'. The ideas within this collection of chapters challenge you to be a clear thinker (revisit Figure 0.1).

With an *eco-caring compass* in hand, one's walking pace may vary during the journey from slow, which allows for serious sightseeing and interactive engagement, to more quickly when small or limited views of scenes are snatched. These 'quick' scenes may be returned to for more in-depth consideration at other times. However, for deeper thinking and fuller engagement, I recommend strolling, ambling and sauntering. To prepare for this journey, you need a planned but flexible approach. So, let's get ready to walk along a professional path filled with leading and managing concepts about early childhood settings and related professional issues. To assist your leader-manager's journey, a number of signposts are placed alongside this path.

Encountering signposts

To support your journey, particular learning or pedagogical features have been created. These features are called 'signposts' and they guide your thinking, engaging and understanding. The signposts that appear in each chapter are explained and described here.

Chapter inspirational quotes

Quotes appear below the title of each chapter. They are samples of fine writing by various authors that are relevant to aspects of early childhood education leadership and management. Sometimes additional quotes are provided within chapters as new Steps begin. Each quote is presented to further spark your engagement as a traveller who is actively thinking about yourself, others and the surrounding Earth. This thinking ought to involve purposely using your eco-caring compass.

Broad concepts

This feature represents a brief overview of each chapter, with an introduction and a few key concepts in question format. These questions form 'Steps' along the whole professional path. Using questions encourages your thinking about various possibilities or perspectives. In each overview, you are initially asked to engage with the questions and identify your current position and aims.

Introduction

Pause and reflect
These signposts encourage you as reader to stop during your journey and 'think about' ideas and issues. You are encouraged to think by exploring, investigating, interrogating, reflecting and much more. At times you are encouraged to share your findings and impressions. There will be challenging opportunities to consider issues such as plans for actions and being an advocate. When you reach this signpost, it will be a time and place for you to pause, pull out *My professional leading-managing journal* and do lots of thinking before documenting key thoughts and reflections which may relate to professional inspirations and aspirations.

Feature professional reflection: Jan's story
In each chapter, a reflection about Jan Carr's professional lived experiences links with the broad concepts. Her stories appear with provocations for you to think about, reflect on in comparison with your own work life, and then write about.

Professional reflection: XXX's story
Additional reflections from early childhood professionals appear in various chapters, particularly Part 2. ECE leaders from Australia and across the Asia Pacific Rim have written these stories. They are extended with provocations.

'Dear Nadine'
For this feature, my friend and academic colleague Diane Nailon models the use of letter writing and correspondence. At the end of each chapter, Di includes her professional story of related experiences, theories and frameworks that link with leading-managing concepts and issues. These letters are both personal and professional; they reflect the past and the present. In essence, Di's letters are a form of chapter synthesis. For a detailed example of such letter writing, readers are referred to the book *Dear Nel: Opening the circles of care (Letters to Nel Noddings)* (Lake, 2012).

A companion website
Additional resources relevant to this book are available online at: www.cambridge.edu.au/academic/leadingandmanaging.

Closing ideas
To recap, your engagement with this book has been likened to taking a leader-manager journey step by step. This Introduction has established a broad map of the book and outlined how to engage chapter-by-chapter, as you follow this professional path. Your journey has now reached one milestone – the end of this map. But first, before moving to Chapter 1, create your personal–professional journal for carrying with you during your journey!

Part 1

Thinking About
People and Places

This section of the book includes three chapters that focus on people in early childhood settings, their interactions with others and the places where they work. In Chapter 1, you will explore concepts to help deepen your understanding of self. This part of your journey includes asking yourself: 'Who am I?' This self-exploration includes a look at leading with managing. In Chapter 2, we explore our language, the powerfulness of words, and communicating for meaning. In Chapter 3, you will contemplate workplaces and the importance of settings and spaces within and beyond early childhood settings.

Part 1

Chapter 1

Understanding self

Socrates advised us 'know thyself' and he claimed the unexamined life is not worth living... Unexamined lives may well be valuable and worth living, but an education that does not invite such examination may not be worthy of the label education.

Nel Noddings (2006, p. 10)

Broad concepts

In this chapter, your journey along the professional leading-managing path encompasses concepts about the self, including both your personal life and your professional life. You are encouraged to think about the following Steps:

- Is 'knowing oneself' relevant?
- Who am I personally?
- Who am I professionally?
- What is leading with managing?

Part 1 Thinking About People and Places

> **Pause and reflect 1.1**
> Before progressing, think about: 'What are my understandings and beliefs about the above questions?' After considering each of the questions above, create an entry in your 'My professional leading-managing journal' by jotting down a couple of learning aims for your engaging with this chapter.

From this first chapter onwards, you will traverse the professional path filled with diverse ideas that are linked with professional experiences, research findings and professional associations. These sources represent multiple professional fields and academic disciplines, including early childhood education, philosophy, feminism, sociology, anthropology, psychology, ethics, human ecology, social justice and equity.

Step 1: Is 'knowing oneself' relevant?

The notion of knowing and understanding oneself may be related to asking oneself such questions as:

- Who am I?
- Who is my family?
- Where do I come from?
- What is my background?
- When (in what times) did I grow up?
- How did I live?
- Who am I now?
- What roles do I have in society?
- How did I get to this point?
- How comfortable am I with myself right now?

Additionally, it will be helpful if you incorporate a qualifier question – 'Why?' – for each of the above questions, as suggested by Noddings (2006, p. 10). For example, revisiting the 'Who am I?' with a 'Why?' forms the deeper question: 'Why am I who I am?' Carefully revisiting past childhood and earlier adulthood experiences can help reveal our present thoughts, values and attitudes, dispositions and habits of mind and indeed result in greater self-awareness. Such a trip back in time may help us understand the impact of the past on our current daily adult lives. This kind of self-study, or memory work, is not about self-interest or self-promotion, nor is it about selfishness (Noddings, 2006). Rather, the purpose of better knowing oneself relates to living and working

Chapter 1 Understanding self

authentically with others. In fact, Amanda Sinclair (2007) suggested 'going back' because 'leadership has a childhood'.

Self-knowing can help us recognise our feelings and thus be better able to understand and meaningfully live and work with others. Having a broad, mindful understanding of oneself can assist a leader-manager with being more realistic about her own abilities or his everyday family or our ongoing professional challenges. But of course, we can never fully know ourselves nor others. Further, we may disagree about what the word 'selves' means. For example, how many 'selves' are there? Mitchell and Weber (1999) suggested the following: private, personal, public, social, political, embodied, individual and collective. We can also ask: 'What might constitute one's ideal self, particularly when creating a vision or image of oneself?' (Boyatzis & Akrivou, 2006) However, even with such questions, it does seem that having a realistic and deep self-knowledge can also help us to better understand others. This kind of self-awareness is vital for everyone working within early childhood settings. Additionally, broader social awareness and authentic professional relationships are vitally important.

Pause and reflect 1.2

According to Foster (2009, p. 103), 'one interesting aspect of children's memory, which remains rather enigmatic, is the occurrence of "infantile amnesia" – whereby most people cannot reliably remember information from before the age of about four years ... One suggestion is that memories of earlier experiences before the age of four may well exist, but in a neural and/or psychological form which means that the individual can no longer access them as memories of specific experiences.'

Quietly ponder your own childhood experiences before recording your early memories as a story. Think about: 'Do I have strong gender, family and/or cultural experiences that have been influential in shaping who I am today personally and professionally?'

Step 2: Who am I personally?

Balancing self

When asking yourself, 'Who am I personally?' you may consider a variety of private and social 'selves'. Here you begin by exploring self as an individual and privately in everyday life. This might involve: just you; your family or extended family with cultural backgrounds; and members of your past and present neighbourhood or community. Of course, self-study encompasses each of us as a social person; this is highlighted in the next Step. Together, the private person and the social person raise a contemporary challenge of balancing self with others, that is, the personal or private with the broader

Part 1 Thinking About People and Places

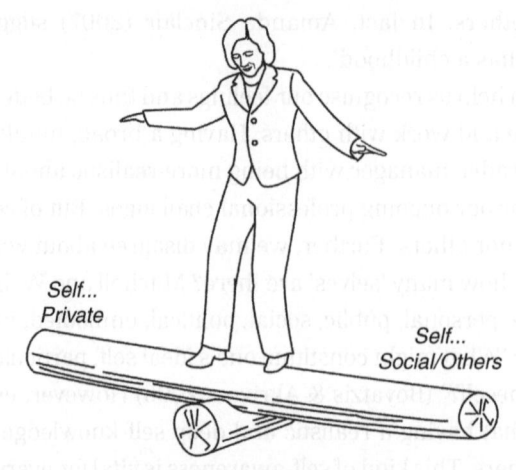

Figure 1.1 *Balancing oneself*

collective or society. Here this balancing is more specifically linked with one's profession and professional position. Refer to Figure 1.1 and think about:

- Where do I stand on the metaphoric balancing log – left, middle, right? When might I move from one focus to another, and why?
- How much of myself do I want to give to being private vs being social?
- In what places might I focus on private self rather than other self?

Dressing myself

With this balancing act in mind, how might you dress yourself at times to represent the private you? Conversely, how might you tip the balance and dress yourself for a social or other orientation or event. Is your clothing the same for these occasions, or different? Why? For example, Sinclair (2007) devoted a whole chapter to 'Bringing bodies into leadership'. Similarly, Mitchell and Weber (1999) provided examples of 'dressing' which are explored further in Step 3. Where do you fit into this kind of balancing act? Let's consider general impressions and perspectives. How private are you? How social are you? Would you define yourself as a 'social butterfly' or a 'wall flower', a bit of both or somewhere in between? What do you think your colleagues' image of you might be? What are your impressions of each of them? Why have you formed such impressions?

Much of our contemporary world seems to be focused on the individual. All around us we can see social value placed on personal desires and competition. I'm sure that you can identify everyday examples in the media, educational settings and sporting events. Pondering oneself does result in some use of the very personal word 'I'. However, even with what can seem like too much 'I and Me' surrounding our everyday lives, it is important to truly understand and know oneself. This is particularly so for

Chapter 1 Understanding self

leader-managers within early childhood settings, as well as for all ECE workplace colleagues. Thus, it is important that the self is viewed as a beginning, so that we can move meaningfully to considering others.

Exploring self

One way to engage in this exploration is to view yourself very personally, while also taking into account context or place, and company or people; in fact, we can hardly view ourselves otherwise. For this exploring you are challenged to do some looking back, as well as contemplating lived experiences right now. This means that it is relevant to identify time and timing as features of your self-exploration and self-knowledge. During such explorations, the breadth of timing will vary. Some of us will spend more time revisiting our past, others will focus on recent and present people and places, and others may consider themselves more hypothetically into the future. To help bring recollections to this moment, you might think about the following during these time-related explorations:

- Your strongest emotions and everyday feelings (for a mapping example, refer to Bansal & Hingorani, 2013)
- Your personal strengths
- Your levels of interpersonal confidence (CREIO, 1998; Consortium for Research on Emotional Intelligence in Organizations, online: www.eiconsortium.org/index.html).

Each of these explorations is a form of personal time-travel across everyday life, where you move between the personal/private and the social/professional.

Reflecting on the past will inevitably involve remembering lived events. The earlier questions might be useful prompts for helping to bring your past to life again and for creating content for any storylines you document. Here, storylines are the narrative threads of your writing; refer to 'telling stories' in the Introduction, and Chapter 2. The idea of considering one's memories in depth, both the usual or everyday and some unique or important past events, can be supported by recording and at times reshaping. For example, Arnold (2005, pp. 29–30) suggested readers might: 'jot down when and where they occurred and who else was involved ... replay the scenario in your imagination and replace the remembered self with your self now. How would the scene change?'

As mentioned above, the idea of taking a focused journey of self-discovery happens alongside relating with others (our 'people thread'), within social settings filled with expectations (our 'places thread'). Zink's (2010) research with high school students included a daily, unguided reflective act of thinking and writing with some sharing. Their sharing was very effective because the self-stories were 'recognisable to others, while at the same time, they recognise[d] the accounts given to them by others' (Zink, 2010, p. 216). This idea of familiarity could well flip our ideas about knowing self and knowing others, so that telling our story 'is not an individual act; it requires the presence

Part 1 Thinking About People and Places

of another and the account is given in relation to them' (Zink, 2010, p. 216). Such an idea is important for understanding our professional ECE selves. This is because story sharing may better inform our thinking about leading-managing and also positively influence our being thoughtful leader-managers.

Pause and reflect 1.3

Stop here and review the Feature professional reflection: Jan's story, on the next page. Which parts of her early life stories are recognisable to you? Consider: 'Do I have similar experience memories?' Do Zink's ideas of self and other 'familiarity' and 'recognisable to others' ring true for any of your childhood experiences when you relate them with Jan's?

Engaging with a stimulus questionnaire is another approach you might consider for exploring yourself and your memories. One useful questionnaire is: *Your identity map* created by the Bangamalanha Centre (Bangamalanha Centre, 2013, np; located on the *8 Aboriginal Ways of Learning* website: www.8ways.wikispaces.com). This questionnaire focuses on:

- Being – living and relating as ontology
- Doing – acting as methodology
- Knowing – thinking as epistemology
- Valuing – believing as axiology.

As a personal and cultural identity tool, it provides four sets of reflective questions about people's ways of being, doing, knowing and valuing. For example, the ways-of-being questions include:

- Where do you belong?
- Who do you belong to?
- How do you know that something is real?

One of the ways-of-valuing questions is: 'What is truth?' Additionally, the guidelines suggest that 'Questioning, challenging and resisting this document is a valid way of engaging with it. Just make sure you're not really doing this as a way to avoid self-scrutiny' (Bangamalanha Centre, 2013, np. Following protocol, I acknowledge the people involved with the *8ways* site, and the site itself. Some of these ideas link with advocacy, which is explored in Chapter 7).

These Aboriginal ways with added Western meanings can be linked to a 'Head, Heart and Hands' frame (Hayward, 2012; McCrea & Ehrich, 1999; Sergiovanni, 1992) and to aspects of embodiment. (As mentioned in the 'Travel Guide' section of the Introduction, 'embodiment' encompasses people's bodies, attributes and other human features, with gender being a key consideration here.) This adult identity tool could be partnered with the 'three Bs' concepts of: 'belonging' as social, others, relating; 'being' as personal, individual; and 'becoming' as future and learning. These 'three Bs' are focused on children in *The Early Years Learning Framework for Australia* (AGDEEWR, 2009 and 2010). By aspiring to the embodiment and sustainability orientations proposed in this book, professionals can link these 'three Bs' directly by undertaking more everyday 'Earthly care' (Elliott, 2014a and 2014b; refer to your compass in the Introduction). In summary, this tool provides you with a platform for jointly sharing personal yet professional views and visions with colleagues, from a leader-manager perspective.

Feature professional reflection: Jan's story

A moment of memories. As a child I had the good fortune of growing up in a semi-rural environment. It was a time when young children were seen to be responsible and able to enjoy the play and freedom of the outdoors. I had the liberty of romping through paddocks in gumboots, catching tadpoles, climbing trees, building billy carts and riding with joyous abandon down a hill with cheers of other children ringing in my ears. I enjoyed the space and place of my childhood. On reflection I clearly remember the memories that inspired me to become a teacher. These are memories of a teacher, Miss B, who had a whole class of young children eager to learn. I recall her intent as she thoughtfully listened and engaged with me as a child. The desire I had to learn and be at school each day was evident for me and all of my peers in her class. I often reminisce about that year when I was aged seven and I knew what I wanted to do as an adult – become a teacher of young children. This teacher was a strong contrast to the school teachers I had the two years prior, teaching with strict and controlling hands and very little joy. Miss B was nurturing, reminding me of my mother; she showed respect, kindness and patience with her young charges. Whilst she created a safe haven and sense of belonging for her class, she had clear boundaries. She also had the ability to develop a love of learning within the environment.

As a child I became aware that the approach to teaching children was a choice. The values and beliefs of a teacher were quite evident to me as a child; they had a huge impact on me and how I viewed learning. On consideration I note that she was one of many teachers and people that have shaped me as an early childhood educator. The skills I have gained, the values and beliefs that are my foundation have been shared with me from a myriad of people in my life.

Our experiences, beliefs and values give us the shape to our life. The desire to be an early childhood teacher was simmering away, waiting for me to find the right path to achieve this dream. With tenaciousness and dedication it became a goal that I worked towards and achieved. As I consider my early professional beliefs and values, I look back and consider which ones I still hold close to my heart. Some of these are: believing in the rights and capabilities of children;

Part 1 Thinking About People and Places

being honest and fair; having high standards and goals; and having persistence. Knowing that setbacks and mistakes are part of learning and growth means that for me reflection and being passionate about my role in working with children is a gift. This is a gift we are given as we influence children's developing beliefs, values and learning (even when days are challenging).

Later on, moving from being an early childhood teacher to being an early childhood leader seemed a relatively seamless process for me. I acknowledge all of the continual learning, mistakes, great moments, mentoring and growth that happened and continue to happen in my career. I believe the abilities of a true leader include leading self through self-reflection, and leading with others. Knowing my own self and my capabilities, plus understanding how they influence me as an educator and leader, brings self-awareness and reflection that is integral to my role as a leader.

*A **provocation**: Jan remembers a specific teacher and her influences that led to Jan's decision to be an early childhood professional. Mitchell and Weber's (1999) first chapter 'Childhood as a memory space: Teachers (replay) school' presented childhood as a key life experience to be recalled. Educators reading the book were encouraged to collectively remember, because everyone has some stories of their primary schooling to share. Mentally and visually revisit your childhood to about the age of twelve by thinking about key people, specific places and special or everyday events. Did you have a 'Miss B'? Can you identify why and how you began your early childhood professional path? What dispositions has Jan written about? Are some of your habits of mind similar?*

Emotional intelligence

Exploring oneself for greater human understanding may be linked with an idea called emotional intelligence. This concept embraces self-awareness, self-management, social awareness and relationship management (for examples, refer to Bansal & Hingorani, 2013; Bruno, 2009; Goleman, 2004; and Sinclair, 2010). Another aspect of exploring self relates to the emotional or value-laden angle of working with and from an 'ethos of caring' (Noddings, 2007 and 2012). Additionally, ideas about 'trust' can be related with 'eco-caring' and extended beyond a human-only, anthropogenic orientation across both personal and professional lives. Trust links with 'ecophilia', which is defined as 'innate intimacy of the body with nature' (Hung, 2008, p. 364).

Working beyond ourselves and with others is at least partly related to the fact that we cannot do everything by ourselves. This idea applies to everyday family life. Similarly, those working in early childhood settings, regardless of their positions and roles, must trust others. Being a personal self with a caring manner for others leads back to the idea of 'trust' as first encountered in the Introduction. However, it is also important to remember that at times there can be distrust or mistrust of others and maybe even of oneself.

Chapter 1 Understanding self

> Trust is at the centre of a whole web of concepts: reliability, predictability, expectation, cooperation, goodwill, and – on the dark side – distrust, insincerity, conspiracy, betrayal, and incompetence.
>
> Katherine Hawley (2012, p. 3)

Pause and reflect 1.4

A key aspect of understanding ourselves concerns the self in place, whether this be natural or human-made spaces. In fact, Nel Noddings (2006) devoted a whole chapter to 'house and home' and explored concepts of shelter, time, organic habits, household tasks, and sharing. These everyday concepts, some of which have embodiment links, can be related to early childhood settings. They mesh with our consideration of various influences on personal feelings of comfort in places and the interactive engagement of both staff and children. Similarly, Paul Lindholdt (1999) focused on sense of place, as noted in the Introduction. He framed students' critical writing by having them put pen to paper in outdoor places. Think about and reflect on dwellings, shelters and places over the years that have influenced who you are now. Jot down a few settings from your past and then link each with the people and events that were important to you at the time. What do these places mean or say about you personally now? How do you think this extended understanding of your personal self might help you better understand your professional self?

Step 3: Who am I professionally?

Clothing the professional, with care

Studying the professional self can be challenging and complex. In fact, this is one aspect of walking a professional path that you may return to at other times in relation to key Steps in later chapters. This section or leg of your journey also moves you to considerations of other people, which means much more than simply not being alone or working alongside someone. 'Allophilia', or liking others because of positive intergroup attitudes (Pittinsky, 2005), can come about when an ethic of caring is in place and shared. It is important to recognise that leader-managers along with other educators may encounter both lighter and darker aspects of human relationships during their collective work. The early childhood workplace, the broader field of children's services and the whole ECE profession are not always easy or rosy! In response to such potentially challenging professional lives, caring relationships, trust and an ethic of care are essential. Thus, for early childhood leader-managers it is suggested that being a 'relational carer' probably is more valuable than just being a 'virtue carer' (Noddings, 2012). This means considering others' expressed needs, which are beyond those needs that professionals might assume about colleagues and children. (Refer to Chapter 7, about being a rights advocate, and think about how these ideas could be related.)

Professionally knowing oneself can help with understanding others. For example, our professional selves and our interactions with colleagues may change as we go back

Part 1 Thinking About People and Places

to revisit ourselves and then come forward, 'reinventing' ourselves (Mitchell & Weber, 1999). To support such personal yet professional revisits and reinventions, we begin by examining the working self, either as an ongoing or occasional leader-manager. Let's do this by 'look[ing] into metaphorical mirrors to acquire self-reflective knowledge, which is an understanding of one's purpose or mission and of one's strengths and weaknesses in relation to that purpose' (Hearron & Hildebrand, 2007, p. 61). Another way you can engage with reinvention ideas and use of 'mirrors' is to metaphorically 'clothe' yourself as a professional (refer to: Mitchell & Weber, 1999, their chapter 'Undressing and redressing the teacher's body'; and Pullen & Simpson, 2009).

Pause and reflect 1.5

Please stop your leading-managing travels here to do some 'dressing' or 're-dressing'. First, refer back to Figure 1.1; it can be related to both balancing your life and dressing the self. This balancing log and act may also reflect a continuum for imagining one's preferred self. You might reflect on your leadership manners and styles, as well as your individual qualities and dispositions (refer to Step 4, below). All these human features contribute to and inform our engaging in wise or not-so-wise interactions and relationships with others.

Next, engage with ideas about being an ECE professional, by:

- drawing a leader-manager
- creating a body-photo essay of a situational leader, and/or
- dressing a doll as positional leader-manager.

Visually move yourself to the social/others end of the balancing log (Figure 1.1) and then 'dress' yourself as a director or coordinator of a particular kind of early childhood setting. Would your appearance vary with specific early childhood positions of leader, manager or administrator? If so, why? Also consider what you would wear as the leader of curriculum, teaching and learning when inside your early childhood setting vs outside this setting when meeting with local government officials. What about dress in terms of men wearing ties, but women wearing scarves? If you are a male ECE professional, think about when might you wear a tie and why. Also, you might find it helpful now to skim the Professional reflection: Leo's story, in Step 1 of Chapter 4. Colours of clothes may also reflect or represent times of gendered choice. The colour pink might be one example (Pullen & Simpson, 2009).

If you create multiple 'dressings', each could reflect a different leader position as well as various types of settings. You could also represent staffing layers from a single setting, or a cluster of services or government departments at local, state and national levels. There may well be similarities and some elaborations. 'Dressing' oneself touches on ideas about status and power among early childhood professionals. It can link with their embodiment similarities and differences related to gender, family background, ethnicity or nationality, etc. (Mitchell & Weber, 1999; Pittinsky, 2005). Record your images and also write a little about why you dressed the same for every situation noted above or why you dressed differently at times.

Chapter 1 Understanding self

Working life

'Working with others' encompasses many aspects of our professional lives and workplace settings. For example, you can engage in: considering issues; uncovering competencies; and revealing ways of interacting and relating. Exploring these will assist you with answering the question: 'Who am I professionally?'

For this exploration, we begin with empathic intelligence. According to Arnold, our empathic intelligence is separate from emotional and cognitive intelligences; thus, 'it is essentially concerned with the dynamic between thinking and feeling and the ways in which each contributes to the making of meaning' (Arnold, 2005, p. 20). Arnold encouraged this dynamic in people through their being sceptical, questioning and being rigorous in daily personal and professional lives. Empathic intelligence has been referred to as an individual functioning system with a number of abilities that include working creatively and using mirroring and affirming. It seems that these abilities can be particularly important for leader-managers in early childhood settings. Arnold linked this theory across personal experiencing and contexts with four relational qualities or attributes for people:

- Enthusiasm
- Expertise
- Engagement
- Empathy.

She also outlined examples of how professionals might put these ways of relating with others into practice. There are similarities between being empathic and various social and emotional ideas and actions that ECE professionals regularly engage with. For example, The Emotional Competence Framework, as well as other theories and models, may help you to more fully understand and engage in framing yourself in terms of: 'Who am I professionally?' (This tool is available in the 'reports' at: www.eiconsortium.org.)

Again, when such relational attributes are wrapped within various worldly influences, they provide a solid framework for helping early childhood leader-managers understand themselves, their close colleagues and their everyday work lives. We can also connect Arnold's 'four Es' (enthusiasm, expertise, engagement and empathy) with the already introduced 'ethos of caring' and considerations of trust. Of course, there is the explicit extension into eco-caring as well. Certainly this professional relating embraces respect for self and others. If we now move to another level, all these ideas may be joined together with people's actions and their underlying experiences. The joining of all these ideas leads to what can be called 'action competencies'. A further extension may lead professionals to the broad educational aim of action competence for sustainability, which has been defined and researched over a couple of decades. The 'winding pathways leading to' this Swedish pedagogical ideal reflect (according to Almers, 2013, p. 125) people's:

Part 1 Thinking About People and Places

- Emotions that can create a desire for change
- Core values within a world of contrasting views
- Trust and faith in other adults.

This idea of action competencies may well be a useful aspect of one's professional persona as a rights advocate (refer to Chapter 7). In summary, our complex socio-cultural attitudes and intriguing human relationships are very much part of answering the question, 'Who am I professionally?'

Pause and reflect 1.6

Arnold (2005, p. 30) incorporated hypotheticals in her book. For example, she suggested: 'Observe a variety of people who demonstrate enthusiasm. How do you detect their enthusiasm? Does it engage you, threaten you or even mystify you?' With embodiment being one of our focal value points across this book, what roles or influences might our bodies and various colleagues' gender play in terms of displaying one's enthusiasm or not? Have a go at sensitively watching a couple of workplace colleagues and a few children's parents. In what ways might being an enthusiastic professional contribute to one's effective leading-managing of early childhood settings?

Values, beliefs and professional self

One's values and beliefs are another aspect of the professional self. They inform our thinking about and coming to really understand ourselves. Within the early childhood education field and profession there are numerous broad and basic values, as well as more specific, complex and even individual values that contribute to defining who we are professionally.

There are established foundations about working with and for young children that encase basic values and essential principles about everyday life in early childhood settings. For both educators working close up with children and leader-managers often at some distance from children, these professional foundations begin from principles related to:

- Acting in a 'precautionary' way (Karliner, 2005)
- Ensuring that we 'do no harm' (Bruno, 2009).

Yet these are not enough. Everyone must also be wise, brave and bold in children's best interests. And so, knowing oneself as a professional goes well beyond acknowledging one's 'basic' beliefs and values about young children, colleagues and families linked with early childhood services. There is an element of professional self-knowing that happens beyond self, along with others. Such relational or interpersonal self-understanding in one's work and workplace can be matched with affect theories, which 'dispute separations between mind and body; and between the individual, their communities and political contexts' (Skattebol, 2010, p. 78). To explain, affect theories relate to emotions and feelings

Chapter 1 Understanding self

and link back to ideas about emotional intelligence. Skattebol's ideas focused on pedagogy and educators (see Chapter 6), while here our focus is positional and situational leader-managers and whole early childhood settings; however, the suggestion that vital critical reflections are couched within a democratic collective is certainly relevant to this leading-managing journey.

Furthermore, values-based professional knowing beyond early childhood 'basics' (often associated with law and service regulations) usually progresses to 'best practice' values and actions. And these are linked with so-called 'quality' or 'high quality' standards or benchmarks. There are documented professional principles and codes as well as government accreditation systems. However, more than a decade ago, Joy Goodfellow (2001) encouraged early childhood professionals to use creative artistry along with 'wise' relational, expert knowledge in their everyday practices. Such wisdom encompassed reflective, affective and experiential abilities within moral and ethical frames (Goodfellow, 2001, p. 5). Such moral higher ground and discerning visions relate to exploring the question of who we are professionally. These frames also intertwine with the particular leading-managing role of being a rights advocate (explored in Chapter 7).

It seems that to fully understand our professional selves (the people focus) and our work lives (the places and practices focus), we must truly understand our values, our moral backgrounds and our ethical positions. Values develop and are then revealed personally and to others in a number of ways. Values may be interpersonal or political, developing early and gradually through (according to Feng & Newton, 2012):

- Modelling and example by others
- Explaining briefly or fully
- Teaching purposely with transformative learning
- Analysing individually or collectively
- Discussing with others.

Pause and reflect 1.7

As a long-time early childhood education professional, I strongly believe that understanding, valuing and modelling moral higher ground is a vitally important aspect of being a children's services leader-manager. Let me put this in perspective for you. This belief is relevant for all leaders regardless of whether their positions are situational and distributed or positional. The professional importance here is based in ethics and equity, fairness, justice and democracy. How would you define 'moral higher ground'? How might you identify being moral or acting morally? How important do you consider this idea for people in early childhood leadership roles? Why? As a leader-manager, how might you explain holding 'moral higher ground' to a new, young staff member? Refer to ECA's 'Code of Ethics' (ECA, 2006) in order to link this issue with various people associated with early childhood settings and ideas about rights advocacy (Chapter 7).

Identity work

With values as a foundation, we can further investigate the challenging idea of uncovering who we are professionally. We might do so by using the notion of identity work along with everyday capabilities. For example, Amanda Sinclair (2010, p. 448) explored leader identity in terms of 'locating ourselves in place and locating a place for ourselves'. She displayed this by writing in two forms, as 'public-self' and 'naked-self', on each page of an article. She described place as 'much more than geography' with emotional features of political, economic and gender relations. The use of 'inspiring stories' in this book draws on this idea. Such identity work is about 'inventing' or 'crafting' a professional self with less ego (Sinclair, 2010 & 2007), by going back but also keeping some present orientation when considering personal, community and professional places along with their influences on self. Of course, it is important to add that we can influence places as well as them having an influence on us.

Identifying one's identity

For you as a traveller moving along a professional path, your focal identity will be as leader-manager working with diverse early childhood settings. It may be incomplete or you may have several faces. This leader-manager engagement with identity may even be more about freeing yourself within relationships than about uncovering a professional self (Sinclair, 2010). Your professional identity can be viewed as more temporary than stable or essential, because people and places are always adjusting and changing; they are never quite the same! This idea of changeability allows us to liken leadership to a form of fantasy (Sveningsson & Larsson, 2006). Think about: 'How stable or temporary and how fleeting do I see my professional identity as being?', and 'How much have early childhood settings collectively changed in the last year?'

Furthermore, getting to know one's professional identity might involve viewing the self as capable or competent. That is, having and displaying various capabilities, even with the normative and at times fragile nature of such self-defining. Here capabilities encompass a professional's attributes, skills, knowledge and dispositions; and, they intertwine with and relate to leadership of self as well as leadership with others (refer to ECA, 2012a; Giovacco-Johnson, 2011). All these temper a leader-manager's everyday workplace actions. Having a value-laden character along with one's personal dispositions and individual habits of mind makes up much of one's total personal–professional identity. How might this being capable or competent relate with the 'action competencies' introduced above? In essence, these ideas take us back to viewing our professional selves through a more socioemotional lens. One vital aspect of this multi-lens approach reflects our professional understandings of people's cultural origins and their life-world backgrounds (Connor, 2011); such a lens might reflect facets like those in a gemstone.

Acknowledging cultural identity

As an important example, the respectful recognition of 'Indigenous Acknowledgement of Country' relates to identity and is encircled by both social awareness and relationship management. All this is couched within emotional intelligence, which was introduced earlier (Bruno, 2009; see: Korff (nd), www.creativespirits.info/; or NSW Department of Local Government, 2007). Recognising and sharing cultural identity can happen every day and be ongoing. For example, when early childhood professionals create a prominent entrance place for an Indigenous art piece along with a relevant, local 'Acknowledgement statement', their settings reflect cultural identity. Sensitivity is demonstrated through the act of displaying these in respectful ways. In practice, an 'Acknowledgement' may be spoken as an event begins, written with a supporting image on an early childhood service's letterhead, or appear in a parent handbook or on a service's website.

For additional practice examples, the website *8 Aboriginal Ways of Learning* (www.8ways.wikispaces.com) provides a variety of culturally sensitive resources. If leaders consider these, then they are endeavouring to lead-manage with true professional understanding of family and cultural diversity. Similarly, but with a children's services focus, SNAICC provides numerous Indigenous child and family resources covering policy, advocacy, tools, projects, training and news (SNAICC = Secretariat of National Aboriginal and Islander Child Care; at: www.snaicc.org.au; SNAICC, 2013). Both organisations help support both positional and situational leader-managers with:

- Identifying: Who am I professionally?
- Thinking about and acting upon cultural competence
- Creating operational principles for early childhood settings with all families.

Moving beyond an acknowledgement, a leader-manager's cultural competence, as part of both professional identity work and mentoring other staff, can embrace cultural safety (Bin-Sallik, 2003) for all families. As an example, Early Childhood Australia (ECA, 2012b) consulted and created the declaration document *Respect, Connect, Enact – A reconciliation action plan for Early Childhood Australia 2012–2016*. ECA expressed regret and committed to organisational leadership actions for the field and profession in terms of relationships, respect and opportunities, with tracking and reporting (www.earlychildhoodaustralia.org.au/about_us/eca-reconciliation-action-plan.html). Other examples related to Australian reconciliation are found in government documents. Such statements and any implementations surely represent broad yet focused rights advocacy (refer to Chapter 7). Taking these actions reflects a professional role that is an essential aspect of early childhood leading-managing.

Part 1 Thinking About People and Places

Respectful recognition and meaningful relationships with people can also go hand-in-hand with moving beyond people to working for the Earth politically, economically, naturally and socially. These actions are highlighted throughout this book using the 'eco-caring compass' icon (refer back to the Introduction). By adopting an essential eco-caring belief or mantra during your journey, you and other early childhood professionals can care for people and for the Earth. This section of pathway returns you as traveller to your values and beliefs and those shared with colleagues.

Pause and reflect 1.8

Refer back in Step 1 to the idea of multiple selves – private, personal, public, social, political, embodied, individual and collective (Mitchell & Weber, 1999, p. 8) – and do some quiet thinking about yourself as a professional: 'Who am I professionally?' Consider yourself in terms of the above 'selves'. Which one best describes you, professionally, now? Next, project into the future – one year from now, in five years – what 'self' might be most potent for you? Why are there potential differences or none over time for you? For each 'self', identify a responsibility that represents ECE leading, managing and administering. For example, this could mean that the 'political' self might: lead a media campaign; manage a meeting with government officials; and administer funding paperwork for reporting to a professional organisation.

Step 4: What is leading with managing?

> ... before I began to study leadership in a serious manner, my knowledge of it was complete. I knew basically all there was to know and I had already spent over a decade practising it ... I should have stopped then, because ever since ... my understanding has decreased in direct proportion to my increased knowledge: in effect, the more I read, the more contradictory appeared the conclusions ... Despite all my best efforts ... the results refused to regurgitate any significant pattern except one banal truism: successful leaders are successful.
>
> Keith Grint (2000). *The Arts of Leadership*. Oxford University Press, p. 1; quoted in Prince (2005, p. 108)

Before moving further along this professional path, let's examine some relevant contemporary ideas about leadership with management and administration. Leadership and leading are complex, contested and ever-changing as both intellectual ideas and everyday actions. In fact, if we review the names of professional journals and books and the titles of academic articles back over the years, such a timeline reveals that today's educational *leader/ing/ership* was more often referred to as educational *manager/ing/ment*, about a decade ago; and prior to that as educational *administrator/tion*. The point is that this complexity and variation reflects our relating and interacting during human encounters. It also means there are almost endless definitions, models, theories and practices. Professionals might find some of these ideas attractive, even useful; however, not all will be worthwhile for early childhood people and places.

Chapter 1 Understanding self

Furthermore, we know that workplace contexts and their intricacies continually influence what leading-managing looks like and how it is expressed and received by leaders and others. Workplaces are home to ever-changing situations.

In the Introduction we explored some ideas about being a leader-manager and doing leading-managing. They were framed as being closely linked to and usually intertwined with the everyday life of early childhood settings; this resulted in the use of these hyphenated double words. However, for simplicity the words *leader, leading* and *leadership* will also be used in the following chapters as various ideas about leading with managing are considered. Although 'listing' is a less than perfect way of introducing important ideas, this approach facilitates a broad overview. Many ideas will be explored further in the chapters that follow. We begin by asking:

- Who can be a leader?
- Who is a follower?
- What dispositions and styles shape a leader?
- What competencies or abilities support a manager?

Who can be a leader and who might be a follower?

If we move forward along this professional path and ponder the key idea that leading-managing is relational work, then interacting sensitively and professionally can be both a solid foundation and a protective umbrella for engaging with people and practices. Firstly, this perspective means that leading and leadership are action-oriented. They encompass collective, trusting interactions among people and their work-positions. However, people's interactions and the interplay between colleagues will vary with their work. For example, work in a setting can be seen in two broad ways (according to Helstad & Moller, 2013), as:

- A division of 'labour' shift and distribution, with labour as roles and tasks; or
- A division of 'authority' change, with authority as legitimate power and legal or assigned responsibilities.

People switch roles, tasks and responsibilities within ECE workplaces. As such, professionals may be a leader of one errand and a follower for another activity. This means that at times colleagues 'travel' between roles using leader-follower 'give-and-take'; this happens as typical ECE workload duties, chores and projects are distributed and divided. There will also be positions and roles that are more set or firm, rather than changeable or loose. Thus duties and roles are either less or more freely exchanged among colleagues.

> We find leadership is a far more complex and contradictory phenomena. Good leaders can do bad things; bad leaders can do good things; and frequently people claiming to be leaders do nothing.
>
> Mats Alvesson & Andre Spicer (2011, p. 3)

What shapes a leader and supports a manager?

The answer to this question relates closely with a person's character, temperament and interactive nature. We might refer to these as one's 'professional disposition'. Positional and situational leader-managers' actions and work are influenced or shaped by their dispositions. Although our worldly views and approaches may differ, contemporary early childhood education professionals often share philosophical foundations that reflect democratic and caring ideas, such as: collaboration, cooperation, ethical principles, social justice, transparency rather than secrecy, empathy, resilience and reciprocity. Such foundations inform and guide both:

- One's leading style or manner of relating with others
- How one manages when getting on with various daily processes and projects.

These managing actions may be combined to form broader roles and responsibilities. In particular, Planning, Organising and Monitoring (POM) frame a significant approach used by many as they do 'things'. This POM approach has been promoted as a valuable one within our economic-rationality-oriented world and also across the ECE field. (For examples, refer to Ebbeck & Waniganayake, 2003; Freeman, Decker & Decker, 2013; Hearron & Hildebrand, 2007; Hewes & Leatherman, 2005.) POM-framing can be a useful tool for thinking about, investigating and engaging with the key roles discussed in Part 2. However, it is important to remember that professional early childhood leading-managing is more often intertwined than separated, even when projects and roles are shared around. There are also many relevant theories and ideas about people's human features; such as their:

- Traits or attributes
- Intellectual and emotional states
- On-the-job behaviours or actions
- Foundational value codes
- Professional prescriptions.

Additionally, government specifications, workplace contexts and neighbourhood cultures contribute to leader-manager personas. Some of these will be considered within the leading-managing roles, including elements of problematising human features within ECE settings.

Leading-managing dispositions and styles

A leader-manager's 'dispositional silhouette' may be reshaped every day, with any number of features having an influence. Here is a sampling of potential influences:

- Gender (Lindon & Lindon, 2011; Mills-Bayne, 2013; Pullen & Simpson, 2009)
- Theoretical leanings or approaches (Waniganayake, Cheeseman, Fenech, Hadley & Shepherd, 2012)

Chapter 1 Understanding self

- Caring actions (Uusiautti, 2013) and servant characteristics (Cameron, 2012)
- Cultural East to West frames (Carroll, 2007; Cleary, 2004; Prince, 2005)
- Positions held and sociocultural context expectations (Cardno & Reynolds, 2009; Choi Wa Ho, 2011)
- Personal qualities, habits of mind or attributes (Costa & Kallick, 2008; Rodd, 2013)
- One's childhood and body (Sinclair, 2007).

An essential disposition influences one's personal life and one's professional persona. Such habits of mind in turn contribute to the swaying of one's interactive style and one's ways of relating in particular directions at particular times and in particular places.

A professional's leading-managing style is about display, about doing or expressing, and about relating with colleagues (Rodd, 2013). Those who separate leading and managing often hold the view that leaders are more about creating a vision, while managers implement that vision and engage with day-to-day events and matters (refer to 'vision' in Chapter 7). Roles can be exchanged and may overlap, so one's style or manner is the actual difference. As such, professional styles may reflect and encompass leading-managing with:

- Care connected with authentic servant/service and transformation (Cameron, 2012; Dunlop, 2008; Uusiautti, 2013)
- Gentle engagement vs direct control (Prince, 2005)
- Active sensemaking or doing leadership with organising (Pye, 2005)
- Intentionality (Waniganayake et al., 2012)
- A 'knack of living with ambiguity' in the workplace (Alvesson & Spicer, 2011, p. 23)
- One focus, as either formal-managerial, collegial-participative transformational distributed, political-transactional, subjective-postmodern emotional, ambiguity-contingency or cultural-moral instructional (Bush, 2011; Coleman, 2012)
- Position, permission, production, people development, and pinnacle levels of non-career-staging (Rodd, 2013).

Leading competence

From this quick trip through what might be called the 'seasonal' nature of leadership with management, you may have identified various 'weather patterns' and different 'geographic climates' that could influence one's travels along a professional journey. As you pondered all these leading-managing ideas, you might have imagined viewing a bright rainbow after some rain or even a few dark clouds before a hailstorm. These differing views and feelings can reflect the essence of all the complexity and even times of confusion that surround what authentic and intentional leadership with effective management is or might be for everyone involved in early childhood settings.

Again, we return to the utility of metaphors at times of confusion and complexity as well as for inspiration and aspirations (refer to Introduction, Chapters 2 and 3). As an illustration, 'dance' reflects many musical moods, body movements and partnering positions; and so, as a noun and verb it works as a metaphor for leadership and its complexities (Ehrich & English, 2013; Krieg, Davis & Smith, 2014). Let's put this thinking into perspective for the early childhood education field. If the everyday world of Western leadership, even educational leadership, is diverse, often controlling and hierarchical, and mainly single-person and product- or outcome-oriented, then maybe Eastern, Taoist or Zen approaches are worthy of review. (For examples, refer to Carroll, 2007; Chakraborty, 2003; Cleary, 2004; Feng & Newton, 2012; Prince, 2005; Uusiautti, 2013; Wong, 2001.) Also, consider these questions:

- Could it be that early childhood educators and leader-managers might relate better with approaches from the East, rather than with corporate approaches and individual models?
- Could such Eastern ideas particularly support managers with identifying and strengthening their professional competencies?

Such thinking might also help leader-managers with 'troubling' (Krieg, Davis & Smith, 2014) and reshaping their beyond-the-fence conceptions and practices for leading-managing outside early childhood settings. Each person's 'troubling' ought to be supported by a traveller's compass with an ethic of eco-caring; and, this tool ought to feature dispositional respect, relevance, reciprocity and responsibility (Markiewicz, 2012).

> 'Leadership' easily becomes everything and nothing. And the use of the term easily oscillates between what everybody does and what only an exceptional group of 'real leaders' do. This means it is not easy to sort out what leadership is and what it is not.
>
> Mats Alvesson & Andre Spicer (2011, p. 9)

Conclusion

This chapter encompasses many ideas about the self, both personal and professional. All these ideas contribute to and influence professionals, especially when in the position of early childhood leader-manager. At this stage in your professional journey, hopefully you have already reached both a greater understanding of yourself and your feelings. This understanding ought to relate to being a more caring and effective person with others. This leading with managing extends selves and relationships with others. The next chapter focuses on the very human ability of communicating within early childhood settings and more broadly.

Chapter 1 Understanding self

Dear Nadine,

Thank you for the opportunity to be an active participant in this book. I welcome the challenge to respond to your ideas and share my insights into some of the provocations that you raise in each chapter. My contributions will draw from the discoveries I have made in my personal and professional life that continue to develop my understanding and application of leader-manager theory and research.

These opening chapters bring 'the personal' to leadership and show us that we need more than just a box full of leadership strategies to use when problems arise. Starting leadership courses and texts by examining one's personal journey and values can be confronting. However I cannot help but think of a high-powered friend who participated in a leadership course based on Stephen Covey's writing. My friend said recently that her successes today are due to the effort she was forced to make at the beginning of the course. She was asked to delve into the personal realm much like the reflective exercises in this chapter. While it was a struggle, my friend's final comment that 'you just can't make the theory work unless you know yourself first' was a testament to her willingness to trust the need to examine her personal story. The insights in this chapter and my friend's experience parallel so many writers from the neo-charismatic leadership paradigm who focus on emotions, values and transformative change.

It has always amazed me how many leadership and management theories there are. It is important to start out into that confusing territory by allowing leader-manager ideas to emerge along the way. I think I finally made sense of them when they were clustered together and put into historical perspective as paradigms. It seems that neo-charismatic ideas about leadership highlight 'the personal' and focus on a person's intense examination into the past through a process of research, documentation and theorising. Daniel Goleman's emotional intelligence is mentioned in this chapter. Goleman has created what he called 'primal leadership theory' which emerged from his reflection on what was missing from other, earlier theories. He made sure that his brain research on emotional intelligence added significantly to what others have found about the need to consider leaders and 'followers' relations. Who we are is influenced by our past, but who we are is also influenced by what we make of it. Like Goleman has done, we can add to the sum of what we are by thinking about how to improve on it.

Many important ideas have been introduced in this first chapter for us to mull over. What re-inventions of ourselves and our ideas will emerge as we research, document and reflect? The journey metaphor is a helpful one.

Until next time,
Di

Pause and reflect 1.9
Which idea in this chapter most influenced your current beliefs, and why?

Chapter 2

Exploring communication

As stated by the eminent cognitive neuroscientist Michel Gazzaniga: 'Everything in life is memory, save for the thin edge of the present.' Memory allows us to recall birthdays, holidays and other significant events that may have taken place hours, days, months, or even many years ago. Our memories are personal and 'internal', yet without memory we wouldn't be able to undertake 'external' acts – such as holding a conversation, recognising our friends' faces, remembering appointments, acting on new ideas, succeeding at work, or even learning to walk.

Jonathan K Foster (2009, p. 2)

Broad concepts

Here your journey along a professional leading-managing path encompasses concepts about communicating authentically, both within early childhood settings and beyond them. You will explore what communication involves, professional ways of communicating and much more. You are encouraged to think about the following Steps:

- Why is communicating with others essential?
- How and why are our words so powerful?
- What does professional communication encompass?

Chapter 2 Exploring communication

Pause and reflect 2.1
Before progressing, think about: 'What are my understandings and beliefs about the above questions?' After considering each of the questions above, create an entry in your 'My professional leading-managing journal' by jotting down a couple of learning aims for your engaging with this chapter.

Step 1: Why is communicating with others essential?

Language is central to people's humanity. Each of us has a language – our mother tongue that was learned informally from infancy while sitting on the knees of family members. Of course, many infants learn more than one mother tongue simultaneously. Additionally, many of today's infants are enrolled in early childhood settings, where they also learn some of their first or second language on the knees of staff. Communication is so deeply intertwined with both our interacting and relating that the three can hardly be separated. This aspect of our humanness is so fundamental, especially in this fast-paced world. Thus, it is essential that early childhood staff consider how to wisely support young children and their burgeoning communications.

For example, this might mean that early childhood professionals create calmer, mindful moments for children to just be, as well as places for quiet talking. Such early childhood settings are a world of human interactions and close relationships between young and older. However, it is important to remember that the contemporary reality of a fast moving world has an opposite effect. Thus, professionals are challenged to meaningfully plan for slowing down everyday life within early childhood settings for both children and adults.

Pause and reflect 2.2
How might this 'slowing down' happen? What approaches can you think of that you and your colleagues might consider useful for creating a slower pace of interacting and relating with one another while actually communicating more authentically? Where might you create a very quiet, intimate place for children? What would you set up in this 'womb' space?

This branch of your path and leader's journey takes you to explorations of various interactive and relational aspects of professional communicating. Both oral and written communications contribute to our everyday interactions within and beyond early childhood settings.

Sharing for meaning

As we talk with another person, we may be sharing an idea, a feeling, an opinion or asking a question. Thus, we are sharing words that have meaning to us as speakers. And the hope or plan is that others understand our words and make meaning from them. Certainly such interpersonal understandings are the aim whether adults are talking together or adults and children are sharing a conversation. In terms of leading-managing situations, comfortable relationships among a staff team may well make it easier for everyone to share ideas, and to honestly and respectfully discuss challenging views and issues.

In some ways it is a wonder that we are able to communicate for meaning as much as we do. This can be particularly true in early childhood settings with a broad collection of staff and many families from widely varying backgrounds and experiences of the world. When such a mixture of people with their varying values and ideas gathers together, it is important for a leader-manager, along with all staff, to be diligent about considering where there is potential for misunderstandings to arise. This is a vital consideration because there are times when one's intended message is not what the receiver hears. How and why do such misunderstandings occur? How can staff be attentive to these possible situations?

There are multiple ways of communicating in different settings. Our communications happen via any number of personal, cultural and professional 'languages'. Thus, for example, we use different phrases and sometimes voice tones with young children in a play yard to those we use when reporting to members of a committee of management at an annual general meeting. Wise words, relevant images and meaningful metaphors permeate work life across the early childhood education field, and they are both vital and influential. Therefore, it seems essential as a situational and/or positional leader-manager that you closely examine and analyse these everyday words, images and metaphors as you encounter them. Such reflections may well help you to be a clearer and more meaningful communicator.

Family knowing, knowing families

A key aspect of communicating authentically within early childhood settings and in the wider community is related to our professional responsibilities and obligations. One such ethical reality is acknowledging the mother tongue and additional languages of all those encountered during our professional work. This professional commitment is broader and more common today because of the global world that we live in. For example, Australia and New Zealand encompass families from nearly every corner of the world; and thus many early childhood settings are very culturally and linguistically diverse. In this context, times may arise when your wise guidance and professional support as leader-manager are particularly helpful for families. This can be especially important when shared communication concerns a challenging issue. These are prime

Chapter 2 Exploring communication

times for staff acceptance of parents as well as for ensuring that conversations are effective and sincere, with any documents being client-friendly.

As an example, you might refer to MacNaughton and Hughes' (2011, pp. x–xi, 198–201) 'A Fairness Alerts Matrix' for assistance with evaluating and monitoring your interactions and relationships. The Matrix serves as a thinking tool for professionals and it encompasses five unfair habits – 'essentializing', 'homogenizing', 'othering', 'privileging' and 'silencing'. These habits may be applied to people in terms of 'grouping' by gender, class, sexuality, language, ethnicity or culture. Putting such habits into perspective means understanding the unfairness of each, and this can assist professionals with altering and replacing them with more just, ethical actions across one's repertoire. The authors' definitions are considered here (pp. 198–201):

- 'Essentializing' – 'Seeing an individual as defined by something deep and enduring (essential) because they belong to a particular group'
- 'Homogenizing' – 'Eradicating differences between members of groups … by assuming they do not exist'
- 'Othering' – 'Seeing yourself and/or your group as the norm, from which everyone else deviates'
- 'Privileging' – 'Seeing yourself and/or your group as more important than anyone else'
- 'Silencing' – 'Making it difficult for an individual or a group to be seen and/or heard'.

With the above Matrix in mind, let's explore the usual reality of early childhood settings. We can begin with meeting and greeting families as a key example of our everyday work lives. Here, it is vital that ECE professionals interact in ways that are respectful of families' socio-cultural backgrounds.

This aspect of respectful leading-managing can be strengthened when all staff understand and acknowledge families in terms of their heritage child-rearing practices and contemporary local community interactions (Riojas-Cortez & Flores, 2009). As such, everyday practices and interactions inform children's 'sense of being within the world around them' and contribute their 'scripts to respond to others and events' (p. 185). Both these ideas are viewed as components of a child's overall socio-emotional growth. Family practices also help young children develop social competencies within their personal 'funds of knowledge – cultural knowledge' (p. 186). The above ideas support the notion that our conversations are deeply intertwined with our ongoing interactions and recurring relationships. They also highlight the importance of professional communications with adults, especially families, and personal interactions with young children.

Part 1 Thinking About People and Places

Pause and reflect 2.3

Think back (through our embodiment lens) to a time and place in your personal life when you were physically uncomfortable. Did this situation influence your ability to communicate with others on the spot? If so, why? Try the approach of 'writing with your ears'. This means talking out loud as you read these questions and then answering them out loud so that you hear yourself. After hearing yourself, record your thoughts. This task encourages you to carefully consider ideas in linguistic steps with the lenses of reading, talking and then writing. What are your impressions of how this approach might be useful for you as either a situational or positional leader-manager of different types of early childhood settings?

Step 2: How and why are our words so powerful?

Our words represent the surrounding social and cultural world. They are more than family-focused examples of communication and usually reflect origins that are broader than a local community. Within the work life of education settings, words and phrases may be linked with personal beliefs, pedagogical stances, political ideas and government influences. In fact, much of the power and complexity of words can lie in their historic origins. An example of where the historic origins of words are examined is Bruce Moore's book, *What's Their Story?: A history of Australian words* – an alphabetical English language resource which includes the very Australian expressions: 'Aussie', 'bush', 'fair go', 'mate' and 'tall poppy'. Similarly, the Australian Society for Indigenous Languages undertakes linguistic research and provides digital dictionaries and other resources (see their website at: www.ausil.org.au).

Within the early childhood education field, a number of organisations and governments have over the years provided resources and documents in multiple community languages. The FKA Children's Services in Victoria and the Ethnic Child Care, Family and Community Services Co-operative in New South Wales are two examples of non-profit organisations that assist staff in early childhood settings and their committees of management or boards of directors. These organisations provide various supports and particular resources, so that professionals can best meet the needs and rights of culturally and linguistically diverse children and families. Having an awareness of such organisations often sits within the responsibility parameters of a leader-manager.

Some hows and whys of words

Even everyday words and phrases can bring forth professional and research ideas about discourse, critical literacy and micro-politics for leader-managers of early childhood settings to carefully consider. For example, as a potential or present leader-manager you may wonder about being a professional in relation to the ideas of being a traveller, travelling through this book and stepping along professional paths. These journey concepts represent a form of metaphor and are typical examples of metaphors that appear in both oral and written communications across the early childhood education field and more widely.

Similarly, how words and phrases are used includes the tone of a person's message, which may sound official or informal. It may encompass meaningful terms of endearment when early childhood educators interact with young children. However, during a telephone conversation with a local food supplier, you will have already created a list of grocery items and planned how to discuss costs and payment. This conversation would be quite different from an in-the-moment chat you might initiate with a couple of three-year-olds as you walk past their wooden block construction. The level of informality that leader-managers and early childhood team members use when communicating with others, including parents, may raise issues about personal and professional communication rules (for example, refer to the sample 'Respectful Communication Policy' provided later, in Step 3).

Some communication rules may relate to embodiment, including gender. When gender is involved, rules can reflect politics, with elements of power and empowerment also intertwined with the tone of people's messages. Another aspect of our professional interactions relates to the level of seriousness of our communications. This involves a continuum of how serious to non-serious or even humorous our words and body language may be. We must, however, remember that both the portrayal of ideas and the understanding of a message by others are of prime importance. As part of her ethic of caring work and her commitment to moral education, Nel Noddings (2003) wrote about happiness and how people seek it in their private and public lives. There is no simple formula about when to use a light-hearted vs a serious tone during professional interactions. Various everyday life features and background experiences will affect what people say and how others respond to that collection of words.

Images

Furthermore, the images and metaphors that are often part of our oral and written communications can be very powerful. Today's world is very visually oriented and so our gaze – the act of looking – can represent power relationships among people. As an example, when looking at a photograph, the looker is allotted 'more power' than the viewed person (Sturken & Cartwright, 2009, p. 111). This 'power' idea links with photographs as anthropological data or even travel images, where the images traditionally played a role in 'establishing difference'. These 'differences' created categories or binaries of both people (us and them) and places (home and foreign).

Part 1 Thinking About People and Places

Pause and reflect 2.4

Think about images for a moment and recall any photographs or drawings that you have seen in the last 24 hours. Were they in a shop window, a newspaper story or advertisement, a television news show, or contributions to a display of children's learning documentation for families in the entrance of an early childhood setting? How might photographs of young children in early childhood settings, including the ways they are displayed, represent 'establishing difference' between children and adults or supporting 'the norm' of how children act and look? Which aspects of this thinking might you relate back to embodiment and sustainability concepts?

Why metaphors?

Metaphors are another aspect of communication that can add clarity to making meanings related to people, ideas and events. In fact, a metaphor provides a comparison between two distinct things. Thus by using a metaphor, we can link an unfamiliar 'thing' with a familiar one as we speak or write. This means that one word carries or describes the meaning of another; and so, metaphors can influence our ways of thinking and even ways of viewing the world. For example, Ehrich and English (2013) wrote about 'leadership as dance', while Boud and Hager (2012) explored the actions of 'acquiring and transferring' one's learning as metaphors.

In terms of professional writing with metaphors, Gareth Morgan's (2006) classic book *Images of Organization* continues to be an excellent source of metaphorical workplace ideas. He wrote that 'metaphor is often regarded just as a device for embellishing discourse, but its significance is much greater than this. The use of metaphor implies a way of thinking and a way of seeing that pervade how we understand our world generally' (p. 4). In this context, professional understandings are vital for early childhood settings because the ECE world is complex, diverse and so very human. Morgan presented nine metaphors of organisational life that ECE leader-managers can think about and relate to. He described organisations as: machines, organisms, brains, cultures, political systems, psychic prisons, flux-and-transformation, and instruments of domination. However, Cornelissen (2005) suggested that organisational metaphors go beyond comparing, as noted above. Just consider for a moment what kind of early childhood setting, including the communication patterns, might be described as a machine or a brain.

As further practical examples, a number of years ago I began asking students enrolled in a university early childhood leadership and management unit to research, think about and create a couple of metaphors. The first cluster of metaphors listed below represents their impressions of the interpersonal *climate* or *emotional feeling and culture* of early childhood settings as organisations. These were sites where they

Chapter 2 Exploring communication

were 'attached at the hip' with a director or coordinator for a five-day professional experience. The metaphors the students came up with included:

- spider's web
- construction site
- forest
- grand symphony orchestra
- road trip
- growing garden
- old mother hen
- parachute
- young willow tree
- staff are ducks on a glassy lake
- home away from home
- the world is listening
- community of practice
- family tree
- cluster of balloons floating into the sky
- rowboat
- scaffolding on building
- square peg fits into round hole
- a campfire
- pyramid builders – not rock pushers
- linking rings
- fusion restaurant and head chef
- happy little beehive
- basket full of dreams
- a power-grid
- ants.

After reading through this list, think about what 'setting feeling' you might link with each of these metaphors. For example if a setting seems very welcoming as you enter, what metaphor might represent this feeling? What if your first impression as you open the entrance door reflects a 'dark side' and creates a concerned feeling?

Part 1 Thinking About People and Places

The second cluster of metaphors listed below was created as a reflection of each student's own *preferred style of leadership* for her/his professional work in the early childhood field. These included:

- bonsai
- liquid mercury sunrise
- Spanish onion butterfly
- the gardener
- spiral staircase
- baby bird leaving nest – spreading wings, ready to fly
- growing seed
- beginning to spring
- willow tree
- lighthouse
- the cloud
- long hiking journey
- sunshine
- step outside the square
- on the road to success
- eye of the wonder
- family community with feminine values
- growing sunflower
- scented candle's light
- from stop sign to roundabout mother

Think about which typical leadership style/s you would match with each of these metaphors. For example, if you believe in a democratic rather than authoritarian leadership approach, what metaphor could represent this style? What about leadership styles that you're 'uncomfortable' with, such as the dictator, an inflexible person, a bad listener? What metaphors would you link with each of these dispositions? Such 'dark' metaphors link with Spicer and Alvesson (2011) and Linstead, Marechal and Griffin (2014).

Pause and reflect 2.5

In the metaphor lists above, it is interesting to notice how often aspects of nature, including plants and animals, were used. Might these selected words have any links to being sustainable? Which metaphors would you link with embodiment?

Chapter 2 Exploring communication

From another angle, Grisham (2006) described metaphors and their use within cross-cultural leadership, with such connections focused on effective communication in contexts encompassing trust, empathy, transformation and power. Thus, effective use of metaphors can assist with professional communications among people (refer to Step 3 below). Grisham also linked storytelling with both metaphors and poetry. For a further example of metaphor use in early childhood settings, read the Professional reflection: Lisa's story, below.

Professional reflection: Lisa's story

Metaphor

My research explored what it means to be a teacher aide in a Queensland Preparatory Year classroom. I was aware that issues of marginality, silence, inequality and disempowerment might challenge aides' perceptions of the value of their place within a school community. This in turn might have jeopardised teacher aides' participation in and sense of belonging to that community. When trying to make more sense of this, I turned to the use of metaphors and imagery.

Ropes are akin to a line and are usually malleable; consequently, they can be seen as a journey metaphor. While searching for information about knots in books, I was intrigued by the vast array of knots. Most knots have a specific use for fishing, hiking, sailing and so forth; others are decorative. While knots are often used to secure ropes together, knots weaken a rope. Rope sizes and conditions necessitate different types of knots. To prevent ropes from fraying, 'small stuff' (cords, lines, twine or string) is often whipped around the ends of ropes.

'Small stuff' was significant to my study as it positioned the aides metaphorically. Teacher aides were marginalised in the research and often in practice. Figuratively, the aides can be seen as the 'small stuff' – that is, thin, weaker strength cordage. Conversely, rope can be seen to represent teachers and principals, who are prevalent, often-heard voices in both research literature and school settings.

I also spent time considering the knot of belonging. I was interested to discover that the figure-8 knot (see Figure 2.1) is also known as the blood bight (Wilson, 1998). To me, the visual imagery of the enclosed figure-8 knot represented a sense of belonging and identity.

It is important to be mindful that while metaphor is useful to bring an idea or concept into the foreground, it may lead to particular viewpoints being privileged or unchallenged. While I found the metaphor of ropes and knots useful to examine or reflect upon some areas of my doctoral research study, I was very aware that my interpretations of knots and ropes might differ from those of others. Knots can be obstructions. While some knots become looser with teasing, many others tighten. Ropes can constrict or bind; consequently, they may also be about conflict or an impasse. I realised that the metaphorical use of ropes and knots had a breaking strain; they could collapse or fall apart at some stage. The use of the term 'stuff'

Part 1 Thinking About People and Places

exemplified this. While discussing their everyday experiences, the aides spoke about their role in terms of 'stuff'. At times they collaboratively organised 'stuff' for children with teachers. Sometimes 'stuff' was shared; at other times, the aides were excluded from 'stuff'. The word 'stuff' captured their expressions and encounters; however, the issues the aides identified as 'stuff' were not small. 'Stuff' was significant. Consequently, using the word 'stuff' in my study did not sit easily with the terminology of 'small stuff.' I discovered that metaphors, like the ropes, also had a breaking strain.

A provocation: *To further explore Lisa's ideas about metaphors in conversation and for meaning, think about all the metaphors you use and hear each day. You might jot these down over a day and then do some comparing and contrasting.*

Figure 2.1 *A figure-8 knot (tied by Alice Sonter, 2013)*

Pause and reflect 2.6

Consider the following sentence in terms of its influence on you: 'As I watched you two think (disagree) together, I learned not only that thinking could be a 'messy road' strewn with 'tricky turns' and 'sudden obstacles' but also that philosophy, at its best, is something that is developed and tested in collaborative relationship with others' (Verducci, 2012, p. 127). How much did the travelling metaphors influence your perceptions?

Now, try designing a metaphor or creating a poem that reflects the importance of professional communicating for leader-managers working with colleagues in a community of practice. As a few hints, think about the words 'team', 'squad', 'flock', 'band', 'chatter', 'listening', 'gossip' ... Or, phrases like 'busy as a bee', 'flat out like a squashed bug'. Interestingly, a metaphor can be used so much in relation to a particular phenomenon that it becomes taken for granted; it is then referred to as a 'dead' metaphor (Heracleous & Jacobs, 2008).

Chapter 2 Exploring communication

Step 3: What does professional communication encompass?

Communication is about conveying messages. It encompasses both the ideas that are communicated and the people that are involved. Our personal, private communications may be the same as some of our professional communications, but there will be differences too. Thus, as a situational or positional leader-manager, think about the 'how and what' of your communicating. This will depend on many things:

- Who the others are (people: staff, parents, government officers, children)
- Where you are (places: centre office, centre staffroom, play yard, public meeting room)
- What you are engaged in (relational and community practices: an informal chat, a parent complaint session, a professional learning workshop, a government review forum).

Forms of professional communicating

There are a number of communication crossroads that are essential for each leader-manager working in and with early childhood settings. Such professional crossroads are about how we convey – talk, write, read – everyday information as well as ideas that are unique or special. In other words, communicating involves sharing messages and also receiving ideas. At a broad or basic level, communication encompasses talking and listening, as well as documenting. Often ideas and information are shared within professional and ethical guidelines, such as Early Childhood Australia's *Code of Ethics* (ECA, 2006). The 'Respectful Communication Policy' presented below is another example of practice guidelines.

Armidale and District Family Day Care Respectful Communication Policy
(Armidale and District Family Day Care Limited Scheme, NSW, 2013)

Rationale

Armidale Family Day Care Limited recognises its responsibility to build and maintain a diverse, respectful workplace, where all partners enjoy an environment in which the dignity and self-respect of each person is valued, and which is free of offensive and derogatory remarks, material and behaviour.

Part 1 Thinking About People and Places

Aim

To ensure that every individual partner in AFDC is treated respectfully and courteously in the workplace.

Partners include but are not limited to Directors, Management, Educators, Families and Children.

Policy

All partners have the responsibility to refrain from participating in behaviour that is, or could be perceived to be, disrespectful in nature.

Procedures

All partners are expected to:

- Model respectful behaviour;
- Recognise and value diversity in the workplace;
- Devote adequate time & attention to listening;
- Encourage the free flow of communication;
- Refrain from interrupting the conversations of others, particularly those between other educators and children;
- Create an environment which supports the resolution of respectful workplace issues;
- Inform all partners that the work environment is one based upon respect;
- Orientate and train all employees regarding a respectful workplace; and
- Monitor the workplace to ensure respectful behaviour is practised.

Employees, Educators and partners will:

- Treat others with respect;
- Respect the rights of all other partners;
- Engage in empathy;
- Recognise and refrain from actions which offend, embarrass or humiliate others, whether deliberate or unintended;
- Try to make coherent and concise arguments, rather than attacking others, encouraging other partners to do the same;
- Recognise the potential for other partners to hold different positions, perceptions and conclusions;
- Raise perceived disrespectful conduct with the person displaying it or with management as soon as possible;

Chapter 2 Exploring communication

- Not make allegations of disrespectful behaviour that are frivolous or vindictive; and
- Make every effort to resolve workplace issues respectfully.

If an issue arises, Management will:

- Recognise and address actions that offend, embarrass or humiliate others, whether deliberate or unintentional;
- Treat each situation as a serious matter;
- Manage all situations towards a resolution between parties if possible, with a view to preserving long-term working relationships, in accordance with the Company's Complaints Handling Policy;
- Provide support to partners who are experiencing the effects of disrespectful behaviour;
- Provide a report of the situation to AFDC's Board of Directors; and
- Maintain strict confidentiality in relation to the situation, instructing other partners to follow suit.

Definitions

'Respectful Workplace'

One that values:

- Diversity and the rights of others;
- The dignity of the individual;
- Courteous conduct;
- Mutual respect, fairness and equity;
- Positive communication between people; and
- Collaborative working relationships.

'Disrespectful Behaviour'

Includes, but is not limited to:

- offensive or inappropriate remarks, gestures, materials or behaviours;
- inappropriate jokes or slurs;
- aggressive or patronising behaviour;
- discrimination and harassment; and
- covert behaviour (inappropriately withholding information and undermining).

Part 1 Thinking About People and Places

> **'Workplace'**
>
> Includes Educator's premises, activities connected with the workplace such as travel, conferences and partners' work sites.
> **Reference:** Longest, B.B., *Managing Health Services Organisations.*
> University of Bristol, Dec. 2012
> **Policy Formulated**: February 2013 **To be Reviewed:** August 2014

Talking

There are many ways or manners of talking. However, how we interact ought to indicate that we are talking 'with' others rather than 'at' them. Similarly, how diligently we undertake our listening influences how others respond to us. Diligent listening also encompasses how well a message is accepted and understood. Even body language can influence interactions and shape the effectiveness or otherwise of a conversation. Body language is considered an aspect of the embodiment orientation throughout this book. Beyond our words, professionals' body language may:

- Express a particular message or display a certain meaning
- Represent a precise feeling – warmth, distance, stiffness
- Impart a specific body impression – facial, hands or arms, whole body.

It is important to remember that when talking, our vocal language and our body language may at times give different messages. For example, as a leader-manager you might be discussing a light-hearted idea with a staff member, but if your whole body is stiff and straight, you may appear uneasy or distant or negative. Conversely, if as leader-manager you and a parent are discussing a challenging issue and you begin smiling or laughing, this could give a mixed message (words vs body language) about how seriously you are attending to the parent and her immediate concern.

Writing

Early childhood services are sites where ongoing and ever-changing written communications occur. Different situations call for different ways of writing. As already noted in Chapter 1, Amanda Sinclair (2010) wrote about 'placing self' in terms of the styles of writing. She presented her ideas or voices twice on each page and 'placed' them above and below a horizontal line. The 'top' story had a more formal, academic style and was typical of a journal article. The briefer 'bottom' story had a more conversational style with the intention of relaying an everyday enactment of the above/first story. Here, you might refer to Di Nailon's 'Dear Nadine' letters at the end of each chapter to explore this personal and professional writing balance.

Chapter 2 Exploring communication

Another example of double writing can be seen in early childhood settings' family newsletters when stories and information are presented in two or more languages. For this writing, staff may create a newsletter layout for multiple languages. Here, the leader-manager of family communications will consider ways of presenting stories. Will our newsletter have:

- A top-half and bottom-half look for sharing information
- A left and right columns presentation, so that English and another language can be easily compared side by side
- A separate page for each language, to assist with uninterrupted reading?

In summary, a sampling of typical professional writing patterns encompasses the following:

- Advertisements for vacant staff positions
- Children's application and enrolment forms
- Children's curricular documentation (see Chapter 6)
- Communications beyond the service (local businesses, government offices; see Chapter 7)
- Family newsletters (weekly, monthly or quarterly)
- Policies (see Chapter 5)
- Position/job descriptions (see Chapter 4)
- Meeting notes (such as: staff planning, regional workshops, government briefings)
- Service handbooks
- Staff notices and guidelines
- Staff stories recorded as conversation discussion points.

Pause and reflect 2.7

What other written documents and tasks can you add to this list? Brainstorm all aspects of writing in an early childhood setting with colleagues; do this from a holistic leading-managing perspective. How would you adjust the format for each document? Who might do the initial drafting of these documents – the positional leader-manager, a situational leader-manager for the project or a small team of staff? Think about how the writing style for each document might vary from a centre's typical newsletter for families. Think about how the following items might vary:

- Format or layout, including type and size of fonts
- Use of tables and/or images
- Kinds of words and phrases used
- Length of references and their use or not.

Part 1 Thinking About People and Places

What else might you do differently when creating a staff policy vs a family newsletter, and why? Which documents would your setting translate into languages other than English? What are a few ways of relating and communicating that focus on meaningful family partnerships (consider talking, writing and reading)?

Reading

In addition to talking and writing, situational and positional leader-managers engage in lots of reading. As a leader-manager, you will read various documents on a daily basis, with some days involving more reading than writing or attending meetings. In addition to reading documents such as those listed above, leader-managers may at various times review:

- Local newspapers for relevant early childhood education stories and topical political news items
- Government inquiry notices, issues papers and reporting documents
- Research publications
- Websites of human service organisations
- Professional association membership information, such as Early Childhood Australia's *ECA WebWatch*, an e-newsletter sent to subscribers fortnightly.

A positional leader-manager may well be the initial reader of the above documents, and be responsible for then introducing them to staff or helping other staff with interpreting and interrogating them.

The computer and more

During your professional journey through this book, and as a leader-manager into the future, you will engage in writing and reading via a computer. You may also talk with others using a computer (social networking, social media, search engines; refer to Pause and reflect 2.8, below). Internet research provides links, resources, stories, images, maps and lots more. Additionally, in recent years, many early childhood settings have created their own websites as family sharing places as well as public marketing spaces.

Because of the public nature of electronic tools plus the potential for hacker interference, it is vital that early childhood settings establish transparent professional guidelines and ethical boundaries about access to and use of these tools. At times there will be well-being issues to consider, such as the exposure of staff and children to electromagnetic radiation related to various wireless devices (IARC, 2011; WHO, 2011). As a leader-manager, you may initiate the development of a social media policy or coordinate the establishment of an Information Technology circle or sub-committee for an early childhood setting or for a cluster of settings. For example, safeguarding children and adults in terms of their identity protection and personal privacy is professionally not only sensible but essential. This safeguarding extends to the physical well-being and emotional safety of both children and staff. This means taking a 'precautionary approach' (refer to *WiFi in Schools Australia* at: www.wifi-in-schools-australia.org).

Pause and reflect 2.8

Research what each of the following e-interactive tools is. Then, create a brief explanation or definition that you could share with families in an early childhood setting:

- Email systems are ...
- Facebook is ...
- Google is ...
- Skype is ...
- Twitter is ...
- A website is ...
- YouTube is ...
- Other e-networking services include ...

Working from your professional lens, create a list of everyday and special uses, advantages, benefits or highlights for various electronic tools and services. Then identify any 'downsides' for each tool; that is, what potential risks or concerns might there be for staff, families and children. Particularly focus on these features from a leader-manager perspective. Be sure to consult your traveller's compass to help you identify pluses and minuses related to leading-managing with computers in terms of both embodiment and sustainability.

Contents of professional communicating

There are so many different 'things' that are communicated during a day and across a week within early childhood settings, as well as outside them. This means that leader-managers are engaged in talking with and writing to people in various places with differing lives and roles linked back to early childhood settings. Other members of staff engage in similar communications. As an early childhood leader-manager, your communication style may vary if you are in a situational role vs a positional role. It may also vary because of your workload.

Within an early childhood setting

Professionals communicate all the time at the micro level as their daily work progresses. As a leader-manager you might communicate with yourself, as you:

- Make everyday work-memory notes
- Note key ideas and messages from phone calls and chats

Part 1 Thinking About People and Places

- Record centre calendar/diary entries
- Document autobiographical professional stories in a journal.

This personal narrative, as part of lifelong learning through writing, varies from work-related life history storytelling that is oral (Hallqvist & Hyden, 2013). You will also communicate with children as they arrive or leave the setting, when you are in a playroom or when they visit the office. Additionally, you will communicate with colleagues:

- As they arrive each day
- During morning tea or lunch breaks in the staffroom
- By engaging in individual chats or consultations as well as team meetings.

Finally, you will communicate with parents when greeting them in the morning, during informal chats at the end of the day and as part of more structured interactions during staff and parent planning sessions or committee of management meetings. All communications with parents and sometimes other family members link with the discussion earlier in this chapter of 'family knowing, knowing families'.

Beyond the early childhood setting

Out in the wider world, professionals communicate intermittently at the macro, more distant level with all kinds of people and organisations. As a leader-manager, you may occasionally communicate with other early childhood settings when:

- Comparing particular policies (see Chapter 5)
- Exchanging staff visits for pedagogical insights (see Chapter 4)
- Networking for joint purchases of housekeeping products
- Planning local ECE advocacy events (see Chapter 7).

At times, you will communicate with local businesses, for example when: seeking quotes for purchasing large kitchen items or child-size wooden furniture; placing vegetable and fruit orders for weekly meals; and arranging staff vacancy advertisements in a local newspaper. At a broader level, you might communicate with organisational people such as: the early childhood setting's insurance company for an annual renewal; a professional association regarding resources or a forthcoming conference; or your bank to clarify various accounts on behalf of your setting's parent committee of management or professional/community advisory board. At the broadest level, there may be times when you will communicate with government officials about rubbish and recycling collections by the local council or current State and National laws related to early childhood education services.

Selling the setting

Each of the above communications may well vary in terms of your words and the tone of voice you use. There may be differences in the timing and length of the interactions and your preparations or follow-up. The famous phrase 'The medium is the message' (McLuhan, 1964) related to 'machine' technologies beyond humans, especially the literacy milieu of media – radio, film/movies, television, newspapers, etc. Today there are so many media sources encompassing, and sometimes even bombarding, our everyday lives. As such, it is essential for leader-managers to both understand and critique these technologies and their particular messages as powerful influences on early childhood settings and the people within. For example, consider the idea of publically 'selling' early childhood settings. This might happen with:

- Parents via newspapers, a website or an information brochure, with the purpose of gaining child enrolments
- Potential staff via a newspaper job vacancy advertisement
- An employment agency on their website, with the outcome of team members being hired.

This selling involves branding settings. An organisational or business brand includes the official name with particular colours and specific font-shapes, and any background spacing or outlines. Often organisations extend their brand or logo with a phrase as a motto and/or a representational image; this also happens for some early childhood settings. These branding items not only create a unique identification for a setting but they can have a unique effect on viewers. Such branding represents one form of public communication and a particular sociocultural discourse. For example, many early childhood settings have 'cutesy' fantasy or fairytale names. These names probably miscommunicate, especially to the broader community, what actually happens inside these settings in terms of children's authentic learning and educators' teaching with nurturing care.

Naming people

Beyond the names of early childhood settings, children and staff are often grouped in learning-rooms that are identified using particular terms or phrases. Many of these room-labels seem to belittle our youngest citizens, with children being clustered by age and then labelled as herds or flocks of native and exotic animals, or as plants. Examples of this kind of naming include children and educators being called:

- 'Kangaroos', 'wombats' and 'blue tongue lizards'
- 'Banksias', 'bottlebrushes' and 'wattles'
- Beyond 'nature' labels – 'pirates', 'fairies' or various cartoon characters.

Such branding realities raise a question for early childhood professionals: What is in a name? Thus, leader-managers might wonder:

- Why aren't young children just referred to as a group of children, possibly with a qualifier adverb or adjective to follow?
- Also, what are the common or normative names for various early childhood staff positions, both historically and now?

If we link back to our embodiment orientation, particularly gender, then the name-branding of ECE settings can be interrogated as forms of social, political communicating and meaning-making. Such investigations may well lead professionals to ask and ponder:

- Where are early childhood educators, their workplaces and children 'placed' in society?
- What are the power/less and voice/silence realities across the early childhood education field?
- Could 'naming' practices for settings, groups of children, and staff positions collectively mean that the field is taken less seriously?
- Might contemporary, mainstream branding trends for early childhood settings contribute to broader community views of the field as less professional or non-educational?

Professional storytelling and story writing

This part of your professional path extends a deeper inquiry into the purposes and value of stories, beyond the brief consideration given in the Introduction and Chapter 1. Here you will explore why you might tell your story to yourself and why you might share professional stories. As examples such stories or 'professional reflections' are included throughout this book.

The idea of telling and/or writing one's story can help an author think more deeply about personal meanings within her or his professional life. Such communications provide an avenue for sharing and comparing autobiographical workplace stories with others as a form of co-learning. This might also be a form of mentoring, which links with ideas in Chapters 4 and 7. Support for these purposes comes from Hallqvist and Hyden (2013, p. 1), who reported the value of narratives for biographical learning based on Biesta and Tedder's (2007) two-way description of 'learning about one's life and learning from one's life'.

A similar personal but professional creation involves 'mirroring'. This is when you compose a reflected best-self-portrait and understand that your portrait may change over time (Roberts, Dutton, Spreitzer, Heaphy & Quinn, 2005). From the beginning of this book, you were encouraged to create *My professional leading–managing*

Chapter 2 Exploring communication

journal for documenting your ongoing ideas and experiences with thoughtful reflections about your inspirations, aspirations and realities. This *journal* could be likened to or supported by a professional portfolio (see: Friedman, 2012).

> Storytelling and leadership are both performance arts, and like all performance arts, they involve at least as much doing as thinking. In such matters, performers will always know more than they can tell.
>
> Stephen Denning (2005, p. xi)

Kinds of professional stories

During your professional life, you will be telling stories orally as a way of jointly sharing ideas with both adults and children. You will also be involved in story writing. This might include:

- Documenting an early childhood setting's pedagogical principles and practices (link with Chapter 6)
- Completing both internal and external reports for various usual and ongoing administrative processes
- Recording your everyday positive or negative highlights with feelings in a private personal/professional diary or journal; yet, some of these ideas may be shared with others.

> Writing is egalitarian; it cuts across geographic, class, gender, and racial lines ... we all have a dream of telling our stories – of realizing what we think, feel and see before we die. Writing is a path to meet ourselves and become intimate.
>
> Natalie Goldberg (2005, p. xii)

Uses of professional stories

Another aspect of professional storytelling involves both situational and positional leader-managers being models for other staff. Role-modelling may encompass encouraging and rationalising storytelling and story writing as two forms of professional documenting and reflecting. This kind of leader-manager encouragement can support other staff members to take empowering steps for their lifelong professional learning. Such an approach links with adult learning and andragogy, which are based around socioconstructive theory with attention to individuals' career paths (see Chapter 4). Telling and writing one's stories might have an evaluative angle that takes account of past and present time features during each self-portrayal. Additionally during co-sharing, team members' stories can contribute to a relationship-rich community of practice. Storytelling as collaborative professional learning may form a shared place for critical challenging, debating and revealing marginal views (Taylor, 2013).

Grisham (2006) provided an overview of leadership storytelling and noted that universally, everyone can tell and understand stories. He also linked storytelling with

Part 1 Thinking About People and Places

both metaphors and poetry (refer back to ideas about metaphors earlier in this chapter). Grisham noted Denning's suggestion that leaders' workplace stories ought to: 'spark action (transformation), communicate who you are (trust, empathy), transmit values, foster collaboration, tame rumors, share knowledge, and lead people into the future' (Grisham, 2006, p. 495; refer to Denning, 2005).

Pause and reflect 2.9

How might you as a situational leader-manager of an annual family-oriented, sustainability-transforming project or event use Denning's list (above) to create a story for your 'introduction' to your first briefing meeting at your early childhood setting?

Relevant storytelling and authentic story writing can add to one's life history as well as one's understanding of self and others. Here, human self-identity can be portrayed as 'fluid, contradictory, and multi-vocal' (Tierney, 2010, p. 132). Autoethnography (Ellis, Adams & Bochner, 2011) and autobiography are other names for the process of telling or writing personal stories or vignettes. Mercilee Jenkins (2010, p. 86) stated: 'I do ethnographic writing for the healing and because I believe in social change, not like the Taliban or fundamentalist Christian talk show hosts, but like Gandhi ... [It] can make a difference in how we know the world around us – past, present and future.' As you read the Feature professional reflection: Jan's story, below, look for her display of the above ideas.

Feature professional reflection: Jan's story

My professional reflection. I began my studies of children at TAFE and continued on to do my BT(ECE) and then my BEd(EC). The path was not always easy with my young family, work and the farm, and so I became very adept at time management and late nights. The more knowledge I gained regarding the early childhood field the more I wanted to know and this is what held the goal firmly in place for me. There were huge benefits for me studying this way as I watched my own children and the children I worked with developing, learning and growing.

I did engage in reflective practices even then, though I did not call it reflection, rather I called it by another name – 'obsession'. Reflection was and still is a strategy that I use often as I consider each day's outcomes. I found that reflecting on myself as well as my practice has become a regular learning and teaching tool. The kinds of questions I ask myself include: Could I have done things differently? What has worked brilliantly and why? As well, my

Chapter 2 Exploring communication

reflecting with the team is done informally daily and weekly, as we look critically at what works well and how we can make positive changes. We now use *Belonging, Being & Becoming, The Early Years Learning Framework for Australia* (AGDEEWR, 2009) and the *Guide to the National Quality Standard* (ACECQA, 2013a) as the foundation of our reflective opportunities. They guide and prompt us to delve deeper and more critically into our practices and processes. Sometimes these reflections are focused on the practices and programs, a child or family, the centre, our community or even nationally.

Advocacy. Additionally I have found that advocating for children's rights has become a huge part of my role as both an educator and a leader. Often advocacy is inspired by reflective practice. Being an advocate for children may come in many forms, from issues regarding health, well-being, safety and development. One recent example of advocacy at our service was the issue of many of the children needing support with expressive or receptive language. Being in a regional town, we noted the very lengthy waiting lists they were on to be seen by community health speech pathologists. We felt that various families may have had difficulties accessing support needed or paying for private sessions. The solution was simple – advocating for the engagement of a private speech therapist in both the centre and in an Indigenous outreach program we run. We advocated for these children and families and received enough short-term funding for assessment and programs to be put in place for them. Actively advocating for what we believe is in the best interests of our children. Our service is families orientated, and our focus on building relationships and supporting families is paramount.

A small snippet. Do we wonder how important we are in the lives of others and how important our relationships are? I was humbled recently when I bumped into a parent from many years ago; she said to me 'Thank you – you may not have realised but you really helped me through a difficult time'. At the time I wondered what I had done all those years ago, and I still don't know that I did anything other than treat her with the kindness and respect that all people deserve.

A provocation: What purposes of storytelling and story writing from above (Step 3) can you identify within Jan's story? As a positional leader-manager, when might you use Jan's story as a writing 'role model' with staff in your early childhood setting? How and why might you use it?

Pause and reflect 2.10

Pause here during this communicating leg of your professional journey. Do some thinking about definitions of leading-managing. As an example, this is one of my working definitions: 'Leadership is a caring moral act of positional or occasional leading for collective learning, for heart-and-soul managing, and for a wellness-climate workplace. Such leading encompasses: one's attitudes, abilities, actions and shared interactions' (McCrea, 2002, p. 10). Now in about 25 words each, write your descriptions of: What is an ECE leader? What is an ECE manager? What is an ECE

Part 1 Thinking About People and Places

follower? What is an ECE partner? What is an ECE administrator? What is an officer or director of a Committee or Board of Management in an ECE setting?

What might you change or add to ensure that you have taken an aspirational account of both embodiment and sustainability orientations? Also, as you travel through other chapters, return to these working definitions, think about them and then over time revise each. This revisiting may be particularly helpful in Chapters 4, 5 and 7.

Also, consider establishing a professional community of leader-manager storytellers for supporting and co-mentoring each other. This community could involve staff from within one setting or several local settings or a small cluster of university students. Such a space and time allows for lots of ethical talking and listening. Because your voices matter, go further by working together on some joint story writing and having a publication plan with collective contributions. For example, Donna Rafanello (2006) wrote about publishing as part of 'Child Care Information Exchange's' Mentor Writing Project in the USA.

Conclusion

Travelling through this chapter, you have explored many ideas about communicating and relating with others. Particularly, there has been a focus on both understanding and using storytelling and story writing every day for all kinds of early childhood education leadership and management. With a background of knowing yourself better (Chapter 1) and having a growing appreciation of multiple forms of communicating and stories (Chapter 2), this professional journey now takes you into Chapter 3 to contemplate workplaces.

Dear Nadine,

This chapter continues an 'invitational' approach to writing about leadership by using a style that lays out possibilities rather than 'answers'. Metaphors are used to describe leadership and sustainability in order to help readers relate to and apply concepts and strategies. In this chapter you have not taken the path most travelled in texts about communication. This is not a 'how to' chapter. There are plenty of books on how to run meetings, use persuasive language, adopt listening skills, write reports, or handle difficult conversations. Instead readers are introduced to the nuances of communicating respectfully in early childhood settings. Rather than simply distinguishing between personal and professional communication, written and oral communication and the use of multimedia formats, you give readers more reflective options by weaving together key messages, illustrations and provocations under three 'Steps'. These fit the complex and intimate nature of leading services that focus on child and family well-being and advocacy. You have highlighted the sociocultural and critical nature of communicating with children, families and staff. Power relationships that often get in the way of successful communication are also addressed. My feeling is that by doing this you are respecting what the National Quality Framework for early childhood services in Australia is trying to achieve. I truly hope that those who read this chapter take up the images, metaphors

Chapter 2 Exploring communication

and stories offered under the 'Steps' to see the many ways that communication occurs and how the communication choices we make will depend on each individual involved, the context and the purpose.

As I read the chapter I could not help but relate to the wide range of communication possibilities that occur in any one day. Adopting a leadership role involves so much communication that it may seem overwhelming. Thankfully the chapter contains examples of just what might crop up, along with very useful literature sources that take ideas and examples further. I still think that it is difficult to go past Robert Bolton's (1979) seminal text *People Skills: How to assert yourself, listen to others and resolve conflicts.* Readers will find that they too relate to some books more than others – perhaps it is because of our personal communication styles (introvert, extrovert, formal, informal, avoidant, assertive). Some sites such as *Sources of Insight* at: http://sourcesofinsight.com/communication-skills-and-presenting-books/ illustrate the extent of communication skills that are valued in the corporate world. This chapter provides a range of insights into how best to communicate authentically through our personal beliefs, understandings and storytelling.

For now,
Di

Pause and reflect 2.11

Which idea from this chapter most influenced your current beliefs, and why? As we complete Chapter 2, also consider establishing an e-mentorship communication process with a colleague. First agree to your sharing and supporting each other by email within an agreed timeline; then, begin your 'Dear colleague' relationship (Boris-Schacter & Vonasek, 2009).

Chapter 3

Contemplating workplaces

Leadership is by people with people and their organizations. It is possible that this human-centered perspective works to distance humans from the natural world ... Is it one of humans over, with or of Nature? ... Nature-centered leaders encourage others to reflect on these relationships.

Spencer Stober, Tracey Brown & Sean Cullen (2013, p. 2)

Broad concepts

Here your journey along a professional leading-managing path has reached a point for stopping to explore early childhood settings and significant organisations beyond them. You will be thinking about the following Steps:

- How diverse are early childhood settings?
- What are some beyond-the-fence contexts surrounding early childhood settings?
- What constitutes an organisation?

Chapter 3 Contemplating workplaces

Pause and reflect 3.1
Before progressing, think about: 'What are my understandings and beliefs about the above questions?' After considering each of the questions above, create an entry in your 'My professional leading-managing journal' by jotting down a couple of learning aims for your engaging with this chapter.

Step 1: How diverse are early childhood settings?

Diverse settings
There is a wide variety of early childhood settings across Australia and internationally. We begin from a contemporary frame of these places and spaces, with some relevant historical perspectives included (Ailwood, 2007a). This 'present-and-past' approach to workplaces may assist professionals when they consider which aspects of settings to protect and what features and practices to change. One consideration about settings relates to their 'naming' (refer back to this concept in Chapter 2). The past-present time dimensions are a relevant leadership and management issue here because the same name can have different meanings and nomenclature across contexts and over decades. Thus, staff, parents, community members and even governments may be confused or misled by the names and labels used for early childhood settings.

Naming places
Let us begin by unpacking names. As an example we could ask: 'What is a kindergarten?' In response, kindergartens in Victoria are primarily for four-year-olds; but in New South Wales, they are the beginning of compulsory or formal school for children turning five. In New Zealand, children aged three to five years enrol in kindergartens. Another question could be: 'What is the symbolism and historic origin, or etymology, of the word "kindergarten"?' To answer this, you might look up Froebel, the father of the 'children's garden' (for this, refer to Gahan, 2007; Irvine, 2013; Press & Wong, 2013; Roberts, 1997). Similarly, the first year of formal primary school in Australia has been called: 'kindergarten', 'preparatory', 'pre-primary', 'reception', or 'transition' (Dowling & O'Malley, 2009). In Singapore there are pre-nursery/play schools for three-year-olds and younger, nurseries for four-year-olds and then kindergartens for five- and six-year-olds.

Collectively, early childhood settings are usually called 'sites for early childhood education' (ECE) (Davis, 2010a; Kagan & Kauerz, 2012; Waniganayake et al., 2012; Waters, 2007). More recently the collective label of 'early childhood education and care'

(ECEC) has been introduced (Ailwood, 2007b; COAG, 2009; Edwards, 2009). As an example, the Australian Children's Education and Care Quality Authority is the independent national body that guides the implementation of Australia's National Quality Framework in all of its complexity. Also, there is the term 'early years', which is used in books such as *Belonging, Being & Becoming, The Early Years Learning Framework for Australia* (or *BBB, EYLFA*) (AGDEEWR, 2009) and *Leading and Managing in the Early Years* (Aubrey, 2011).

Furthermore, there have been attempts over the years to linguistically bring children's education and care together by using the term 'educare' (Hallet, 2014). I still prefer 'ECE' and its variations, such as: 'early childhood educators'; 'early childhood education profession/al'; 'early childhood field'; early childhood pedagogy'; and 'early childhood systems'. There is an ideological aspect to these namings. This preference relates to my view of 'early childhood' or 'early education' as inclusive of and encompassing both children's learning and their caring and being cared for. Within this view, children's everyday education and routines are intertwined and collected together within a pedagogical lens (refer to Chapter 6). However, at times there still seems to be a care vs education divide and debate (Rodd, 2013). These ideological and practical challenges mean that some educators and community members view education through a more formal lens; that is, with the view that children's learning and teaching is not inclusive of various everyday routines and well-being care, which are vital aspects of ECE. For example, the phrase 'Education is Care, Care is Education', which was created for invitations to a book launch (McCrea & Piscitelli, 1991), encompasses this particular orientation.

Beyond the care vs education debate in Australia, there is a history of normative sociocultural impressions of women's roles in the home and their involvement in the community. Here you might consider referring back to your guiding compass in the Introduction and its orientation for 'exploring embodiment'. There are also historic service-type variations that have influenced the current forms of early childhood settings. Examples of this include a diversity of: staff training and qualifications; children's age groupings; regulatory requirements; and, parent fees vs levels of government funding (for specific examples, refer to Brennan & Adamson, 2014; Mellor, 1990; Press & Wong, 2013; Sims & Hutchins, 2011).

Thus names and the naming of early childhood settings are an important aspect of site or place identification and transparency for those working within them and also for community members viewing from outside. Words can create confusion and so misinform people, or words can create a crystal-clear impression in people's minds. This is because 'a name carries with it much more meaning than just one or two ideas. [There is] personal experience with that word, [and] our culture's interpretation' (Jaskulsky & Besel, 2013, p. 39; also refer back to Chapter 2).

Types of places
We have reached a point for asking: 'What are all the types of early childhood education services?' In contemporary Australia, the settings that young children attend are predominantly childcare centres and kindergartens or preschools. However, there are other types in Australia and New Zealand, such as:
- Family day care schemes or home-based services
- Playcentres
- Multifunctional Aboriginal children's services (MACS)
- Mobile multi-purpose services
- Integrated children's centres.

There are many resources that outline examples and details about this diversity of services. (For examples, refer to AGDEEWR, 2009; Boyd & Ailwood, 2007; COAG, 2009; Hewes & Leatherman, 2005; Waniganayake et al., 2012.)

Childcare centres may be called 'early learning centres' or 'children's centres' and historically many were referred to as a 'crèche', 'day nursery' or 'nursery school'. Most childcare centres offer enrolments for infants to five-year-olds and they are open for families to use for eight, ten or even twelve hours each day, usually from Monday to Friday. Many childcare settings are referred to as 'long day' or 'occasional' services; this terminology reflects Australian Government types of funding. Occasional childcare centres may be open for about ten hours a day but offer fewer hours and/or few days of service for each young child. Childcare centres are important for young children's learning and care. However, they are also important for parents who have young children and are trying to meet their work commitments. In fact, the original Australian *Child Care Act 1972* (Commonwealth Consolidated Acts, available at: www.austlii.edu.au/au/legis/cth/consol_act/cca197275/) and current Federal and State commitments, including finances, are fundamentally based on women and their workforce participation, more than they are foundationally focused on young children and their education (Ailwood, 2007c; Logan, Sumsion & Press, 2013).

Kindergartens or preschools may also be called 'early learning centres'. Such Australian settings may be community-based and non-profit or they may be owned and run by a person or commercial business for profit. Following on from above, the term 'kindergarten' is the most common historic name, going back to early beginnings in the late 1880s in Australia's capital cities. This establishment involved a 'Free Kindergarten Movement', Kindergarten Unions, and Kindergarten Teachers Colleges or Kindergarten Training Colleges alongside actual centres that young children attended (Mellor, 1990; Press & Wong, 2013; Roberts, 1997). Today, the kindergarten also appears in Singapore as a key type of early childhood education provision (Ang, 2011) and in Europe as a forest kindergarten or, as in Zurich, Switzerland, a 'Waldkindergarten' (view site

Part 1 Thinking About People and Places

at: www.edutopia.org/early-childhood-outdoor-education-waldkindergarten; Knight, 2011; and refer forward a few pages for 'forest kindergartens').

The following is a list of different kinds of early childhood settings whose meanings and purposes you could research:

- preschools or kindergartens
- childcare centres
- family day care schemes or home-based services
- playcentres
- hospital-based ECE services
- multifunctional Aboriginal children's services (MACS)
- mobile multi-purpose children's services
- Indigenous playgroups
- on-farm care
- nanny services
- integrated children's centres
- work-based children's services

Pause and reflect 3.2

Working from your previous studies and any workplace experiences, create a description or definition for each of the early childhood sites listed above. Do some comparing and contrasting of the setting names in countries beyond Australia and New Zealand. Think about how much these service types intertwine vs have distinctions, both now and in the past. What leader-manager responsibilities might you have as an educator or as a positional director to help community members to better understand the nature of early childhood settings and their names?

Settings as landscapes

During your professional journey, early childhood settings are viewed as 'professional landscapes' within multilayered contexts that are similar to Urie Bronfenbrenner's bioecological systems theory. (For examples, refer to Bronfenbrenner, 2005; Hearron & Hildebrand, 2007; Prior & Gerard, 2007; Rogoff, 2003; Sims & Hutchins, 2011; refer also to Introduction.) A sustainable lens can be added to this framework (Littledyke & McCrea, 2009; McCrea & Littledyke, in press; Stanger, 2011). The image or metaphor for exploring professional landscapes fits with the idea of you as a traveller going on a leadership and management journey through this book. Such landscapes are influenced by: government policies; forms of management or governance (who manages them); as well as any particular philosophical stances that staff members may take.

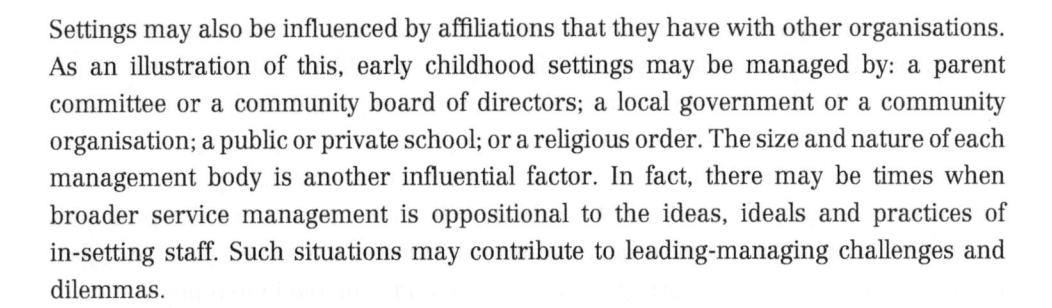

Settings may also be influenced by affiliations that they have with other organisations. As an illustration of this, early childhood settings may be managed by: a parent committee or a community board of directors; a local government or a community organisation; a public or private school; or a religious order. The size and nature of each management body is another influential factor. In fact, there may be times when broader service management is oppositional to the ideas, ideals and practices of in-setting staff. Such situations may contribute to leading-managing challenges and dilemmas.

Settings and philosophies

Historically, key philosophical stances and cultural orientations within the early childhood education field have developed from foundations such as:

- Maria Montessori
  (Eissler, 2009; Feez, 2010 & 2013; Lillard, 2005)
- Rudolf Steiner/Waldorf
  (MacNaughton & Williams, 2009; Shell, nd)
- Reggio Emilia
  (Edwards, 2009; Katz & Chard, 2000; Malaguzzi, 1987; McLachlan, Fleer & Edwards, 2013; Sims & Hutchins, 2011)
- Aboriginal worldviews
  (Herbert, 2013; Markiewicz, 2012; Martin, 2007a & 2007b; Miller, 2010; NSW Department of Local Government, 2007; Qld Department of Education, Training & Employment (QDETE), 2013; Sims, 2011b; SNAICC, 2013; Summerville & Hokanson, 2013; Wooltorton & Bennell, 2007)
- Te Kohanga Reo
  (the total immersion te reo Maori whanau-family program for mokopuna in New Zealand; NZ Ministry of Education, 1996; Ritchie, 2013 & 2012)
- 'Forest' kindergartens and 'bush' or 'beach' kindergartens
  (forest in Sweden, Denmark, Scotland, Great Britain: Knight, 2011; Maynard, 2007; Sandberg & Arlemalm-Hagser, 2011; and bush in Australia: Dorrat, 2011; Elliott & Chancellor, 2013).

Being both foundational and contemporary, such philosophical and theoretical positions inform various educational components of early childhood settings. These components may encompass: the philosophy and policies; staff education and their ongoing professional learning; everyday pedagogy with curricula and learning-and-teaching cycles; educational resources; indoor and outdoor layouts and designs. (For examples, refer to Arthur, Beecher, Death, Dockett & Farmer, 2012; Edwards, 2009; MacNaughton & Williams, 2009; Widger & Schofield, 2012; also refer to Chapter 6.)

Setting furnishings and resources

The design of early childhood settings is influenced by contemporary views of the young child and childhood, as well as by various State, National and international normative guidelines and requirements. And of course, there are historic community and professional ideas that inform at least some of the indoor and outdoor spaces created within today's early childhood settings. Basically, when an early childhood setting is established, neither the indoor spaces nor the outdoor places are totally empty.

So, what are the usual furnishings and resources, and why are they provided? As an Australian example, the *BBB, EYLFA* (AGDEEWR, 2009, p. 14) practice-principles include 'creating physical and social learning environments that have a positive impact on children's learning'. This principle is explained and explored in that publication in less than a page, with comment on the feel, purposes and nature of both indoor and outdoor learning spaces. The related Australia-wide legal documents are the *Education and Care Services National Law* with the *Education and Care Services National Regulations* (Ministerial Council, 2011). However, a specific listing of expected furnishings and resources was not provided in the *Regulations*; rather 'Part 4.3 Physical environment' regulation #105 was written in repetitive language and lacked any details regarding indoor or outdoor spaces to assist those consulting this legal document.

It is true that a 'list' can be reductionist, hyper-rational and normatively limiting; however, a list can also provide useful broad guidance as a starting point for those seeking advice and direction. This double view of professional guidance with it being very general vs more explicit can be explored through such power lenses as domination and control by governments alongside resistance and/or freedom of professionals (Ball, 2003; Ball & Olmedo, 2013). This idea might vary from professionals struggling for support to them having helpful, transparent information. Furthermore, we can ask: 'What might be a relevant or most useful balance of such power relations and communications for early childhood settings, especially as educators become more engaged and professional?' Both guidance approaches do usually offer further references and links to other ideas and sources.

As an example, the third aspect of the Australian legal puzzle was the establishment of the *National Quality Standard*. The 'Quality Area 3 Physical environment' extended the educational furnishings statements from that set out in the *Regulations*. This extension of professional guidelines was provided in the *Guide to the National Quality Standard* (ACECQA, 2013a), which encompassed overviews, questions, aims, assessor approaches and further readings. All the above ideas are relevant and actively applied when a team of staff cooperate to create a *Quality Improvement Plan* (*QIP*) (ACECQA, 2013b).

Other settings' guidelines

A guidelines and legal comparison task can be undertaken beyond Australia. In New Zealand, the Ministry of Education provided a dual document encompassing *Licensing Criteria for Early Childhood Education and Care Centres 2008* and the *Early Childhood Education Curriculum Framework* (NZ Ministry of Education, 2011). Within this booklet, readers were also referred to both the *Education Act 1989* and the *Education (Early*

Childhood Services) Regulations 2008. The Ministry booklet broadly outlines furnishings, resources and children's curriculum requirements in qualitative and quantitative terms – 'sufficient', 'suitable' and/or 'appropriate'. Similarly, Singapore's Ministry of Education is responsible for early childhood settings (Ang, 2011) and the Early Childhood Development Agency oversees regulation and development. The Singapore Ministry developed a number of *Nurturing Early Learners* (*NEL*) curricular resources. The key document is *Nurturing Early Learners, A curriculum framework for kindergartens in Singapore* (Ministry of Education Singapore, 2012). A mother tongue languages resource also supports both parents and educators.

Which resources?

Early childhood educators and leader-managers may ask: 'What furnishings are relevant for early childhood settings?' As a leader-manager, you might respond to this question by undertaking an environmental and situational analysis with other staff. Such an analysis would include reviewing furnishings, learning spaces and education resources. Within a well-established early childhood setting, this can be a particularly valuable approach (Crowther, 2011; Sims & Hutchins, 2011). Additionally, using an Appreciative Inquiry lens may well extend the value of this exploration for everyone (online: http://appreciativeinquiry.case.edu).

Indoor furnishings begin with child-size tables and chairs often near low, moveable shelving units that display and store hands-on learning materials. Children's everyday learning materials encompass such essential items as: a full set of wooden unit blocks; creative arts consumables; picture books; manipulative materials; and natural and human-made artefacts. Outdoor places usually consist of natural features such as sand, water, soil, plants and paths. There are also flexible open spaces for redesigning with various whole-body manipulative resources and for lots of movement by children.

If a setting follows a particular ECE theory or philosophy, then some furnishings and learning resources will be individualised to reflect those values and related aims. For example, Steiner settings will have child-size furniture and many learning resources made from wood, often with curves and bark along with pale coloured cotton fabrics. These resources are natural and rustic (Bone, 2005; Shell, nd). They will be supported by natural, wild outdoor spaces and edible garden places. Whereas, a Montessori early childhood setting will display many specialised learning resources for children to 'do it myself'. Some examples are:

- Sensorial materials – pink tower, wooden smelling bottles
- Practical life items – dressing frames, functional child-sized household cleaning tools
- Mathematical objects – number rods, sandpaper letters and numbers (Eissler, 2009; Feez, 2013 & 2010; Lillard, 2013 & 2005).

Part 1 Thinking About People and Places

A setting with a sustainable living–learning philosophy will incorporate both pedagogical features and daily practices that are sympathetic with Early Childhood Education for Sustainability (ECEfS) (refer to Chapter 6 for other pedagogical matters and examples). In fact, there are hints that this ECEfS belief-approach might happen more easily in early childhood settings than many currently believe. This is because generally women seem to be more aware, more concerned and more active when environmental issues arise (Sakellari & Skanavis, 2013). Examples of such ECEfS decisions might include:

- Pedagogical features like – creating children's edible gardens; establishing natural wild places; incorporating natural pieces of shells, rocks and wood; balancing when to just observe natural things and when to carefully collect a few; blending in children's acts of community citizenship that engage economic, social and political issues; integrating place-belonging concepts and responsibilities; and, encompassing Indigenous wisdom sentiments within relationships and interactions. (For examples, refer to ACECQA, 2013a & 2013b; AGDEEWR, 2010 & 2009; Aquash, 2013; Armstrong, 2013; Bone, 2005; Cutter-Mackenzie & Edwards, 2013; Duhn, 2012; Edwards & Cutter-Mackenzie, 2011; Elliott, 2014a & 2014b; Kinsella, 2008; Lee, 2012; McCrea, 2008; Pratt, 2010.)

- Daily practices such as – installing a solar hot water system; considering water tanks; making 'food first' among a setting's ECEfS commitments; establishing an energy policy centred on using more natural light; ensuring light bulbs are the most efficient (LED), and meaningfully turning on lights; using forest-friendly paper products; engaging with the 'three-Rs' (reduce, reuse, recyle) across all operations of the whole setting, especially by reducing in the first place and then reusing; maintaining green cleaning practices in the office, kitchen and playrooms, and all outdoor spaces. (For examples, refer to Almers, 2013; Australian Ethical, 2014; Davis, 2008; Davis, 2010b; Davis & Elliott, 2014; Duncan & Bartle, 2014; Edwards, Moore & Cutter-Mackenzie, 2012; Karliner, 2005; McCrea, 2006; McNicol, Davis & O'Brien, 2011; Pramling Samuelsson & Wagner, 2012; Taylor, A., 2013.)

Pause and reflect 3.3

Think about being a newly appointed educational leader who is asked to create a shopping list for purchasing all the standard early childhood learning resources. The context is a new setting with infants to five-year-old children. What would you include? Also, think about when and how you would consult with colleagues; who beyond-the-fence you might consult; how you would go about identifying pedagogical justifications for purchasing various children's learning resources over others, for a parent committee of management; and in what ways you might encourage colleagues to link these learning resources with your setting's educational philosophy and the contemporary curriculum guidelines. When considering these questions, also refer to Chapters 4 and 6 and 'National Quality Standard (NQS)' (ACECQA, 2013a; Cheeseman, 2012).

Chapter 3 Contemplating workplaces

People within settings

Of course many people interact within early childhood settings. There are young people – the children – and adults, being either staff members or families. Parents and other community members may initially contribute to a setting by delivering and picking up children; however, they can have much more involvement, as you will explore gradually in the following chapters. The staff working within an early childhood setting may take on many positional roles: assistant working with children, cook, cleaner, room leader, teacher, educator, accountant, gardener, office administrator, bus driver, assistant director, coordinator or director, etc. There are also those working in family day care schemes, with such position titles as: business manager, coordinator, child development officer, and home educator.

Roles

Further discussion about staff and staffing issues appears in the next chapter. Your whole professional journey through this book will include many examples of adults taking on leader-manager roles or positions. The last four chapters of the book are framed by a broad leading-managing approach and they encompass four key professional roles:

- Team stakeholder
- Policy designer
- Pedagogy creator
- Rights advocate.

At an early childhood setting level we might even call these professionals 'micro-landscape' leader-managers, with their micro or near work reflecting one or two of Bronfenbrenner's nested circles (Bronfenbrenner, 2005; Sims & Hutchins, 2011). Professionals can also be considered from a role-relationships angle, such as getting along, disagreeing with negotiating and mentoring empowerment. The ability to get along with others is vital and appears to be simple. Human interactions, however, encompass both engaging positives and challenging situations. This is where we balance disagreeing and negotiating with others, along with carefully noting the strength or tone of our encounters. As professionals move beyond just getting along, the idea of empowering one's self and others comes to the foreground. As you might imagine, becoming empowered involves both power and the political. Look for examples of getting along, disagreeing, negotiating and empowering in the Feature professional reflection: Jan's story, below.

Part 1 Thinking About People and Places

Feature professional reflection: Jan's story

Empowering relationships. One of the most foundational skills I have learnt in leading a centre is about being flexible and fluid. A key lesson for me has been acceptance that the day may not unfold as planned, yet to calmly accept this for what it is. This also means having an understanding that when working with people I have to be willing to change and adapt, to listen carefully and accept what is. For me relationships are essential and foundational to everything else that happens. For example, we see that within the landscape of the centre, consideration must be given to different people and the relationships that are cultivated. Relationships with families, children, the team, other professionals and support services may vary in the early childhood field. I aim to find the right balance when building respectful relationships, by giving consideration to culture, age, ability and personalities. I see my role as a leader constantly adjusting to allow for these changes. At times I find my role as a leader can extend to being an advocate, counsellor and listener, teacher, mentor and friend, negotiator or boundary setter, budgeter or organiser, but underlying all of these is an ethical professional.

Encouraging voice. One area I feel strongly about is how to advocate for and yet encourage everyone to have a voice. To do this I incorporate the idea of equity rather than equality into my leadership practice. What I mean by this is that everyone should not have an equal platform but rather a varied equitable platform that allows each to achieve equality. The focal idea here is that through equity we can give those that need support an extra helping hand to achieve equality. Another aspect of creating empowering relationships is ensuring all stakeholders are heard. Anthony Semann once said at an 'Unpacking Conference' in Sydney: 'It is not the loudest voice that should always be heard.' This statement resonated with me, especially in regards to the diversity within my centre. So often we do only hear the loudest voice in a group and the quiet voice goes unheard. One way I get around this within our team is to set up opportunities for educators to express themselves. This might be finding moments to connect and chat with them in an informal way, and ask for their thoughts on a situation. At times this may include being a voice for the quiet ones. At meetings another technique I use is to encourage the quieter educators to share their thoughts on an idea first before the rest of the team. The agenda item that we are talking about might be in regard to a policy or practice and I might say: '[educator's name], what do you think about . . . ?' I find this simple technique does work – all team members are then heard and empowered. I also use this practice when making a point to ask quiet or less confident families for their feedback, or even when working with those quieter children. By modelling the importance of the opinions or thoughts of the quieter ones – child, parent or educator – this personalised questioning seems to raise each person's standing in the group. This approach also nurtures the confidence and self-identity of the quiet voice. Similarly, collaboration within our team is vital. It encourages educators to have a voice, be part of any changes, and take ownership of the

Chapter 3 Contemplating workplaces

choices made and the implementation of these choices. It gives our team a greater sense of unity.

A provocation: Review Jan's 'encouraging voice' ideas and think about one or two additional ways that you as a positional leader-manager like Jan might further empower your quieter staff members. Share these ideas with your colleagues for their feedback and impressions.

Influences and interacting

Within a framework such as the Bronfenbrenner one, everyone moves back and forth from themselves to outer influences and organisations (refer back to 'roles' and also note the next Step, below; Rogoff, 2003; Swick & Williams, 2006; Ungar, Ghazinour & Richter, 2013). Another relevant thought for this segment of your professional path is the idea that settings influence people *and* people influence settings. These influences can be supportive, but they can also be concerning or problematic. This is where professional agreements can be reached and professional dilemmas can be addressed as early childhood staff members engage in wise, critical comparisons. For example, comparative ECE processes (Tayler, 2007) may relate to:

- Identifying theoretical frames
- Noting different readings of policy
- Distinguishing interests, trends and concerns of the time (also refer to Kolb, 2008; Krieg, Davis & Smith, 2014; McLachlan, 2011; Pye, 2005; Widger & Schofield, 2012; Wong, 2013).

Asking deep questions (Tayler, 2007) during these investigations can be a useful approach, as it can help you and other participants explore oppositional ideas and practices in meaningful ways. From my perspective, it seems that all these processes ought to have a collective and reflective aspect, which a key leader-manager might encourage and guide.

Pause and reflect 3.4

Pull out your traveller's compass and consider some physical setting dilemmas and challenges that you might face as the designated 'educational leader' ('NQS'; ACECQA, 2013a) of a kindergarten or preschool. Use 'green' and 'rosy' coloured lenses (see Introduction for compass with two orientations – embracing sustainability and exploring embodiment) to guide your story writing about such issues. Also note how you would negotiate with other educators when discussing these place and space issues at a curriculum planning meeting.

Part 1 Thinking About People and Places

Step 2: What are some beyond-the-fence contexts surrounding early childhood settings?

This step along your leading-managing path encircles many beyond-the-fence workplaces that directly or indirectly relate with early childhood settings. Although these sites and the people within them are external to ECE settings, they still influence leading and managing.

Workplaces beyond-the-fence

Again, an ecological systems or Bronfenbrenner-like model encompasses the various organisations that link with early childhood settings (Stanger, 2011). These different kinds of organisations or workplaces include:

- Layers of government – local, state and federal
- Professional early education linked organisations
- Other educational sites and services
- Professional membership organisations
- Local businesses.

Australian government links

The traditional three layers of Australian government all have strong guidance roles and usually have various support links with every type of children's service. At the local government level, this will be in the form of town and rural planning links with early childhood settings when new sites are proposed or renovations are considered. Local governments administer public water systems and waste collections with recycling. They sponsor community libraries and neighbourhood parks. Some local governments run a cluster of early childhood settings, where they own the land and buildings as well as hire and manage staff. When this is the case, there is usually an overarching council person who coordinates and facilitates both staff and settings. Within many councils, this person has an early childhood education qualification and is responsible for broad leading and managing.

Pause and reflect 3.5

You might be wondering about the nature of children's services and their links with local government beyond Australia. If you are, this can be a stopping point on your professional leading-managing path to again comparatively look outside Australia. Review any similarities and variations, and do so with a leader-manager lens. Do you know the historical roles of the local council where you currently live or work, in terms of their provision of children's services?

Chapter 3 Contemplating workplaces

The various Australian States are central to the provision of early childhood education. They fund kindergarten/preschool education, usually for four-year-old children. Until recently, States independently set and implemented regulations for various early childhood centre-based services, at times including family day care schemes. More recently, the *Victorian Children's Services Act 1996* and the *Children's Services Regulations 2009* applied to most but not all early childhood settings in Victoria. This was the case for every Australian State or Territory until the Council of Australian Governments (COAG) agreed to a partnership called the 'National Quality Agenda' in December 2009. This encompassing countrywide reform for the benefit of young children happened within a 'productivity agenda'. The ensuing National Quality Framework (ACECQA, 2013c) came into effect in January 2012. It included a *National Law* (*NL*) with *National Regulations*, the *National Quality Standard* (*NQS*) (ACECQA, 2013a & 2013b), and the establishment of ACECQA. One key result was an Australia-wide uniform standard for most early childhood services. Within this national legal framework, each State or Territory established a 'regulatory authority' with responsibility for approving and monitoring as well as assessing quality within the *NL* and *NQS* parameters of services (ACECQA, 2013c). States may also take responsibility for investigating complaints or concerns about services plus advising services about 'best practice' (Gowrie Victoria, 2013).

The Commonwealth of Australia is a federal constitutional monarchy with parliamentary democracy and British Commonwealth membership. As you will have already noted during your professional journey along this leading-managing path, the Australian Government has a history of deep involvement with various aspects of the early childhood education field (for examples, refer to Ailwood, 2007a; Brennan & Adamson, 2014; COAG, 2009; Logan, Sumsion & Press, 2013; Press & Wong, 2013; Wangmann, 1991). Currently, this commitment begins with the legal *National Quality Agenda* and the Framework agreement with States and Territories as noted above. The Commonwealth also provides funding for the direct operation of childcare centres, family day care schemes and out of school hours programs (OOSH). In the past, the Australian *Child Care Act 1972 (Cwlth)* set the scene for:

- Defining quality spaces for children and the quality and quantity of staff (Logan, Sumsion & Press, 2013)
- Providing funds for children's services.

This particularly assisted mothers to re/join the workforce and parents to undertake VET and university studies. The Australian Government also established the National Childcare Accreditation Council and the mandatory *Quality Improvement and Accreditation System* (*QIAS*) for childcare centres across the country (from 1993–2011; go to 'NCAC archive' within the ACECQA website at: www.acecqa.gov.au/ncac-archive; Wangmann, 1991). The *QIAS* provided a national step forward for some

Part 1 Thinking About People and Places

early childhood settings beyond the existing State regulations (McCrea, 1989). Many people, programs and resources influenced the development of *QIAS*; these included:

- The NAEYC voluntary accreditation system for early childhood programs in the United States (Bredekamp, 1987; NAEYC, 2010, 2007, 1998 & 1991; Sciarra, Dorsey, Lynch & Adams, 2013, p. xi)
- The Queensland 'voluntary accreditation' consultancy process and documents (McCrea & Piscitelli, 1991, 1989a & 1989b; Press & Wong, 2013, p. 69; Waters, 2007, p. 122). The Queensland consultancy *Handbook* was later adopted with cultural adaptations and language translations for use in Vietnam in 1995 and Hong Kong in 1996.

The *National Quality Standard* replaced *QIAS* with renewed processes and numerous documents from 2012, with *NQS* applying to virtually all kinds of early childhood services across Australia, rather than primarily childcare centres.

Other governments and organisations

For comparing and contrasting beyond Australia, you can review other countries' governmental structures alongside their work for and with children's services. (Refer back a few pages to Tayler's (2007) comparative approach as a frame for these investigations; see also Cornelissen, 2005.) For example, Singapore is a sovereign republic, city-state and island country, as well as a member of the British Commonwealth like Australia. There is no local government layer; however there are community development councils with mayors. Similarly, Fiji is a Pacific island country with a parliamentary republic government, including a number of municipal local governments with mayors. New Zealand is a third government worthy of children's services comparisons.

Additionally, there are international organisations and guidelines or agreements that cross-link national countries and their governments. For example, the United Nations (UN) as an international inter-government organisation was founded following the end of World War II by more than fifty countries with a broad commitment to world peace. A number of the UN's key 'arms' relate directly to young children and families around the world; these include this sampling:

- UN Educational, Scientific and Cultural Organization (UNESCO: https://en.unesco.org)
- UN Children's Fund (UNICEF: www.unicef.org/about/)
- World Food Programme (WFP: www.wfp.org; and related Food and Agriculture Organization of the UN: www.fao.org/home/en/)
- Office of the High Commissioner for Human Rights (www.ohchr.org/EN/Pages/WelcomePage.aspx)
- Office for Children and Armed Conflict (www.childrenandarmedconflict.un.org)
- Commission on the Status of Women (www.un.org/womenwatch/daw/csw/)
- Commission on Sustainable Development (http://sustainabledevelopment.un.org).

Chapter 3 Contemplating workplaces

Pause and reflect 3.6

Where do children's services fit into the government layers of Singapore and Fiji or New Zealand? Think about investigating beyond the southern Pacific Rim to other countries and their commitments to young children. What kinds of early childhood leading-managing roles and positions exist in Scandinavian or European countries? Finally, review online at least one 'arm' of the UN that you think might provide international views and perspectives relevant to your current studies and work with young children at a whole-setting level.

Professional engagements

Professional micro-links

Early childhood staff members interact regularly with any number of professional organisations at a micro or near level. Three examples of such bodies would be the historic collection of:

- KU Children's Services in New South Wales
- C&K in Queensland
- FKA Children's Services in Victoria.

For more than a century, the above organisations have provided general assistance and guidance for early childhood educators, leader-managers and whole settings. They also coordinate specific support units. For example FKA has a long-established Multicultural Resource Centre, and C&K includes an Aboriginal and Torres Strait Islander Programs Unit with the Dhagun-Gur Resource Library.

Additionally, across Australia the six Lady Gowrie Centres continue to cater for a variety of everyday aspects of early childhood settings. These include staff professional learning events and pedagogical resources, as well as offering their own daily services for local children (Press & Wong, 2013). Furthermore, organisations like Community Child Care Co-operative in New South Wales and Community Child Care Association in Victoria are State-specific peak bodies with membership primarily through early childhood settings, with some individual professionals also joining. They create multiple resources such as newsletters, journals and fact sheets, and they also cater for staff professional learning needs. As a situational or positional leader-manager within an early childhood setting, there will probably be times when you will interact with these organisations or similar ones, both as a leader and on behalf of other staff. One of these organisations might be a place where you professionally volunteer and act as an advocate (link with Chapter 7) or you might work within one as an early childhood leader-manager. Following on with a sampling of professional links, but beyond these examples, consider: What comparative professional bodies exist in other Australian States and in other countries?

Broader education links

There is another layer of beyond-the-fence workplaces that often links early childhood settings; these include various education sites and services. One example of such linking happens with local primary schools, as educators and leader-managers help families negotiate children's transitions from an ECE centre to beginning formal school. Similarly, a leader-manager may arrange on-site observation visits with local high school teachers in order for teenagers to learn about young children in educational contexts. Settings that enrol children with additional needs and rights will probably establish ongoing links with specialist professionals and services. The relevant professionals might be a special education teacher, a physiotherapist or a speech therapist. Additional broader-education links might be established with universities, TAFE colleges and/or other VET providers, particularly:

- As existing staff members undertake further ECE studies
- When higher education students visit early childhood settings to complete their professional experience days.

Pause and reflect 3.7

Think about what other broader beyond-the-fence education workplaces might link with early childhood settings. Create a listing of possibilities and explore how you as leader-manager might liaise and work with them on behalf of your workplace.

Professional macro-links

A further professional link for early childhood educators and leader-managers might be established through individual or centre membership with Early Childhood Australia (ECA; Press & Wong, 2013) or similar professional associations within Australia or beyond. For those leader-managers with sustainability leanings, specialist engaging, resourcing and advocating can happen via the New South Wales Early Childhood Environmental Education Network or through Environmental Education in Early Childhood (Victoria) or the Queensland Early Childhood Sustainability Network. Even the countrywide Australian Association for Environmental Education has an Early Childhood Special Interest Group.

For those leader-managers committed to ensuring sensitive and relevant settings for all children, professional links may well be created with organisations such as:

- Ethnic Child Care, Family and Community Services Cooperative – a NSW state-wide peak organisation, which focuses its work on children and families from Culturally and Linguistically Diverse (CALD) backgrounds
- Australian Research Alliance for Children & Youth, which focuses on holistic well-being.

Chapter 3 Contemplating workplaces

Local business links

Early childhood settings interact with many community businesses during each twelve-month period. There are routine consumable purchases to arrange, such as: food items, toiletries, office supplies and children's art resources. Each of these consumables can involve several local businesses. For example, the purchase of weekly or fortnightly food stores usually means linking with a butcher shop, a vegetable and fruit shop and a supermarket. This is also an important stopping point for reconsidering and aspiring to sustainability (refer back to 'Which resources?' in Step 1). Besides purchasing, early childhood settings have payments and disposals to attend to, with each of these creating more organisational links beyond-the-fence. As a financial support, ECA's *Getting up to speed – Digital business kit for Early Childhood* could be a valuable resource for this leading-managing work. Then there are business links that extend past the local community.

Pause and reflect 3.8

Think about all the other businesses that leader-managers in early childhood settings might interact with regularly and occasionally. What kinds of businesses have you identified? Which of these linking contact relationships might you share with other staff so that they act as situational or project leader-managers? Brainstorm these businesses and organisations with colleagues to extend this into a team-collective listing of local and broader contacts.

Feature professional reflection: Jan's story

Looking outside the service and building relationships. Advocating for our centre, families and rural-regional communities is an aspect of leadership that I have developed over the years. Initially when I began my early childhood career, I concentrated all of my efforts within the centre. In those first few years, I felt my only role was to nurture the children and families under 'my wing'. I would say my view slowly changed as my awareness of my role and confidence in my leadership practice grew. We have a high number of Indigenous children enrolled in our centre, and our service is highly regarded in the local Aboriginal community, based on a long history of building strong relationships. Also, our usual children's services run additional programs within the local Aboriginal community that are aimed at helping empower families. Following are two examples.

Exploring centre needs. One evening when I was supposed to be sleeping, I was considering the Aboriginal boys at our service. I wondered how they expressed themselves through their behaviour, and then I had a light-bulb-moment. We needed a strong Aboriginal male role model to help guide our boys. It was then that the birth of the 'Strong Man Program' happened. I shared this idea with everyone I knew, asked for advice, and then began the task of submission writing, constant telephone calls and 'begging for funding'. After many, many hours, weeks and months of seeking, we were supported by both State funding and a private organisation. An Aboriginal youth was hired for the role, and he remains with us today. This program continues to successfully operate into its fifth year, with amazing outcomes for our whole community.

Exploring community needs. Another program we advocated for was 'Parents in the Park', a Friday morning playgroup. After receiving a grant to purchase a trailer and resources, we went into the local Aboriginal community and set up in the park. After that we were back on the funding merry-go-round until DEEWR supported us with the funds to run this program. Funding is sought yearly in order to continue this invaluable service.

Each week we set up at a local park about five kilometres from the preschool. We operate this program in conjunction with the 'Linking Together Centre', which is an Indigenous support agency offering many community programs. Our program certainly steps outside the box, as we provide both parent education events for families that choose not to go to an early childhood service and a direct outdoors play-learning service for children. We identified that there were children and families that decided not to utilise a conventional service. Through this program we bring in support networks, schools, community health staff and other organisations. Families and children explore their offerings, develop relationships with others, and foster their own personal inclusion as relevant. Our feedback from the Aboriginal Education Consultancy Group (AECG), as well as from Elders, partners, support networks, educators and the broader community, has been positive.

What are other possibilities for everyone? Our next aim is to create a gathering place that is for our centre families but also other families in the local community. In conjunction with this, we have identified that there are no public nappy changing or breastfeeding facilities in our town of 15 000 people. And so we asked, could we provide these together with a space for networking? A gathering space would provide opportunities for coming together for: meetings; making new relationships; forming networks; and gathering information about child and parenting supports. It could be a space for meeting therapists and educators. And importantly, such a gathering place ought to be physically beautiful, with indoor and outdoor spots for quiet reflection.

Advocating in many ways. We subtly advocate for children's right to play, through our daily educational program and practices. We also advocate more intentionally through the way we view our role, and then more actively, explicitly out in the wider world. As a leader, I am part of a community and an advocate for children and families. One of the most important skills I have learnt is that if I believe in the possibilities for change, all I have to do is dig my heels in deep, be persistent and keep asking. I like to believe this is professional advocacy; otherwise it might be recognised as stubbornness!

A provocation: As you identify Jan's ways of advocating, think about how comfortable you would be right now doing the same things. Are you professionally ready to believe in and take such actions? If you feel you are not ready, note what you might investigate or who you might consult with to help you be more confident and committed. Would having a mentor or coach assist you with your advocacy aspirations (link with Chapter 7)? What about forming a professional support network?

Chapter 3 Contemplating workplaces

There are histories for all the workplaces that interact with early childhood settings. There are also contexts that influence the contemporary views and practical realities of defining and studying a children's services leader-manager. Thus, a 'macro-geography' leader-manager will have multiple broad roles and diverse relationships with families, community cultures, governments and companion organisations. This complex world of people, influences and settings can lead to dilemmas and challenges for both situational and positional leader-managers, and at times for all other staff members.

Step 3: What constitutes an organisation?

All of the workplaces noted in this chapter are organisations. They have major social context features and factors that result in two-way influences. Children's services are often considered human service organisations, yet labelled 'institutions' rather than services by others (Dahlberg, Moss & Pence, 2001; Ebbeck & Waniganayake, 2003). As portrayed in Step 2, some of these links beyond-the-fence are broader than other human services. The nature or essence of an organisation is an important aspect of leading-managing both the site and the people within.

Setting ambiance

In fact, the people within an organisation and those visiting it can 'feel' that place or space. Such feelings are often referred to as the climate or cultural ambiance of a place. The idea of early childhood settings as places that can be healthy or unhealthy for the staff working within them is not new. Years ago, Paula Jorde Bloom (1988, p. 1; Bloom, Hentschel & Bella, 2010) wrote about measuring organisational climate: 'Each program's personality and characteristics certainly affect the quality of the work life ... Theorists refer to this distinct atmosphere ... as *organizational climate* ... The use of a weather metaphor does seem appropriate, because some centres seem to be distinctly sunny, warm, and nurturing; others are stormy and unpredictable.'

She created a short, informal questionnaire, 'Assessing organizational climate', for individuals, and the '*Early childhood work environment*' survey for informing a collective centre profile report (Bloom, 1988; Bloom, Hentschel & Bella, 2010). Later Bloom, with others, outlined a social systems perspective or model for early childhood settings; the interrelated parts or components of an ECE system/organisation were people, structure, processes, culture and outcomes (Bloom, Sheerer & Britz, 1991; Bloom, 2005). As such, an external environment encircled ECE organisations; this would be like the beyond-the-fence links noted in Step 2 and reflects the outer layers of Bronfenbrenner's nested circles. Since the late 1980s and early 1990s, others have continued to research and describe early childhood settings in terms of being unique human organisations. (For examples, refer to Aubrey, 2011; Bruno, 2009; Lindon & Lindon, 2011; Sullivan, 2010.)

In terms of feelings and emotions, people's relationships and interactions intertwine with settings and result in broad impressions or perceptions of place; these may differ from reality. Such intertwining of human interactions with settings contributes to nuances that make organisations unique. For example, an early childhood organisation may appear:

- Welcoming to all
- Quite organised but more distant for parents
- Full of changes for staff who then feel either steadiness or uncertainty.

Establishing an evaluation capacity and culture within early childhood settings may well assist staff with revealing anticipated and unexpected feelings about the place, as well as learning from both child and adult perspectives (McCoy, Rose & Connolly, 2013). Let me put such organisational feelings into a real-world perspective for you. Creating an organisation chart that displays the formal decision-making style and structural flow of an early childhood setting can help everyone to be clearer about how staff actually relate with one another. For example, Bruno (2009) noted three types of organisational structures – hierarchy, flat and hybrid – that represented moving from top-down-deciding to shared-deciding to team-deciding with reflective guidance and mentorship. This clarifying of people's role-positions and their layers of responsibility may also help reveal the true, everyday climate of a setting (Sciarra et al., 2013).

Workplaces as organisations

Every workplace can also be understood in terms of organisational concepts and theories, models and frameworks. For example, Edgar Schein (1992 & 1990) created a conceptual model of workplace settings with various cultural levels. These were labelled: visible artefacts, governing values, and basic or underlying assumptions. More recently with the changing world in mind, Schein (2010) expanded the concept of complex cultures into a deeper model encompassing multiple organisational phenomena, such as:

- Behavioural regularities
- Group norms
- Espoused values
- Formal philosophy

Chapter 3 Contemplating workplaces

- Rules of the game
- Climate
- Embedded skills
- Habits of thinking, mental models, and/or linguistic paradigms
- Shared meanings
- 'Root metaphors' or integrating symbols
- Formal rituals and celebrations.

Yet, Schein (2010) maintained his three earlier levels of culture for organisational study or analysis. There are also 'linguistic turn' ideas and models that highlight communication as constituting organisations, with important elements of relational power (Leclercq-Vandelannoitte, 2011; also refer back to Chapter 2).

Organisational metaphors

Workplaces as organisations may be viewed or identified and experienced through descriptive or associative metaphors. For example, the 'embodied realism view' of an organisation offers a hands-on experiential and spatial angle to understanding both settings and interactions (Heracleous & Jacobs, 2008). Similarly, 'connectivity' as a metaphor for links within and between human interactions of organisations has been proposed as a salient alternative to 'culture' (Kolb, 2008; also refer to Cornelissen, Oswick, Christensen & Phillips, 2008; Jacobs, Oliver & Heracleous, 2013; Morgan, 2006; and again refer back to Chapter 2).

Above, early childhood settings were outlined as potentially displaying: welcomingness; organisation but distance; or changes with uncertainty. Settings can also be experienced in terms of creating a sense of place for people, and so a return to topophilia meanings may be useful. As metaphorical examples, these impressions or feelings can be matched with images, and the labels might be:

- for a welcoming site – a 'cosy home' or a 'warm open fire'
- for an organised, distancing site – a 'fence between'
- for a changing site – an 'out of control merry-go-round'.

For early childhood settings and the professionals within, the concept of being an organisational leader-manager is very relevant. A few theories and frameworks have been noted here to help guide and support early childhood leader-managers, as they deepen their understandings, heighten their beliefs, and authenticate their actions for young children and the human organisations they frequent. Consider Jan's organisational metaphor of family representing her centre, described below.

Part 1 Thinking About People and Places

Feature professional reflection: Jan's story

A family workplace. When I consider our centre and the people within in it, I think of it as a family in a very special and magical space, where the possibilities are endless. I wonder if the magic is the people, the relationships, the place, the history, the influences of the past, the possibilities of the future or a combination of all. But I see it every day in the smiles, eagerness, caring and joyfulness that comes through our doors. I see this spirit of family: from our dedicated and hardworking educators who make a point of going that little bit further to provide that something special; and from the willingness of our families to help the centre and other families within it. I feel a sense of gratitude to be working in the early childhood field and to have the opportunity to share these early years with the children and families. Recently, one of our four-year-old girls said to her mother 'I need a photo of our family to bring to preschool, because we are all a family here too'. Like her mother, I was touched by her view of the importance of us in her life; the importance of strong, beautiful and respectful relationships and a sense of belonging to this place that is shaping her view of the future.

Every day I see the value of relationship-building in the early childhood field as I work with children, families and community. I believe the most important time to be building these relationships is in every moment. Having a combination of positive expectations combined with an ethical view is the key to respectful relationships. Building relationships, in our view, is not just the educators with child, family or community. There is also the importance of all stakeholders building relationships within our centre. Examples are: introductions between families and educators; and taking our children out into the community to learn about how to engage with others. It might be as simple as saying 'thank you' to a bus driver who has delivered them to an excursion, or responding to a personal greeting when walking through town on an excursion. A recent, really touching example of relationships within our centre relates to fundraising we have been doing for a family in need. These ongoing fundraisers have shown us the deep sense of community within our service. The remarkable thing is that the money and support were given with love and generosity from many of our families and children as well as the community. Such giving is clearly evidence of a sense of belonging and being part of something bigger than ourselves.

A provocation: *If you were asked to identify another metaphor for Jan's centre, what might you decide on and why? How does your metaphor link with, extend or differ from Jan's 'family'?*

Chapter 3 Contemplating workplaces

Pause and reflect 3.9
At the end of Step 1, you were asked to imagine being a leader-manager of children's learning by identifying physical setting challenges. Now imagine yourself as the director (the positional leader-manager) of a whole children's centre. In your work with a committee of management, you have been delegated the task of initially identifying all the beyond-the-fence contacts that your workplace engages with. How might you go about gathering these contacts from all the centre records and documents? How would you engage other staff in the teamwork of completing this identification process? What format might you use to organise and display your findings for the committee members?

Conclusion
This chapter encompassed many ideas about early childhood settings and various beyond-the-fence sites. Your contemplations of numerous micro or near settings and macro or wider settings closes for now. These places and ideas serve as another guide along the way to leading and managing across four key but broad roles in the Part 2 chapters.

Dear Nadine,

The insights presented in this chapter regarding the history and the use of language to describe practice, structures and policies in early childhood education provide a rich canvas for our work in early childhood settings today. By asking the reader to decide 'what's worth keeping and what's worth changing', this chapter provokes the need to more fully understand the sources of early childhood maxims that we so often take for granted.

Once I would have said chapters like this, that describe the bigger picture of early childhood education, held little for our everyday work with staff, children and families. I would have wanted to read more about the 'nitty-gritty', and 'recipes for success'. With time and hindsight I now know that the big picture, Bronfenbrenner's exosystem, affects all aspects of our decision-making about leading and managing our services. This chapter helps us to see the landscape before we begin painting it. I found that the chapter allowed us to locate who we are and where particular early childhood services sit in the landscape. Illustrating the various early childhood service types, traditions and policy backgrounds in Australia and internationally added a great deal of colour, shape and texture to what otherwise might have been a very bland canvas, with readers only being familiar with a small number of local settings.

I was heartened by references to early childhood education in other places. Beliefs, customs, economics and politics certainly do influence why policy decisions are made. Finding out about similarities and differences opens our eyes to what we do and what could be. The OECD worldwide early childhood education profiles (2006 & 2001) played a major role in the early childhood policy and practice changes in Australia during the last few

Part 1 Thinking About People and Places

years. The timing of the OECD Reports alongside the emergence of brain research that focused on the significance of the early years had a profound effect on making governments take notice. However, I think the global influences on change are more subtle as well. Personal global experiences at an individual or micro level have contributed to changes we see in the sector today. I wonder how many of us have had our early childhood practices influenced by what we have experienced in other places. I know my work in Papua New Guinea, Singapore and China still makes me question many of my early childhood beliefs that I previously had taken for granted.

Readers can look for personal and global influences in the development of the National Quality Framework. The research, ideologies and evidence-based practices generated here and internationally provide a sound basis for our adoption of the NQF. However, the policy was also shaped by personal endeavours. Several authors of the *BBB-EYLFA* who wrote about their intentions for the *Guide* provide additional insight. Jennifer Sumsion and her colleagues (2009) commented about their intent to champion both critically reflective practice and social justice; these ideals illustrate the role that individual and collective beliefs play in policy-making.

I suggest that readers might use this chapter's NQF discussion to frame their understanding of early childhood leadership in terms of the advocacy role we each play in making sure the intentions of the framework are embraced. This will necessitate our thinking deeply about the language we use when describing what our current policies are asking of us. Indeed our professional conversations around the NQF and related issues such as the education and care historical divide will be significant for moving our agenda forward. This chapter offers much food for thought.

Regards,
Di

Pause and reflect 3.10

Which idea from this chapter most influenced your current beliefs, and why? Record your personal feelings, inspirations and professional thoughts in your 'journal'.

Part 2
Thinking About Practices as Roles

Building on your understandings of people and places, you will now spend time exploring four professional roles: team stakeholder, policy designer, pedagogy creator and rights advocate. Each chapter includes a broad outline of one role before encouraging you to scrutinise and reflect deeply on it. You might wonder, why these four roles and not others? These focal roles reveal much about how early childhood settings function and how both positional and situational leading-managing happens.

It is important to remember that the 'team' of staff are vital participants and contributors to everyday life in early childhood settings. Without staff there would not be settings for children to attend and families to interact with. Designing 'policy' initially involves the integration of people's philosophical or theoretical views and their workplace positions. Furthermore, creating a 'pedagogical' scene for young children is really the essence of early childhood settings. Finally, 'advocating' for all kinds of human rights reflects serious and beyond-the-fence professionalism.

Part 2

Chapter 4

A professional role – a team stakeholder

Compassion means 'cumt passio', suffering-with... In compassion, the distance between you and the other is crossed... In compassion the other and the world are realized as your very self.

S. Rao (comp./ed.) (2002, p. 95)

Broad concepts

Here your journey along a professional leading-managing path encompasses concepts about being a team stakeholder or a person focused on staff and staffing. You will be thinking about the following Steps:

- What are the leading and managing facets of a team stakeholder role?
- Which staffing responsibilities are key?
- Where do rights and rules fit into staff sharing and workplace give-and-take?

Part 2 Thinking About Practices as Roles

Pause and reflect 4.1
Before progressing, think about: 'What are my understandings and beliefs about the above questions?' After considering each of the questions above, create an entry in your 'My professional leading-managing journal' by jotting down a couple of learning aims for your engaging with this chapter.

Step 1: What are the leading and managing facets of a team stakeholder role?

Team and stakeholder
This chapter begins with an exploration of what we mean by 'team' and 'stakeholder'. Pausing here on your professional pathway gives you a little time to think about: 'How would I explain or define being a "team stakeholder"?' A team is a collection of people, but it is also much more. For example, forming and being a team implies interactions, relationships and shared commitments. There are sports teams, community service teams (usually called committees), and there are education teams. Within early childhood settings the collection of all staff is often referred to as a 'team'. Teams and their teamwork do not just happen; they have to be worked at. It takes time for people to share, engage and solidify their ideas and relationships. Teams also grow and change over time, as the surrounding world alters and as staff members come and go from a workplace. Some people are called 'team players', especially when they collaborate and willingly contribute to the common good.

Is a team member a 'stakeholder'? This label originates from the two words within. There are those who 'hold' or have a 'stake' in things, which is usually a positive interest or involvement in ideas, actions or events. Years ago gold miners 'staked' claims, and in today's business world stakeholders often have financial concerns and embrace economic affairs. Similarly, our jobs might be 'at stake' if policies change and funding is reduced. So, for this leg of your professional journey, everyone will be some kind of team stakeholder by just working in an early childhood setting. Additionally, parents or other family members may be volunteer or honorary team members and stakeholders; furthermore, sometimes broader community citizens join early childhood teams.

Roles with actions
Moving beyond the labels, let's look at being a 'team stakeholder' as a focal role across a whole setting. When, as positional leader-manager, the director or coordinator enacts a team stakeholder role, her/his adult-oriented or staff-related actions may be informal or formal, and some may be shared. By clustering related actions together, a particular

Chapter 4 A professional role – a team stakeholder

set of 'role actions' is formed. In terms of staff and staffing issues, the relevant 'role actions', either individually or as a set, can be viewed as a form of 'workforce lifecycle', moving from the birth of a new position within a setting to phases of 'childhood', 'adolescence' and later 'adulthood' during one's employment, and then a 'death' as one leaves a position and workplace. A team stakeholder role will usually include multiple staffing actions, such as those listed here:

- Identifying vacant or new positions – team and committee
- Selecting new staff members – committee recruitment processes
- Establishing and maintaining authentic relationships – leader and team
- Guiding and supporting staff – leader and colleagues
- Mentoring or coaching staff – leader and colleagues
- Ongoing planning, regular feedback reviewing, and periodic monitoring of staff in terms of their responsibilities and everyday actions – leader focusing on strengths and talents
- Creating daily/weekly staff rosters – leader, deputy leader and team
- Negotiating staff professional learning plans, both experiences and events – all staff
- Discussing position redesign, career options and paths – all staff
- Mediating resolution of conflict relationships and challenging issues – leader and committee officers
- Meeting with staff regularly about setting issues and celebrations – leader and team
- Listening, chatting informally, even personally with acknowledgement of colleagues – leader and team
- Ensuring staff workplace health and safety – leader and board or owner.

Ability repertoires

For leader-managers to accomplish these 'role actions' in responsive and insightful ways, each will have a background with a unique 'ability repertoire'. A leader-manager's repertoire will consist of her/his professional characteristics, competences and talents. There are many abilities that might cluster uniquely for each professional, such as: planning, organising, being fair and consistent, role modelling, listening, mediating, delegating, thinking, innovating, facilitating, consulting, keeping promises, and acting with integrity.

As a support for leader-managers, Hewes and Leatherman (2005) suggested a three-layer administrative process that may be useful for those in positional, distributed or situational roles. The first layer of this model began with a triangular arrangement of 'Planning' (happens before), 'Operating' (happens during) and 'Evaluating' (happens after). Then, two exemplar processes were noted for each of these:

Part 2 Thinking About Practices as Roles

- P – policy making and organising
- O – directing and supervising
- E – assessing and analysing.

At the third layer, any number of daily, weekly or cyclical tasks could be identified as examples of undertaking the six 'action-ing' processes as listed above. Illustrating these second layer processes to third layer tasks might involve the following:

- Policy making can happen when staff engage in jointly developing food learning standards
- Assessing can happen when the designated educational leader engages in reviewing educators' child observations with them.

Let's put these processes and tasks into a broad professional perspective for you. This means that each person will understand her/his 'ability repertoire' or clustered talents, and as a professional will display role actions in ethical and wise ways.

Furthermore, beyond the 'role actions' listed above, there are other 'role actions' or leading-managing competencies that may be displayed within early childhood settings. These also link with staff and their workplace engagements. For example, finances and insurance equate with many budgeting and accounting activities for someone within settings (refer back to Chapter 3 and ECA's online *Digital business kit*). One key routine task related to finance is paying staff members' salaries and their on-cost benefits. This nuts-and-bolts action is primarily administrative. Furthermore, it is widely accepted that staff costs comprise the biggest proportion of every early childhood setting's budget. (For examples, refer to Brennan & Adamson, 2014; Bryant & Gibbs, 2013; Hearron & Hildebrand, 2007; Hewes & Leatherman, 2005.) A second example of staff 'role actions' links with the facilities as designated spaces and places provided for educators within every setting – a staff common room, the office planning space, toilets with shower, a library and resources area, an outdoor relaxation place, etc. (Click & Karkos, 2011; Hearron & Hildebrand, 2007)

With a focus on staff and staffing, let's begin with foundational practices. A positional leader-manager or another designated staff member will focus on ensuring that specific adult-child ratios are maintained and that staff members possess various qualifications that are up to date. These practices are in accordance with professional standards and legal requirements. As illustrated in Chapter 3, the *National Law* (*NL*) with *National Regulations*, the *National Quality Standard* (*NQS*) (ACECQA, 2013a & 2103b), and the establishment of ACECQA form the backbone of legal requirements for Australia. The educator-to-child ratios vary with the ages of children and group sizes within early childhood settings. Similarly the necessity for an early childhood teacher is linked with children's ages and groupings. For more information about this, refer to *Education and Care Services National Law and National*

Chapter 4 A professional role – a team stakeholder

Regulations, regulations 123 and 129. There are links with various 'Quality Areas' of the *National Quality Standard*, particularly 'QA4: Staffing arrangements'. As an example, definitive guidance is outlined in 'QA2: Children's health and safety' regarding educators' responsibilities surrounding children's reasonable supervision, their risk protection and other foundational practices. To extend these ideas further, you could compare Australian requirements with those in New Zealand and elsewhere around the world.

Pause and reflect 4.2

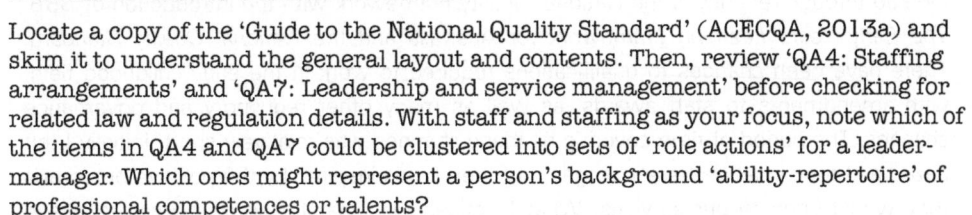

Locate a copy of the 'Guide to the National Quality Standard' (ACECQA, 2013a) and skim it to understand the general layout and contents. Then, review 'QA4: Staffing arrangements' and 'QA7: Leadership and service management' before checking for related law and regulation details. With staff and staffing as your focus, note which of the items in QA4 and QA7 could be clustered into sets of 'role actions' for a leader-manager. Which ones might represent a person's background 'ability-repertoire' of professional competences or talents?

Now consider other places and their lenses on staff and staffing in early childhood settings. What State or National laws, regulations, standards and accreditation systems and/or processes exist for early childhood settings in the Pacific Rim – New Zealand, Singapore, Hong Kong – and beyond, for example: Sweden, England, Latin America, Caribbean countries (Vegas & Santibanez, 2010)? Also, what professional early childhood bodies or organisations exist in these countries; and what standards and/or codes of ethics do they work with?

Let's pause here so that you can read and think about the next Feature professional reflection: Jan's story. This one is about herself, staff and staffing issues.

Feature professional reflection: Jan's story

My roles and beyond. An early childhood director has varied responsibilities within the role of 'leader'. I see my role as a leader as more of a collaborator, facilitator and organiser, encouraging others to look towards the future with a collaborative aim towards our goals. Warner described the key components of leadership as having passion, vision, perseverance, partnership and courage. I also believe creativity, flexibility and humour to be important aspects of leadership. As I consider the centre and educators' long-term goals, I look at how I can support these centre hopes. I ask myself: 'Who and what do I need for each goal to make this work effectively?' I also wonder about which team member can contribute to working towards a particular goal and consider how I can assist them.

Part 2 Thinking About Practices as Roles

Team. Working with a diverse team of educators requires acknowledging each educator's values, beliefs, abilities and knowledge. It means consideration is given to both individual personalities and a shifting context within the centre. Some of this information can be learnt through formal staff appraisals and meetings, while so much can be learnt when listening and observing staff in action. This means that building long-term collaborative and respectful relationships within the team is vital.

Professional learning. Finding opportunities to enhance professional learning either through staff development events or mentoring can result in growth and change. I see this growth as being an asset to both the mentored and mentor as well as having benefits for the whole team and centre. As an example, one of the challenges we have worked through recently is the National Quality Framework with the introduction of BBB, *The Early Years Learning Framework for Australia* and the *National Quality Standard*. There have been changes to qualifications required to work in the early childhood field, with amendments to staff awards, as well as many other regulatory and governance changes. The period of time covering all these changes was relatively short. Initially I felt dazed as I took in all of these changes; but then I was inspired by the positive outcomes they would bring to our services. What I noticed was that for some educators, these changes seemed to be overwhelming initially, and some were just against them. Through ongoing professional development and discussions at both our in-service and externally, I am proud to say our educators are becoming capable and competent in their roles and with all the changes.

A provocation: Above, Jan identifies leading-managing roles for herself as a positional director. However, she also explicitly identifies that other staff have active roles. Her example is about major national changes across Australia as they relate to their local workplace. She says that creativity, flexibility and humour are vital for leading. Can you locate parts of her story that reflect these talents? How would you define these three aspects of being an early childhood leader? Think about how you could link your ideas with concepts across this chapter.

People's positions

This chapter is about adults who work in and with early childhood settings. You will remember that staff were introduced as the human aspect of settings in Chapter 3. In addition to the 'role actions' presented above, staff are hired for particular role-positions: assistant working with children, cook, cleaner, room leader, teacher, gardener, office administrator, bus driver, assistant director, coordinator or director. There are also those working with family day care schemes, with such position titles as: business manager, coordinator, child development officer, and home educator. Most settings have a part-time or casual accountant, and this person usually works with an office administrator or a committee of management treasurer, at least at annual

Chapter 4 A professional role – a team stakeholder

financial reporting times. In terms of understanding one's position, early childhood settings will have a collection of position descriptions, with each containing unique and vital staffing information, which may include the following:

- Title or name of position (with date last reviewed)
- Location of daily work and overview of organisational context
- Reporting to/accountability
- Classification of position (for pay and benefits; union, award, etc.)
- Primary purpose of position (essence statement)
- Listing of key responsibilities (including uniqueness from other positions)
- Selection criteria and descriptors (relating with key responsibilities)
- Special requirements. (For ECE, this could include: working with children checks; links such as a Code of Ethics (ECA, 2006) or a code of conduct (refer to Australian National Regulations, regulation 168); and any travel expectations within one's workload.)

Regular review of position descriptions may happen in conjunction with various routine reviews of policies. Some services establish an annual calendar of cyclical review for policies based on a defined life-review timeline, such as every twelve or eighteen months (link with Chapter 5). Position descriptions may be reviewed as staff vacancies occur. This helps ensure that listed responsibilities and resulting 'role actions' meet the current staffing gap within a setting.

Educators

Within Australian early childhood settings, every staff member working directly with young children is now called an 'educator' (AGDEEWR, 2009, p. 45) and under the *Education and Care Services National Regulations* there is one designated 'educational leader' for each setting (Cheeseman, 2012; Ministerial Council, 2011, Part 4.4, regulation 118). Legally the educational leader is defined as holding a professional practice leadership role, rather than being a 'responsible person'. Additionally, various sections of the Australian *National Law* and *National Regulations* highlight three required positions of 'responsible person' – approved provider, nominated supervisor and certified supervisors (Vic Govt, Dec 2011, available on ACECQA website – *National Law*: Sections 162 and 164; *National Regulations*: 168 and 173). One 'responsible person' must be present and ultimately in charge of every early childhood setting at all times. Your professional journey could be richer if you pause and think here – do some comparing and contrasting of required child-contact and leading-managing positions in other countries.

Part 2 Thinking About Practices as Roles

Directors and coordinators

Beyond the legal labels for key early childhood setting positions, there are historical and customary leading and managing appointments in Australia and beyond. These positions may be either:

- *Designated or positional*, such as – director, coordinator, assistant director, manager
- *Situational* – team leader of specific event, project manager of major enterprise, acting coordinator of setting.

Pause and reflect 4.3

Refer back to Chapter 2 to 'Pause and reflect 2.10' at the end of Step 3. What leader definition did you create? Now, how would you 'define' leadership with a staffing-focus (again in about 25 words)? What might you include and leave out of a dynamic working definition about yourself and colleagues? Would your momentary definition vary for positional leading vs situational leading roles?

How the role of team stakeholder is created, reformed and displayed may vary for numerous sociocultural and local geographic reasons. As noted elsewhere, ideas about our bodies and one's gender are one influence. Whether people identify any gender-oriented variations or not, gender could reflect on their positions within a team as contributing leader-managers or as designated 'authority' persons. Here, Leo Prendergast shares his story of working within a team and encouraging team players.

Professional reflection: Leo's story

'Being a team'

One of the things I learned from my first 'not too successful' experience as a Director was the need to have the team with me rather than seeing myself as leading and the team following. But, by my second try at being a Director, I remember another quite experienced worker being surprised when I positioned myself as part of the team. I shared in the work – the joy, the cleaning up and the disasters. She said that she had spent the first six months of working with me just waiting for my explosion and starting to blame her and others for things that went wrong. That had been her experience of 'Directors', and she thought it went with the territory.

I thought a lot about this view of a Director, and it seems to me that young early childhood teachers usually spend a whole career working with just a few other teachers; and then, they are often thrust into leadership early on in their teaching career. They are lucky if they ever have a real mentor. Even learning from an experienced teacher as a role model over a

Chapter 4 A professional role – a team stakeholder

sustained period can be rare. In contrast, many primary teachers are posted to a school where there are dozens of other teachers, with many being quite experienced. Thus, they have many years to learn, to observe and to be mentored before reaching a leadership position. No wonder so many young early childhood teachers, myself included, have struggled initially. We try so hard to 'lead', when we can be far more effective leaders by positioning ourselves as part of the team.

This led to a decision I made early in my career as a Director to pay so much attention to team building. I have stuck with this over the years. For example, I like to roster staff to work across all tasks in the service and to work with all other staff. That means on occasions both the qualified teachers working together in one room while there are perhaps two educators with a Certificate III working together in another room. On the surface and in the short term, this arrangement might not be the best thing, especially if those two Cert III staff have never been in such a position before; however, in the longer term it makes our program stronger. The two teachers get to work closely together and learn from each other. The Cert III staff have chances to take on more responsibility for a while; and, in my experience, it makes them all stronger and more effective team members.

As my Director experience grew, I was most influenced by situational leadership theories (Blanchard and others; for example, Blanchard & Hodges, 2003) – coaching and mentoring less confident staff and ensuring training for the confident but less competent staff. I still try to move all staff to a point where, as leader, I can delegate to as many of the team as possible. But then comes the hard part, of course – being able to let go as leader. If I want another member of staff to take on responsibility, I have to 'give' them rights to make decisions. And further, I feel that as leader I then have to stand by those decisions, even when I personally may have made a different decision. If I want that delegation to work and to be effective for the other team member and the program, and also reduce my workload, then it has to be two-way. There are both responsibility and rights for the other team member, and the knowledge that I will support them and their decisions. I have found that so many fellow team members, when given the chance and support, do rise to the occasion.

In summary, I remain uncertain whether my being a male has had any real effect on my journey as an early childhood education leader. I have read often enough the things written by or reported from other males in the early childhood field. Most seem to see themselves sitting outside the mainstream; and so, they report that being male was/is a defining characteristic. While I have no doubt that initial reactions to me from many others within our profession and field are based on my gender, I think that factor fades very quickly. I think most people are open and respond far more to colleagues' perceived competence and knowledge. Sure, their first response might reflect that I am male; but, I like to think that any initial feelings quickly give way to responsiveness. That is, I am a competent early childhood teacher and Director. Such a competency view is the more important and enduring response that I hope for and usually get.

A provocation: *Leo's story seems to reflect the essence of this chapter – the idea that everyone is and can be a team player and a serious contributing stakeholder. Thus, each may*

Part 2 Thinking About Practices as Roles

> engage in situational leading-managing from time to time, if not more consistently for longer-term projects and events. Have you heard of a team that shares/shared tasks and roles as much as Leo describes? In this space Leo did not explicitly outline how joint respect and trust and such developed across the centre's team; so think about: 'What might Leo have role modelled, said and done during everyday events to encourage each team member's confidence and willingness to "have a go"?' and 'How has Leo probably interacted and related with other staff members to encourage this everyday situation?'

Pause and reflect 4.4

Refresh your thoughts about embodiment and the current imbalance of women and men working across the early childhood education field. Next, consider the designated position of director-teacher of a preschool or kindergarten for three- to five-year-old children. What do you see/feel/believe ought to be the priorities for a person in this role? Create a list of four or five key responsibilities, support each with a brief justification or rationale, and include professional literature references for future reconsideration.

Step 2: Which staffing responsibilities are key?

Many responsibilities

When all the responsibilities for whole early childhood settings are identified and considered, a rather large collection emerges. As noted in Step 1, all aspects of staff and staffing are focal and are really the starting point. Other responsibilities for settings can then be highlighted and undertaken; and of course, staff are intimately involved in these. These beyond-staffing responsibilities encompass leading-managing the following within settings:

- Fiscal system
- Facilities (refer to Chapter 3)
- Documentation and policy system (refer to Chapter 5)
- Health and safety system
- Food services
- Educational program (refer to Chapter 6)
- Family connections (refer to Chapter 2)
- Community and public affairs

Chapter 4 A professional role – a team stakeholder

- Accountability and legal requirements
- Professional and advocacy practices (refer to Chapter 7).

Ways of supporting staff

One major responsibility for all early childhood settings is maintaining a comfortable interpersonal climate or cultural feeling. A meaningful workplace can bolster staff members as they undertake their responsibilities and contribute to the successful overall running of a place. A communications-focused approach within organisations can be supportive. With meaningful communicating taking place in a workplace, the oral, written and gestural forms reflect the idea that 'communication is constitutive of organizing' (Leclercq-Vandelannoitte, 2011, p. 1248; also refer to Elliott, 2005; Gerrissen & The Red Thunderbird Agency, 2009; Running Wolf & Rickard, 2003; Umbreit, 2003; Warner & Grint, 2006). This means that a setting operates the way it does because of how communications are valued and happen. Beyond establishing a welcoming place that is saturated with respect and trust, there are numerous ways to sensitively and positively communicate and support colleagues every day.

Relational communicating

Of course, how team stakeholders relate, interact and communicate are top priorities for everyday life in early childhood settings and for any authentic leading of them (refer back to Chapter 2). With these priorities, it can also be useful to extend our understandings of emotional competencies and other abilities. Studying Gandhi as a real person in a real world at the time provides a biographical/story example of the complex interplay of self and service (Bansal & Hingorani, 2013; Chakraborty, 2003). It is suggested that these writings be reviewed with a critical questioning lens (Eacott, 2013) or even some historic Aristotelian wisdoms (Grint, 2007). Such lenses also help readers avoid more heroic or charismatic masculine leader influences, which offer little relevance to contemporary early childhood educators, leader-managers and whole settings.

Surrounding and building upon our meaningful communication, there are human internal feelings and dispositions or habits of mind, as well as the catalyst of motivation. There are a number of now classic theories about human motivation, with Maslow's Hierarchy of Needs being a focus (Marotz & Lawson, 2007). Sims and Hutchins (2011) adjusted Maslow's 'needs' into 'rights' for young children. If a leader-manager's interactive and relational ways do influence the 'tone' of a setting, then a broad cooperative, sensitive, calm approach is suggested. There are many personal/professional attributes or qualities that shape one's ways of relating and thus a person's 'tone'. As an illustration, one's ways may encompass the authentic display of: integrity, respect, openness and trust, strong work ethic, sense of humour, adaptability, vision. (For examples, refer to Costa & Kallick, 2008; CREIO, 1998; Gordon, 2014.) Having the confidence to really believe in certain early childhood conceptions and principles and then act upon them

Part 2 Thinking About Practices as Roles

can also reflect one's 'tone' (refer to 'moral higher ground' in Chapter 7). Thus, it is vital that all early childhood leader-managers are strong enough to act with wisdom, rather than simply acting without doing harm. Making use of various theoretical offerings can assist professionals personally and cooperatively. Some illustrative offerings include:

- A strengths approach (The Strengths Foundation at: www.thestrengthsfoundation.org; Feinstein & Kiner, 2011)
- Appreciative inquiry assumptions (Appreciative Inquiry Commons at: http://appreciativeinquiry.case.edu)
- Leadership 'community of practice' groups (Wenger-Trayner & Wenger-Trayner, nd; at: www.wenger-trayner.com/blog/leadership-groups-for-social-learning/)
- Leading-managing with Habits of Mind characteristics (Costa & Kallick, 2008; at: www.jtbookyard.com/uploads/6/2/9/3/6293106/ebook-_learning_and_leading_with_habits_of_mind_-_16_essential_characteristics_for_success_2008.pdf)
- Using de Bono's (1987) *Six Thinking Hats* and Gardner's theory of nine types of intelligence (at: www.howardgardner.com/multiple-intelligences/; for examples, refer to Goleman, 2009; Goleman, Bennett & Barlow, 2012).

These theory-with-practice resources are helpful options that can support and guide leader-managers during day-to-day workplace interactions. Additionally, professionals will contribute by attending to their language, their interactive manner and their ethical etiquette when working with others. The above points provide relevant approaches, examples and strategies for team players during shared professional planning and learning. These frameworks can also be useful when staff participate in learning sessions beyond-the-fence. In essence, these offerings provide theoretical and practical assistance for leader-managers as they communicate with and support other staff members during both joyful and challenging times.

Leading for learning, learning for leading

Staff members' professional learning occasions, both within their workplace and at sites beyond-the-fence, might be meaningfully extended by working through some of the above theoretical positions. Additionally, deeper learning from everyday professional practices can happen, by:

- Engaging with confronting questions, such as: Ask 'How?'; Ask 'Why?'; Ask 'What might be?' (Robertson, 2013)
- Engaging in repertoire-extending practices that also analyse workplace environments (Boud & Hager, 2012).

Similarly, the notion of 'leadership for learning' (LfL) as whole setting educational processes provides another suite of questions. These are about relating and learning in a 'community', and this can happen even in settings with an authoritative leader

Chapter 4 A professional role – a team stakeholder

(Marsh, Waniganayake & Gibson, 2013; for background about 'LfL' refer to Macbeath, 2006). If team stakeholders collectively considered and responded to such questions, they could then create a shared agenda of locally relevant professional learning issues to explore over time. For a deeper understanding of how valuable collective sharing can be, a team of staff could become trailblazers, touring various Indigenous ways. There are historic and contemporary ways. Several are outlined here:

- The Australian Institute of Family Studies' e-resources site called *Knowledge Circle*. This is an Aboriginal and Torres Strait Islander focused portal for support workers, with important guiding principles (at: www2.aifs.gov.au/cfca/knowledgecircle/)
- The *8ways* site encompasses cultural interface protocols, a cultural analysis tool, and ways of learning (www.8ways.wikispaces.com)
- Talking circles have a long history with indigenous North American peoples, including First Nations in Canada and Native Americans. Traditionally all ages shared in a circle representing the interconnection of people, earth, moon and sun. A talking stick moves from person to person. Through teaching, listening and learning, knowledge, values and culture were passed around and passed on (Gerrissen & The Red Thunderbird Agency, 2009; Running Wolf & Rickard, 2003; Umbreit, 2003; plus, 'Talking Circles' at: www.firstnationspedagogy.ca/circletalks.html and 'Talking Stick' at: www.stipo.info/Artikel/The_story_of_the_Talking_Stick). The importance of a circle and circularity resulted in their use in a model of leadership (Warner & Grint, 2006)
- A final illustration of shared or social learning is 'communities of practice' (at: www.wenger-trayner.com/theory/; review other 'tags' near the end of this sub-site). The 'leadership groups' were noted above (Wenger-Trayner & Wenger-Trayner, nd at: www.wenger-trayner.com/blog/leadership-groups-for-social-learning/). The authors created seven evocatively named leadership group processes: agenda activists; community keepers; critical friends; social reporters; external messengers; value detectives; and organisational brokers. These could be particularly useful roles and processes for advocacy across the early childhood education field (link with Chapter 7).

Pause and reflect 4.5

Investigate at least one of the shared learning ways presented above. Think about how you might try it out with colleagues. How would you initially raise the idea of talking, sharing and learning in a different way with colleagues? Also, using one of these ways, consider your inspirations and aspirations: when, where, with whom, what issues and ideas?

Part 2 Thinking About Practices as Roles

Parents and others

As a relevant example, we can review and think about family connections as they link with staff and all the staffing issues explored so far. Parents and other community members may initially contribute to settings by delivering and picking up children. However, they can have much more involvement, and may even take on 'team stakeholder' by being:

- Member of the committee of management
- Volunteer in the kitchen
- Helper in a classroom with children
- Planner for fundraising events
- Ethnic storyteller
- Co-curricular planner.

In essence, there are many ways for parents to become everyday partners with educators as they collaborate with and for children. (For examples, refer to Bruno, 2009; Eaton, 2008; MacNaughton & Hughes, 2011; Prior & Gerard, 2007; Rodd, 2013; Sims & Hutchins, 2011; Waniganayake et al., 2012.) Furthermore, as one framework for interacting with families, the ECA (2006) *Code of Ethics* outlines 10 professional ways. Of course, it is vital that early childhood staff and especially those in leading-managing roles use both a family background lens and an ethnic diversity lens when they review the *Code* and various family resources. (For examples, refer to Fluckiger, 2013; Hallet, 2014; Miller, 2010; NZ Ministry of Education, 1996; Ritchie, 2012; SNAICC, 2013.) Such professional challenges link with cultural competence and the essential nature of communicating meaningfully, as explored in Chapter 2. For another helpful framework, leader-managers could go back a few years to Roslyn Elliott's (2005) 'Model of Communication Accretion Spiral'. The model was created to represent reciprocal communications spiralling upwards and outwards as staff and parents interact over time. Elliott's linking of conversation-content stages with Maslow's hierarchy may be expanded from needs to rights of adults (Sims, 2011a; Sims & Hutchins, 2011).

Pause and reflect 4.6

Think about how you might incorporate a sustainability, 'green lens' orientation and practices into key responsibilities listed in various position descriptions. One way to explore and address this leading-managing challenge is working from a community engagement framework or model. Such a beyond-the-fence perspective helps ensure that some staff responsibilities are defined with a touch of outward-looking and broader responsiveness. This means attending to ideas and possibilities as your compass is consulted for the bigger picture and macro layers of society and the Earth.

Chapter 4 A professional role – a team stakeholder

Two relevant frameworks that may assist you here are: firstly, the inform, consult, involve, collaborate, empower levels of participation (International Association for Public Participation Australia (iap2), nd); and, secondly, a wider world engagement grid with crossed-frame for a nature-centred leadership stance; this means people's values and actions move west to east from servant/charitable participant to activist/reflexive participant and also move south to north from reflective novice to expert (Stober, Brown & Cullen, 2013; link with your eco-caring compass and its orientations). These ideas also link with policies for early childhood settings (refer to Chapter 5) and being a rights advocate (refer to Chapter 7). Record a few ideas, processes and practices that seem to you to be most relevant for being such an ECE leader-manager of a whole setting.

Step 3: Where do rights and rules fit into staff sharing and workplace give-and-take?

You might wonder where staff rights and rules really fit into daily life in early childhood settings. We begin from the point that everyone in an early childhood setting brings individual professional and personal qualities to the workplace. Similarly, staff members probably have some limitations or less experience within certain aspects of the daily life in a setting. Understanding team stakeholders' strengths and experience, or lack of experience, can be especially relevant when times of great change are afoot. This is important in terms of leader-managers both supporting and guiding colleagues, especially during these times of change.

Rights

This aspect of being a team stakeholder relates to everyone. There are local, professional, state, national and international layers of law that may apply to all staff within early childhood settings, and the honouring of and adhering to such legal statues often becomes a key responsibility for one person. This could be a director or coordinator (whose position description covers a generic duty of care for staff, child and family rights) or the president of a committee of management or chair of a board of directors. At the broadest Bronfenbrenner layer, the United Nations' *Universal Declaration of Human Rights* from 1948 is the key example (at: www.un.org/en/documents/udhr/). In order to explore broader international and even national laws related to human rights, leader-managers ought to consult their eco-caring compasses and engage in serious orienting and viewing into the distance.

In most cases, the everyday workplace rights of early childhood educators are located within State acts and legislation. As examples, there is a broad duty of care for everyone. There are workplace health and safety laws covering risk management and prevention as well as hazardous chemicals. There are union worker agreements

Part 2 Thinking About Practices as Roles

about position titles, pay and benefits. Such rights and legislation apply to everyone working in a State or in most countries. Focusing on the early childhood education field, we return to things like the Australian *National Law* and *National Regulations*, which in essence outline what adults in various roles must do for ensuring that they provide basic protection, do no harm and meet their duty of care for young children. This results in children's basic rights being honoured (again, refer globally to the UN or UNICEF for both the *Declaration of the Rights of the Child* (1959) and the *Convention on the Rights of the Child* (1989/1990)). More locally, the Australian Human Rights Commission now incorporates a National Children's Commissioner (Mitchell, 2014). Rights represent moving toward and trying to ensure equity and social justice for people (refer to the rights advocate, Chapter 7). An important point here is the fact that where there are rights there are also responsibilities; these vital 'two Rs' usually fit like hand and glove.

Pause and reflect 4.7

Which workplace professional rights do early childhood team members have now that did not exist thirty, fifty or one hundred years ago? One hint is to consider the influences of gender and also young children being the focus for offering early childhood education, rather than society in general or women working. Consider how you might work in a small team with different members to investigate micro to macro layers of government and explore various rights of staff and parents.

Struggles

There are everyday workplace pressures and challenges, with some staff being affected and influenced more than others. Of course there is the ongoing dilemma of meeting one's professional responsibilities alongside various financial and temporal constraints. It seems that there just isn't enough money for the year or hours in the day to engage in the most ideal practices across every aspect of early childhood settings. Some of the usual setting challenges that positional leader-managers and other team members face encompass:

- Questionable retention and turnover rates
- Emotional and physical stress and burnout
- Uncertainty about change
- Physical layout of spaces
- Resistance to changes
- Job diversity and satisfaction
- Employment compensation, equity and security.

Chapter 4 A professional role – a team stakeholder

(For examples of these challenges, refer to Aubrey, 2011; Marotz & Lawson, 2007; Rodd, 2013; Waniganayake et al., 2012.)

There is also the human reality that people have frailties and dark sides; and these may be magnified, even encouraged, by 'dark' interiors within a broader organisation. Harassment and bullying are serious, negative professional behaviours that affect people very personally (Daly, Byers & Taylor, 2004; Linstead, Marechal & Griffin, 2014). These misconducts might be isolated and more individual, but they cannot be ignored in any workplace. A setting that explicitly displays the valuing of people can soften these challenges. Such valuing might happen by recognising professional efforts and facilitating team respect. By doing so, difficult staff may become more amiable and good-natured. This is most likely to happen when challenging colleagues are regularly exposed to socialness with humour (Kenny & Euchler, 2012) and they experience explicit exemplars of their workplace purposely attending to everyone's well-being. For positional leaders, learning to recognise struggles and dilemmas may well help them to cope and to respond more capably to others (Cardno & Reynolds, 2009).

Rules

A rather obvious starting point here is for leader-managers to fully understand duty of care, the Precautionary Principle and do-no-harm policies. These key stances ought to be the basis when establishing rules for early childhood settings. They can also be the foundation for people's interactions. In both positional and situational positions, all leader-managers are some kind of role model for colleagues. A person's role modelling may happen unknowingly or else definitively with full awareness and intent to guide others. As an example, some staff rules within early childhood settings may arise from beyond-the-fence; however, leader-managers still have responsibility for them. Here, we can consider the meaning of all staff being 'fit and proper' as highlighted in the Australian *National Law*.

- How might this relate to checking and dealing with any criminal history issues (*NQS*, QA7 and *National Regulations*, r. 16]?
- What might this mean if a traveller dons professional lenses to view the ECA (2006) *Code of Ethics*?

Settings will have in-house rules about use of places and spaces as well as rules about local staffing decisions linked with particular personnel backgrounds, experiences and qualifications defined legally beyond-the-fence. Settings will have statements about people's confidentiality (*National Regulations*, rr. 181–4) and the privacy of organisations. The list of local rules related to team stakeholders will vary with types of settings, their size and key sociocultural surroundings.

Part 2 Thinking About Practices as Roles

Pause and reflect 4.8

Identify an aspect of rights, struggles and rules that you find intriguing and worthy of further exploration. Who might you share this knowledge with, and in what setting? Create a poster for communicating with your team and display it in the staff common room (look up hints for effective poster making).

Conclusion

As you travelled through this chapter there were all kinds of team stakeholder bridges and roundabouts, some smooth, wide roads and a few narrow side tracks with several bumps and potholes to negotiate. As presented here, the professional role of team stakeholder includes everyone. However, there are times and places, with particular professional practices and people, when team stakeholder means one leading-managing person with certain authorities. As your journey continues, the next 'sign-post' indicates that being a policy designer is also a key professional leading-managing role within early childhood settings.

Dear Nadine,

This chapter deals with complexity head on. Early childhood environments are complex, and we do need to recognise and accept this before we take up leadership roles. The leader–manager–administrator trilogy of positional roles that was identified in the chapter can contribute to our forgetting that we (including the leader) are all 'stakeholders' in early childhood teams. Having a useful definition of 'stakeholder' will help readers to reflect on who it is that early childhood settings serve. As long as we all have a stake in keeping children at the core of what we do, then we will build, network and participate in staff, family, professional and wider community teams. This chapter impressed upon me the importance of each of us playing their part as a fully contributing team member. I often use Belbin's team roles to identify the skills we each bring to the team, or the roles we may need to play in order to keep the team functioning (see: www.belbin.com/rte.asp?id=8 for an overview of Belbin roles; Cook & Rouse, 2014, pp. 40–1).

An important feature of the chapter is that it supports both those who are new to a leadership role, and experienced leaders, as they expand upon theoretical and practical strategies for engaging with staff and families in authentic ways. Reflexivity is at the heart of professional learning and development, and early childhood education is a relational activity. It is the art of facilitating critical conversations that really matters. The need to consider human rights and ethical practice cannot be overestimated. Ethics are at the core of how we engage with others. Some 'child friendly city' work I have been doing lately sent me scurrying back to children's rights literature mentioned in this chapter. It is encouraging to

Chapter 4 A professional role – a team stakeholder

know that these underpin all of the legislated and policy frameworks that we operate under in Australia.

This chapter provides a timely reminder that the mandated 'rules' and 'guidelines' developed under the National Quality Framework originate in children's rights. We know we have to abide by the 'rules', but when we apply a 'rights' perspective we are taking a 'principled' position. It is always worthwhile to go back to the original charter (www.unicef.org/crc/files/Rights_overview.pdf) and envisage their application in our lives, and children's lives here and now. I think that the partnerships with parents alluded to in the chapter are well served by making the NQF rules and guidelines visible. They establish a base line of trust and confidence in our overarching system. From there it is up to us and our staff team to maintain a 'duty of care' with children, families and each other. As we are reminded throughout the chapter, living our values (including eco-caring values) is fundamental to enacting positional and relational leadership roles in early childhood education.

It was a 'heavy' chapter, so I am pleased that the Feature professional reflection: Jan's story related the need for humour along with the other important values that she holds. For me, humour is the reality check I often need. I noticed reference to the need for good humour when addressing the more difficult times. Humour does rub off on others and contributes to an encouraging culture. Our many and various leader roles can cause us to take ourselves too seriously, especially when we are under pressure. I guess that keeping a sense of balance and prioritising what is important are the keys to success.

Cheers for now,
Di

Pause and reflect 4.9

Which idea in this chapter most influenced your current beliefs, and why? Record your personal feelings, inspirations and professional thoughts in your 'journal'.

Chapter 5

A professional role – a policy designer

Policy ... moves beyond the dictionary definition and is construed as a multi-faceted, multi-dimensional social and political phenomenon which includes a cycle of strategies bound by time, resources, players and performances with dynamic and often contested political sites.

Ann Farrell (2001, p. 241)

Broad concepts

In this chapter, your professional journey takes you to the challenging hills of this leading-managing path. While considering policy from the heights of agreed values, you may look up for further inspiration. You may look back down, viewing gaps across the profession as a valley. You may even look forward along the horizon for creative insights, meaningful aspirations, future dreams and ethical visions. There are professional rewards to be gained from this kind of investigation. As you read this chapter, you will be thinking about the following Steps:

- What are the leading and managing facets of a policy designer role?
- What policies are needed and why?
- How are policies created and cared for?

Chapter 5 A professional role – a policy designer

Pause and reflect 5.1
Before progressing, think about: 'What are my understandings and beliefs about the above questions?' After considering each of the questions above, create an entry in your 'My professional leading-managing journal' by jotting down a couple of learning aims for your engaging with this chapter.

Step 1: What are the leading and managing facets of a policy designer role?

Policy designer
A policy designer is actively engaged in an early childhood setting and usually collaborates with others. Rather than referring to this role as a policy 'writer' or 'author', 'developer' or 'documenter', the noun 'designer' implies that those involved are more creative and original, rather than just being functional or mechanical. This ought to mean that any resulting policies have been more carefully conceived and thus professionally sketched. Designing policy involves encountering values, ideas and ideals alongside everyday practices. Design also involves thinking about and responding to lots of questions. Investigating the policy designer role encompasses both positional and situational leader-managers. There will also be times when this leading-managing project of policy work is centred with others as a collective within early childhood services. However, in essence, for policy work to be suitably relevant and educationally effective, this development must be undertaken with:

- Due attention to authentic relationships among contributors
- Serious consideration that policy topics and themes are in-context, sensitive and meaningful
- An eye looking for continuous transformation of ideas and society.

Knowing what a policy is
Part of understanding what a policy is also involves knowing what a policy is not. At the early childhood setting level, a policy is a formal written statement, a professional guideline of what, how, who and when. For your leading-managing journey, you might think of policies as a collection that forms the local 'road map' for a setting. At broader agency or government levels, a policy is an official document with required or expected guidelines and structures, and sometimes processes for that organisation or other groups that the organisation has some responsibility for. Larger than a local 'road map', these kinds of macro policies could be viewed as an atlas with pages of maps, or a globe rotating on an

Part 2 Thinking About Practices as Roles

axis. It is important to keep both local and beyond-the-fence policy work in perspective, because: 'rather than being value-free, policy is value-laden and resides within a defined value stance' (Farrell, 2001, p. 243). This means establishing a balancing act for the design of reasonable and wise professional policy portfolios for early childhood settings, while also critically reflecting on existing policies and various broader demands for policy. This consideration encompasses both local and beyond-the-fence policy portfolios, with both influencing the daily goings-on across the early childhood education field. Initiating such an important balancing act is certainly a leading-managing responsibility; a team member might undertake this with others or on their behalf.

Policies are also temporally bound. They are created at certain points in time within particular sociopolitical cultures and places. If we return to the idea of macro policy as a physical globe, the sociopolitical context could be represented by the axis of the globe. Thus, policies are often reviewed, revised and sometimes abandoned as time passes and places have a change of heart. This altering climate of policy work happens within early childhood settings and at beyond-the-fence places. Changeability occurs at all layers of government for political and economic reasons, as well as within associations, organisations and businesses. Thus, definitions of policy vary, particularly when they have an educational focus rather than a business one.

A policy is a policy, is a policy, is not

The following is a sampling of definitions of 'policy':

> Put simply, a policy is 'a statement on how the centre will run and the way that decisions will be made'.
> (Bryant, Semann, Slattery, Madden & Gibbs, 2009, p. 260)

> Describes the guideline or rule to be followed. A policy states your agreed beliefs on a range of topics relating to the service provided, gives a framework for decision making and ensures consistent practice.
> (McCormilla, 2012, p. 4)

> Once decisions have been made about the mission statement, policies – that is, a set of coherent guidelines, systems and approaches – can be determined using strategic thinking and decision-making. Policies support the fulfilment of the vision and leadership philosophy.
> (Rodd, 2013, p. 129)

> ... a statement of intent that can guide decision-makers about how to direct resources to achieve an intended outcome.
> (Waniganayake et al., 2012, p. 21–30)

> Written policies, procedures, and rules encourage consistent and timely decision making, while discouraging those decisions made without sufficient information. They constitute a blueprint.
> (Hearron & Hildebrand, 2007, p. 95)

> Public policy can be defined as the authorised rules and regulations by which organisations and bureaucracies function. Policies, in effect, establish the parameters that guide coherent decision making by personnel.
> (Ebbeck & Waniganayake, 2003, p. 136)

Chapter 5 A professional role – a policy designer

Governance includes the structures, processes, and policies that enable a system to function consistently, effectively, and efficiently. Second, policy often addresses specific issues, programs, or funding systems and distinguishes clean lines of authority.

(Kauerz & Kagan, 2012, pp. 88–9)

Understanding the purposes of policies

The above policy descriptors provide relevant clues about why we 'do' policy work and how policy at one level contributes to policy and practices at another level. One aspect of understanding the purposes of policy is being able to identify when a policy might be needed at the local service level or more broadly within government. Having relevant policy portfolios within and for the early childhood education field can mean that settings are recognised as being more professional. This idea is very important for the field even today, particularly if we consider the history of women and young children and their places in society and education (refer back to embodiment, kindergarten, care vs education, and naming tensions, in Chapters 2 and 3).

Each early childhood setting establishes what are referred to as 'governing or long-term policies', which reflect broader whole setting aspects such as financial considerations, personnel systems and governance structures and parameters (Hewes & Leatherman, 2005). Similarly, 'operating or short-term policies' are created to define the boundaries of everyday procedural practices; examples would include most of the *NQS* policy requirements boxed below in Step 2. Wisely leading and managing the design and administration of policies can benefit early childhood settings. These purposes encompass numerous professional actions, such as:

- Acknowledging and attending to legal requirements with transparency
- Identifying and considering potential operational risks
- Delineating appropriate everyday consistency, with reasonable flexibility
- Explicitly informing families and the community of professional and legal reasons behind various educational principles and practices
- Establishing visible common guidelines for staff teams, particularly for challenging times
- Purposely researching, critiquing and framing authentic equity and social justice principles for everyone
- Making decisions about setting facilities and features that might be handled in more timely ways
- Communicating ideas and negotiating misunderstandings in simplified and less emotional ways
- Ensuring that working documents are routinely reviewable and cooperatively adjusted, rather than 'set in stone'. (For examples, refer to Bryant & Gibbs,

2013; Chen, Nimmo & Fraser, 2009; Harris & Manatakis, 2013; Herbert, 2013; Mevawalla, 2013; Whitington, 2014.)

Building a background – the philosophical basis of policies

As you journey into policy work along this professional, leading-managing path, it will be important to stop and again focus on who you are and what you and others believe in. This is also a time to consider who might be involved in policy work. Consider how much and when a staff team, children and families and members of the local community might contribute. Early childhood policy work can begin with people forming a community of practice and revealing their personal–professional belief systems, which encompass primitive, authority and derived beliefs (Rivalland, 2007). Of course, it is vital that positional and situational leader-managers are sensitive to what others value about young children, their early education and family life. Thus, identifying personal and professional beliefs and values and cooperatively sharing these helps establish a more solid foundation for then creating a negotiated overarching philosophy. In addition to establishing a whole setting philosophy, some early childhood teams create a distinctive pedagogical philosophy that focuses on young children's everyday living and learning within that place. For example, some contemporary philosophical positions about young children are linked back to historic people like Maria Montessori and Rudolf Steiner, as well as the town of Reggio Emilia in Italy (Widger & Schofield, 2012; refer back to Chapter 3 and link with Chapter 6).

Returning to a broad encompassing philosophy, this becomes the background lens for designing legally required and professionally informed policies. The particular beliefs that a team decides on for informing basic or required policies will be reflected in careful selection of linguistic descriptors (adverbs, adjectives, phrases, theoretical or professional references). When a policy portfolio reflects a unique belief approach, it also takes account of rights, struggles and rules. Within this context, it is important to note that every early childhood setting in Australia is required to have a whole setting philosophy (refer to *National Quality Standard*, QA7). In support of this expectation, there are many examples of overarching philosophies and pedagogical stances that staff teams can review, critique and build from. (For examples, you might refer to Arthur et al., 2012; Bryant & Gibbs, 2013; Cook & Rouse, 2014; Lee, 2012; McCormilla, 2012; Waniganayake et al., 2012.)

Engaging with theoretical or professional frameworks can facilitate a team's philosophical thinking. For example, professionals might create a collaborative philosophical statement by using an interactive process with many 'Cs' – consult, consider, collaborate, create, carry out, celebrate, champion and change. Another framework that may assist teams with their thinking about beliefs and then creating a philosophy is

Chapter 5 A professional role – a policy designer

the 'practical theory of educative leadership' from Duignan and Macpherson (1992). This framework of three broad realms included encompassing activities and probing questions. Engaging with the activities and questions can turn this model into a reflective guide that leader-managers and colleagues might use when creating a philosophy and designing policies. The details of the model are outlined below (Duignan & Macpherson, 1992, p. 183):

- *A realm of ideas* with reflective practice, plus philosophical activity (what is right?) and planning activity (what is significant?)
- *A realm of people* with cultural agency, plus political activity (what is the dominant theory of social reality?) and cultural activity (how are new shared meanings mediating practices?)
- *A realm of things* with material actions, plus managerial activity (what is achievable?) and evaluative activity (are new practices efficient and effective?).

Looking at a sample early childhood philosophy can assist you with understanding and applying these realms. A philosophy phrase could be: 'We provide a wide range of natural and culturally diverse material.' This phrase represents one part of an accepted, official community discourse; however, during interviews, staff volunteered their ideas about natural materials as teaching tools, but not for multiculturalism (Rivalland, 2007). For our purposes, a team of educators with a leader-manager could both speculate about why culturally diverse materials were omitted and interrogate the 'natural materials' fragment of philosophy. Relevant questions might include:

- What is right about incorporating nature?
- How did natural materials provided as learning and teaching tools initially mediate existing practices?
- What kinds of learning about and engagement with nature can be achieved when natural materials are embedded into curricular resources?
- Why would staff fully ignore half of this philosophical statement?

Pause and reflect 5.2

If you were the situational leader-manager and the designated educational leader, how might you set up a community of practice project for investigating relevant policy options with colleagues? (Also refer to Chapter 6.)

Think about what you believe might be the first couple of priorities for someone leading a project to redesign a setting's policy portfolio. It may be helpful to interview a few directors or coordinators to gain an array of useful ideas. Then, you might brainstorm these ideas with colleagues in order to decide on initial follow-on tasks. Why do you feel these are important first steps?

Part 2 Thinking About Practices as Roles

Step 2: What policies are needed and why?

At this stopping point on the leading-managing path, you will consider local policies within early childhood settings. Additionally, your understanding of policies will broaden out beyond-the-fence.

For early childhood settings

If existing policies from a selection of Australian early childhood settings were examined, researchers would uncover all kinds of themes and issues. There would be variations in layout formats and actual wording, with particular attention to adjective qualifiers. Many early childhood education topics would be reflected in every setting's policy portfolio. This commonality, or what may be referred to as 'normative angle', would relate to contemporary government regulatory and financial systems (such as COAG and ACECQA). Key principles from professional affiliations may also be influential (such as ECA or the Lady Gowrie Centres). Similarly, variations in the wording of normative policies as well as unique policies may intertwine with specific values held by staff, families and/or local communities. In such cases, special interest organisations will be helpful and influential. External, sociopolitical influences highlight the need for serious and considered leading-managing when designing a policy portfolio. This sensitive and wise leading-managing ought to explore 'why this policy?' and attend to collective contemplation with professional lenses that look for the ethical and equitable, the socially just with moral higher ground (link with Chapter 7). These professional, value-laden contemplations take us back to the chapter beginning where the policy designer was cautioned about needing the strength and ability for climbing up hills to reach a panoramic viewing platform – this can be thought of as the moral higher ground aspect of a policy portfolio. In Chapter 2, a 'Respectful Communication Policy' was displayed, and it is exemplary of the professional lenses noted above.

More specifically, when Australian early childhood settings are designing and reconsidering policies, they are guided, at least initially, by the *National Quality Standard* (*NQS*) (ACECQA, 2013a) and the intertwined *National Law* and *National Regulations*. At the broad whole setting level, 'Quality Area 7: Leadership and service management' includes 'Element 7.3.5: Service practices are based on effectively documented policies and procedures that are available at the service and reviewed regularly' (ACECQA, 2013a). This Element relates to *National Regulations* 168–72 and the required policies (refer to the box below). For

Chapter 5 A professional role – a policy designer

comparison, consider if the National policy in New Zealand is similar, both historically and now.

> ### 'NQS', QA7, Element 7.3.5 – the required policies are:
>
> **1)** For all ages, all service types:
> *1.1 health and safety policies and procedures, including:*
>   Delivery and collection of children
>   Excursions
>   Refusal of authorisation for a child to leave the service
>   Dealing with infectious disease
>   Dealing with medical conditions
>   Emergency and evacuation
>   Health and safety, covering: nutrition; sun protection; water safety; first aid
>   Incident, injury, trauma and illness
>   A child-safe environment
> *1.2 staffing policies and procedures, including:*
>   A code of conduct
>   Determining responsible person
>   Participation of volunteers and students
> *1.3 relationships with children policies and procedures*
>   Including interactions with children
> *1.4 service management policies and procedures, including:*
>   Governance and management of the service, confidentiality of records
>   Enrolment and orientation
>   Payment of fees
>   Dealing with complaints
> **2)** Specifically for family day care services:
> *Additional to above are policies about:*
>   Assessment, approval and reassessment of residences and venues
>   Engagement or registration of educators
>   Keeping a register of educators
>   Monitoring, support and supervision of educators
>   Fit and proper assessment of educators and assistants and adults residing at residences
>   Visitors to residences and venues
>   Provision of information, assistance and training to educators
>   Engagement and registration of educator assistants

The Feature professional reflection: Jan's story, below, acknowledges the Australian *NQS* but also provides an example of going beyond requirements.

Part 2 Thinking About Practices as Roles

Feature professional reflection: Jan's story

Leading and policies. The National Quality Framework broadly guides our practices and the quality of services that we provide. In the *National Quality Standard*, Quality Area 7 states: 'Good service leadership and management should have well-documented policies, procedures and records, shared values, clear direction, and reflective practices to enable the service to function as a learning community.' This encompassing statement gives direction to part of the leader's role. Policies are an important part of any service and they require ongoing focus. When do we design a policy? Often in the past, policies were developed to deal with arising issues or regulatory requirements. They were more reactive rather than proactive; and they were looked at with a regulatory and governing lens of expectations for services to abide by.

At our centre we continue to update and bring in new policies based on the new *National Regulations* and *National Law*; but, we now are looking more proactively at policy development to enhance the centre's broad direction and incorporate our philosophy more actively through our policies. This means that we want to clearly state our combined beliefs, values, purpose, practices and links within our community. We want our policies to clearly link with our philosophy.

For example, while building relationships within the team, we are considering place. While our intentions are nurturing relationships with our children, families, community, we also look at nurturing our centre, our environment. As we move toward the future, our focus is on how we not only look at the long-term goals and a vision of the centre but also on the way that our centre impacts on our future world and our children's future. This has meant an ongoing policy commitment to various sustainability practices and continually redesigning an engaging natural environment for our children to experience and explore.

As another policy designing example, we recently raised money for an unwell child from our service and his family. We worked together with another small group to achieve an outstanding financial result. Not long after this time, we heard of another child and family in need of support in a smaller outlying community. This brought up many questions that were shared within the team at a meeting: Does this family have a support network? How can we support others in need in our community? If we fundraise every year, can we support those that really need a helping hand? This was discussed at a meeting and afterwards until we had a basic structure for our ideas and what we wanted our future practice to be. A very capable student-teacher was asked if she could develop the draft for this fundraising policy. (Usually, as centre director, I would complete this drafting process and present an initial policy.) This draft policy was distributed for educators, families, children and our whole organisation's board to review. After this process of feedback, we will have our new fundraising direction and it will reflect a practice of sharing our resources and goodwill. Such a policy means that we are proactively looking at our position in the community, along

Chapter 5 A professional role – a policy designer

with our roles and responsibilities about how we support families within our broader community, not only those in our centre.

A provocation: *What is the most inspirational aspect of Jan's story? If this example of leading-managing policy work has stirred your professional interest, why is that?*

Within organisations beyond-the-fence

Engagement as a policy designer involves professionals in going outside and beyond-the-fence of early childhood settings. A policy designer critiques public or external policies and relevant legislation as part of a process that then informs policy content at the setting level. Critiquing policy may be a team-oriented task, as staff members ponder such issues as: context of children's rights; rules for sensitive interactions; and governance of a learning organisation. A more specific construct that builds further from children's rights and social justice beliefs is social inclusion (Wong & Turner, 2014).

ECA and ARACY (Australian Research Alliance for Children and Youth) provide organisational samplers of Australian policy beyond-the-fence. As a national, membership-based professional association with peak-body status across all layers of government, ECA consulted widely to develop a value-based and principled reconciliation action plan (2012b; available online). ECA's commitment was declared through identifying key threads within the plan; these helped make it a reality and create a difference in communities. The threads encompass relationships, respect, opportunities, and tracking with reporting. These threads closely resemble the 'Four Rs framework' for research work with and in Aboriginal communities: respect, relevance, reciprocity and responsibility (Markiewicz, 2012).

As a broader-than-early-childhood organisation, ARACY's *The Nest* was designed as a national child and youth well-being plan, with an action agenda and guiding framework (ARACY, 2013). This organisational policy included a short shared-vision statement that expanded into measureable outcomes or goals. Referred to as key 'result' areas for young people, these encompassed:

- Being loved and safe
- Having material basics
- Being healthy
- Learning
- Participating
- Having a positive sense of culture and identify.

Part 2 Thinking About Practices as Roles

Similarly, ARACY's *The Nest* encompassed six operating 'commitment' principles for guiding collaborative implementation of this agenda through improving, promoting or reducing actions.

Both these organisational action plans included varying terms and alternative processes from early childhood settings. They represent 'guidelines', 'platforms', and even 'manifestos'; and, these can be other names for policy. Additionally, both documents considered issues and topics that are very relevant to young children's lives as they interact within early childhood settings. Thus, both could contribute to the thinking of professionals as they create philosophies and design policies. These two documents might also inform leading-managing actions for rights advocacy (refer to Chapter 7).

For a comparative global perspective at the broader government and non-government organisation layer, the New Zealand Ministry of Education and the US Centre for the Study of Social Policy (CSSP) offer relevant resources, including principles, documents and policies. The New Zealand *ECE Educate* site states bilingually: 'Our vision is to provide a collaborative space where early childhood educators can share, reflect on, and be inspired by quality teaching practice' (p. 1; at: www.educate.ece.govt.nz/). The site does deliver on this stated vision in many ways.

As another instance, all of CSSP's policy work has been guided by broad principles; these are: equity; results; two-generational strategies; comprehensive and coordinated solutions; community co-investment; and using research and evidence. Their work included policy briefs and policy documents; one example is: *Policy Matters: Setting and measuring benchmarks for state policies – Improving the readiness of children for school* (Kagan & Rigby, 2003; at: www.cssp.org). With such policy work as background, Kagan, Tarrant and Kauerz (2012) outlined the movement of principles from a system-level planning process to the policy matters level. The guidelines begin with a stem that the planning process had to:

- Be inclusive, transparent and influential
- Be driven by current research and a Theory of Change
- Account for the realities of each state's policy and political context
- Result in a set of actionable priorities
- Have an afterlife.

As a European example of beyond-the-fence policy work, the Irish Office of the Minister for Children traced out a comprehensive set of diversity and equality guidelines (Murray, Crooke & O'Doherty, 2006; at: www.dcya.gov.ie/documents/childcare/diversity_and_equality.pdf). The document began with definitions and included an introductory 'journey' metaphor with a policy context of focal Irish and international agreements and legal acts. Aims and objectives were then noted, with hints about how to use the document. The first substantive section asked adults to reflectively explore values

Chapter 5 A professional role – a policy designer

and attitudes. This was followed by consideration of goals for working with children and development of a relevant policy portfolio. The document included a sampler of philosophical ideas and policy supports. In summary, all the above guides could help team stakeholders frame their decisions about everyday practices. In a team, such professional decisions might happen as colleagues do comparing and contrasting, confirming and changing with relevant research findings and organisational examples.

Pause and reflect 5.3

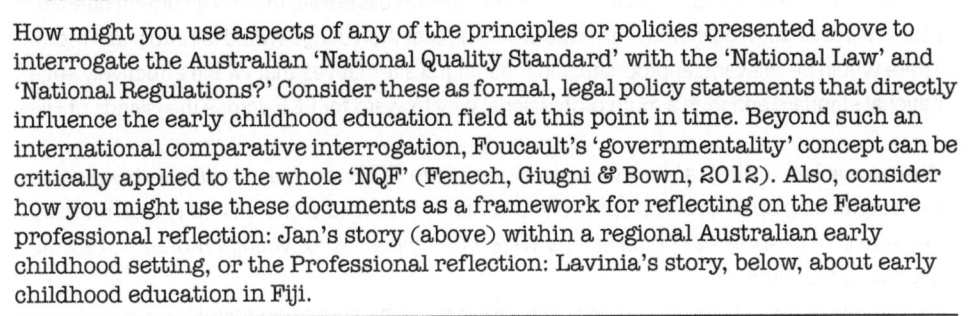

How might you use aspects of any of the principles or policies presented above to interrogate the Australian 'National Quality Standard' with the 'National Law' and 'National Regulations?' Consider these as formal, legal policy statements that directly influence the early childhood education field at this point in time. Beyond such an international comparative interrogation, Foucault's 'governmentality' concept can be critically applied to the whole 'NQF' (Fenech, Giugni & Bown, 2012). Also, consider how you might use these documents as a framework for reflecting on the Feature professional reflection: Jan's story (above) within a regional Australian early childhood setting, or the Professional reflection: Lavinia's story, below, about early childhood education in Fiji.

Professional reflection: Lavinia's story

In Fiji, the Early Childhood Education sector of the Ministry of Education comes directly under the Primary Education Unit. The government provides only some assistance through the provision of grants to teachers and donations of equipment to assist with children's learning. This arrangement places sole responsibilities for local, everyday early childhood education on communities, as they manage and run centres.

Within this context and sector-task, as officer-in-charge (1999 to 2000), I viewed the broad running of Early Childhood Education in the country. This role included: overall development with drafting and revising of the ECE policies; and the regulation of early childhood services along with setting standards for the infrastructure. My role encompassed considering and conducting professional development for teachers, as well as conducting ECE awareness programmes in urban and rural communities. An example of an important policy was the 'Provision of Establishment and Registration of Preschool Centres'. Here, I had to liaise with educational stakeholders and the Ministry of Health together with the Ministry of Education's Human Resources Department. The policy was drawn up as a deterrent to the many people who had been trying to set up preschools in any manner for the sake of making monetary gains at the expense of children. The policy was approved and is still being implemented today as a form of 'precautionary principle' in the best interests of young children.

Part 2 Thinking About Practices as Roles

As an officer-in-charge of ECE, planning, designing, organising and monitoring the administration of all aspects of early childhood education was most tedious. The challenge for me was monitoring all aspects of my work in the position, and therefore I could say boldly that quality was missing. It was a stressful work environment. There was a lack of human resources; and so, the burden was rather too heavy for only one person. In fact, at least three people were needed. If this staffing level had been established, there would have been a sharing of tasks across three broad areas: one to manage curriculum, one to manage the administration 'bit' and another for the community 'bit'.

Even now, I believe that to solve this challenging workplace role, there is an urgent need for ECE in Fiji to be fully legislated. The hope would be that then things would fall into place more. There would be relevant, appropriate and meaningful alternatives that would effectively set a national standard and thus a more professional way forward for ECE across the islands of Fiji.

A provocation: In Lavinia's story, she outlines all the ECE work that could have been done, even continuing until now. You can feel the continuous pressure on her, and you can identify her sense of despair that better things were not happening for young children across the country at that time.

As you pause here during your professional journey, think about two things:

1) *If I were in her shoes, what would I plan to discuss with my direct supervisor in the government department about the unrealistic workload I am dealing with? Create a list of three to five key points about the position.*

2) *Staying in this ideal-world-moment, consider National-government-level policy options and identify what might be the most important first policy to be enacted. Doing research and chatting with colleagues both initially and as you reveal your thoughts can be worthwhile.*

Pause and reflect 5.4

As you will have noticed during your travels to this point in the chapter, policy portfolios are an essential component of contemporary early childhood settings. They are also part of the operational structure of most organisations and government departments that interact with early childhood professionals and their workplaces. Yet the headings, the word choice and the physical look of policy portfolios vary greatly.

The phrase 'what policies are needed' once again raises the tension of meanings – are policies 'needed'? This means, are they: required, obliged, demanded, desired, wanted, depended on, necessary, essential, justifiable? Consider: When are policies a professional choice and staff decision based on higher order values and ethics? In other words, when do they go beyond 'required' as in basic or foundational? Can adding particular adverbs and adjectives to a foundational policy really turn it into more than basic (refer back to earlier ideas about this in Step 1, and link with Chapter 7)?

For example, Wyong Shire Council on the central coast of New South Wales established a community vision statement with sustainability principles of: 'Think

Chapter 5 A professional role – a policy designer

holistically, act responsibly'; 'smart, local, adaptable'; 'care for nature'; 'good processes, improved outcomes'; 'work together; lead by example' (2013; at: www.wyong.nsw.gov.au/environment/). How might these brief phrases help inform your policy planning and designing, if your staff team decided to add a holistic sustainability perspective to a setting's policy portfolio?

Step 3: How are policies created and cared for?

What does a policy look like?

Some policies are written in a sentence or two, others are extensive templates with consistent components. Let us consider some examples. The Armidale and District Family Day Care policies, including 'Respectful Communication', have a fairly consistent template. There are minor heading variations because of development over time and by different team members (refer back to this policy in Chapter 2). As the policies are routinely reviewed for content relevance, an agreed uniform template will be applied into the future. This will happen gradually in accordance with an established spread-of-time calendar that acknowledges the workloads of both scheme staff and volunteer members of the Board of Directors. Current templates are on official letterhead and include each policy's title followed by: purpose or aim or rationale; definitions as necessary; short preamble or brief policy statement; full delineation of procedures; sources (references, including State laws, *National Regulations*); related ADFDC policies; dates of current re-writing with original formulation date and future reviewing.

We can go back about twenty-five years to explore the path of policy work across the Australian early childhood education field (Baxter, Gelenter, Ryan & Weingarth, 1988). The *Keeping on Track* folder was created to address major challenges that directors and others faced at the time during their everyday administration and management of early childhood settings. Using historical lenses, we can uncover the sociopolitical times and note that this manual predated the establishment of the National Childcare Accreditation Council with all its staff, supports, documents and processes for the Quality Improvement and Accreditation System for childcare centres (NCAC and QIAS, in 1993; historical materials are located at: www.acecqa.gov.au/ncac-archive). Thus, it was a particularly helpful guide that assisted directors, coordinators and committees over the years with meeting basic State regulations and going beyond them. For example, the policy section provided a process for developing a centre-wide philosophy for underpinning policies. Additionally, a model for designing and displaying policies was outlined with three components: aim, explanation and implementation. This template still has value in terms of:

Part 2 Thinking About Practices as Roles

- Guiding what ought to be included in a policy
- Supporting those engaged in policy work.

About ten years later, a fourth revision of *Keeping on Track* (Gibbs, 1999) provided a general review of 'How do we go about writing policies for the centre?'. Two options were suggested: either starting from scratch and brainstorming; or beginning with a sample policy and altering it. Development stages were outlined and these included the steps: examine the issue/topic; collect information; brainstorm with others; draft and ratify a policy; and implement it. Today, there are many resources outlining policy templates and samples that leader-managers can seek out and share with colleagues.

Taking responsibility for policy work

When a team of staff is responsible for designing a policy portfolio, they will engage in many 'lead-plan-organise-monitor' tasks that happen collectively as a whole project with acts of administering, managing and leading (refer to McCormilla, 2012 and PSC Alliance website for useful booklets, fact sheets, policy tips and examples). Everyone will do some considering of organisational parameters and limitations. There will always be controls and limits related to finances, ordinary business dealings with the community, and usual maintenance of resources, buildings and yards. These realities influence which policies are established. Similarly, the design of policies can influence organisational features. On a more sociopolitical level and a cultural awareness basis, policy designing takes account of people's rights, the usual human struggles, and broader rules and requirements. Team members may lead, manage or administer various tasks. Key examples include:

- Someone will responsively *administer* – setting the meetings, gathering reliable resources, creating an agenda, recording brainstorming and decisions, etc.
- Someone will actively *manage* – chairing the meeting, suggesting links to legal requirements, noting potential risks, reviewing current documents, tabling professional and research literature, noting the existing policy review schedule, noting timeframes, arranging an input-review-feedback process for drafts, etc.
- Someone will sensitively *lead* – negotiating differing opinions and ideas, asking critical questions, offering critical issues, encouraging quieter colleagues, challenging others to reflect more, synthesising new ways, translating research findings, encouraging involvement of others beyond staff, etc.

Caring for and about policy work

Of course, once a policy is planned, designed, reviewed and edited, it is put into practice. This involves documenting and implementing with follow-on tasks. Each policy enters a recurring cycle of professional attention and ethical care; and so, a whole policy portfolio is gradually revamped and updated (refer to the list below; link with

Chapter 5 A professional role – a policy designer

Chapter 7 on advocacy). Aspects of caring about policy work and caring for policies are firmly linked with leading-managing change within early childhood settings. This leading-managing is also about responding to and advocating about broader changes beyond-the-fence.

Professional attention to a policy cycle encompasses:

- monitoring use
- interpreting professional positions
- reviewing currency
- revising as values and laws adjust
- consulting stakeholders' current views
- re-negotiating meanings of phrases
- upholding required practices
- evaluating effectiveness
- interrogating research findings
- maintaining relevance
- critiquing existing and new government standards.

Pause and reflect 5.5

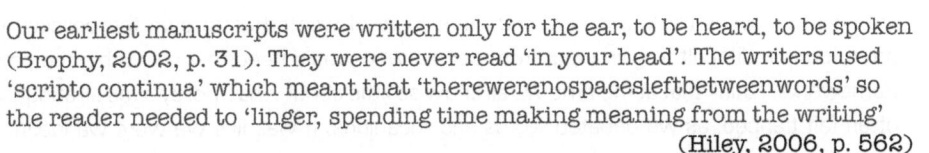

Our earliest manuscripts were written only for the ear, to be heard, to be spoken (Brophy, 2002, p. 31). They were never read 'in your head'. The writers used 'scripto continua' which meant that 'therewerenospacesleftbetweenwords' so the reader needed to 'linger, spending time making meaning from the writing'
(Hiley, 2006, p. 562)

Consider Hiley's words and do some wondering about the written structure of education policies. Review both local setting policy formats and broader organisational or government policy templates. Also note that obviously, formal policies are not poetry, nor are they intended to entertain readers. Identify how the form or format of an ECE policy does/does not help readers with understanding both the intent and purpose of it.

Conclusion

Your travels through this chapter were initially described as a hilly challenge of understanding and designing policies. This process ought to result in personal, professional and team satisfaction. You have now been up hills and down into valleys exploring the many ways that a policy designer works and what such project work entails. This section of always-unfinished track can be affected by seasonal and climate changes that originate close by or come from afar. At times you will embrace the weather and its

Part 2 Thinking About Practices as Roles

changes; however, there may be times when you will resist an onslaught of elements by clinging to a precautionary principle for young children and taking an ethical stance for the profession. Both these actions can be couched within one's lifelong emotional competence (Bansal & Hingorani, 2013) and potentially represent advocacy (refer to Chapter 7).

As you leave this section of professional path and journey forth, continue to reflect on the notion that a policy designer's work is about changing ideas and taking a stance. In essence, designing a policy portfolio happens as shared interpretive actions. This interactive process includes situational and distributed leading-managing, with all contributing visions and thus cooperatively influencing each other. This means that dynamic relationships and sensitive interactions are features of the humane climate surrounding such a professional role. Policy is a vital track off the main professional path. This path can be rough and uneven, yet ultimately it should contribute to the best interests of young children and to our collective professional 'common good'. With wisdom, leader-managers can influence practices now and into the future.

Dear Nadine,

This chapter took me back to my earliest leadership roles in early childhood when I tried hard to work with staff, parents, children (when possible) and community members to develop or re-visit policies. At that time I knew that working with others would make policies and attendant practices more relevant, and more 'ours'. I wanted us to own the policies, yet often found it difficult to gain input from people who would need to work within the policy frameworks. I think that at the time we all knew so little about what 'policy' was all about, we often felt trapped, as we debated words and meanings. It was like we were wandering in circles in a valley (to use one of the journey and landscape metaphors in the chapter). We just wanted people living on the peaks around us (in government or peak organisations) to save us all this trouble and simply give us policies to follow.

If I remember rightly, on the occasions when we collaborated well, usually on policies about which we were most passionate, we fell into the three roles described in the chapter as administering, managing and sensitively leading the policy process. On these occasions the load was shared, with different individuals taking responsibility for the tasks associated with one or more of the roles. In hindsight I would have loved to have the roles and tasks clearly identified and laid out here. I guess muddling through was fine at the time because we did address our core philosophy and beliefs in an attempt to live our ideals through the policies we constructed or reviewed. I wonder how many of the readers will find themselves muddling through policy processes when they first start out. Perhaps the thinking about policy ideas in this chapter will make it a little easier.

Lavinia's story provides insight into the frustrations associated with having the power to design policies yet being hampered by lack of resources which would ensure that the policies could be enacted successfully. We can so readily think that policy designers at the State or

Chapter 5 A professional role – a policy designer

national level have an easy time. Sadly they do not. I guess that compromise often sits alongside the ideals that we have for the policies we might design and what we actually achieve. I wonder how many of the examples of policies that were shared in this chapter fall short of what some individuals involved 'really wanted'. Sumsion et al. (2009) point to the impact we would like to have on policy and the compromises that are often necessary (refer back to 'Dear Nadine' letter in Chapter 3 for the first reference to this source).

This is an honest chapter on policy. Policy is not presented as an easy 'fix' to remedy what is going wrong in practice. There are a number of signposts presented in the chapter for achieving a collaborative approach to creating polices. The need to conduct a situational analysis 'for' policy, and also to conduct an analysis 'of' policy is recognised. The chapter highlights the need for understanding the big picture, including current discourses about early childhood and how these have informed the layers of policy that we need to attend to on a daily basis. Readers are made aware that policies, at all levels, are always in tension and in a state of flux. The attention to these details provides what is needed for leaders in early childhood settings to design authentic and rigorous policy with others. I wish I had this guidance to call upon in my early days.

Cheers,
Di

Pause and reflect 5.6

Which idea in this chapter most influenced your current beliefs, and why? Record your personal feelings, inspirations and professional thoughts in your 'journal'.

Chapter 6

A professional role – a pedagogy creator

> We recognise that we are both co-products and co-producers of this moment and that the best we can do is offer glimpses.
>
> Richard Edwards & Robin Usher (2008, p. 14)

Broad concepts

In this chapter, your professional path widens to a well-marked and maintained four-lane highway, with side paths that are firmly gravelled and well-trodden by foot and bicycle traffic. The size and condition of this travel route represents the centrality or key purpose of early childhood settings. As young children are the centre point, everything that contributes to their well-being and authentic learning is pivotal. All other aspects of these settings as presented throughout this book exist as contributors to young children's living and learning. Young children are the central purpose of all ECE work. In this chapter, you will be thinking about the following Steps:

- What are the leading and managing facets of a pedagogy creator role?
- Which responsibilities help frame children's learning?
- Who is involved in children's learning?

Chapter 6 A professional role – a pedagogy creator

Pause and reflect 6.1
Before progressing, think about: 'What are my understandings and beliefs about the above questions?' After considering each of the above questions, create an entry in your 'My professional leading-managing journal' by jotting down a couple of learning aims for your engaging with this chapter.

Step 1: What are the leading and managing facets of a pedagogy creator role?

Being an effective and authentic pedagogy creator involves engaging with many people, various educational places and diverse curricular models and practices. Both positional and situational leader-managers are usually active participants in all aspects of early childhood pedagogy. Generally, pedagogy relates to children's educational experiences beginning with adults' philosophical ideas, moving to other learning steps and teaching processes, and finally to the everyday interactions and experiences within early childhood settings.

Pedagogy creator
This chapter begins from a consideration of pedagogy creators in the broadest sense. Following the pattern set in previous chapters, we start by exploring these two words. Firstly, it is important to remember these words are part of the socially constructed and socially situated discourse of early childhood education and have a long history. The word 'pedagogy' was used years ago and then it fell out of favour or fashion, at least in Australia. Young children were 'cared for' and 'exposed to free play activities'. They 'participated in learning experiences' and there were 'planned weekly programs'. There were building and playground guidelines with required furniture and equipment/resources lists. In fact, I worked from such documents when I was a Preschool Adviser in Victoria during the late 1970s. The words 'learning', 'teaching', 'programme plans' and 'curriculum (learning/discipline areas)' were components of Kindergarten Teacher College courses (refer to Press & Wong, 2013). There were guideline samplers for planning, documenting and implementing; however, these were not formal or official documents at the time. 'Pedagogy' did firmly and normatively re-enter Australian ECE discourse in the early 2000s. This happened with the publication and wide distribution of *Belonging, Being & Becoming, The Early Years Learning Framework for Australia* (AGDEEWR, 2009; Kennedy, 2011; Semann & Soper, 2012). Significantly, at the same time, ECE discourse meanings shifted dramatically when it was noted that everyone working directly with young children was an 'educator', but not a 'teacher'.

Part 2 Thinking About Practices as Roles

The language of pedagogy speaks of 'early childhood educators (and their) professional practice, especially those aspects that involve building and nurturing relationships, curriculum decision-making, teaching and learning' (AGDEEWR, 2009, p. 9). This is now the official or standardised working definition that helps guide all Australian early childhood staff in their daily work with young children. Within the normalising *National Quality Standard*, Quality Area 1 is labelled 'Educational program and practice' with definitional discourse encompassing: learning, curriculum, the program, learner, routines and documentation (ACECQA, 2013c). The adult actors as educators 'design' and 'deliver'; they even 'plan', 'respond', 'document', 'evaluate' and 'reflect'; however, they do not 'teach'! Pause here to think about:

- Who is a teacher?
- How are ECE teachers defined, described and discussed elsewhere around the Pacific Rim and beyond?

Such *NQS* definitions and documents support and guide fundamental agreements for educators related to 'doing no harm' to others, otherwise known as 'the precautionary principle'. (For examples, refer to Ball & Olmedo, 2013; Collins & Ting, 2014; Karliner, 2005; Mevawalla, 2013; Tickner, Raffensperger & Myers, nd.) The *NQS* also frames a professional commitment to 'common good' features for everyday caring routines and authentic learning. As such, these fundamentals are underlying and basic. Professionals ought to go beyond them to create authentic and meaningful learning environments (link with policy and advocacy, in Chapters 5 and 7). As already noted, policy actions contribute to baseline positions and they can move towards wise practices with young children. With this in mind, there are key responsibilities and certain dispositions that both positional and situational leader-managers take on in order to realistically facilitate wise pedagogical practice among staff. Similarly, within *NQS* Quality Area 3: 'Physical environment', the above ideas of 'doing no harm' and for the 'common good' are extended beyond humans (also see Elliott, 2014a). The relevant QA3 Standard is: 3.3 – 'The service takes an active role in caring for its environment and contributes to a sustainable future' – and two specific elements offer further guidance (ACECQA, 2013a). In general, government positions and related documents simultaneously represent a form of sociocultural power and control of the field vs ECE professionals having some agency (see Chapter 7). These government items are examples of institutionalising education, which also happens within other layers of education and to educators.

Pedagogy can also mean, a 'planned and deliberate process whereby one person helps another to learn. This is what first peoples did through various formalised rites of passage, from child to adult to elder' (Kalantzis & Cope, 2008, p. 6). The challenge for any pedagogical leader-manager lies in balancing existing normative guidelines and legal standards with contemporary wise professional statements, relevant theoretical models and germane research findings. From an ECE professional perspective on pedagogy and being a creator of it, the idea of curriculum as 'simultaneities' could be a useful framework for leader-managers and other educators. Six simultaneities form an interactive vision for educators to work with; this curriculum or pedagogy is then considered in terms of structure, process, content, teaching, learning and activity (Hussain, Conner & Mayo, 2014). Such pedagogy includes curricular disciplines and it has both some structure and some openness for changes to happen with children and adults.

Being a pedagogue

Early childhood educators are a 'mixed lot' across each early childhood setting, especially with their assorted qualifications, varying job titles, array of daily tasks and, of course, their personal sociocultural backgrounds. Because of such staffing arrangements and the dilemmic nature of what pedagogy is and could be, leading-managing within early childhood settings becomes crucial. In this chapter, these pedagogy creators may also be called pedagogues. Furthermore, both positional and situational colleagues ought to be actively engaged in shaping all aspects of pedagogy. Positional leader-managers might particularly work beyond-the-fence, on behalf of a staff team, with leaders from other settings. A positional leader-manager or a designated situational leader could well interact with leaders and managers from macro-level organisations that are also involved in ECE pedagogy creation. This may be an 'educational leader' or another member of the team for each setting (Cheeseman, 2012). Some of these interactions will be professional learning events, where leadership intertwines with collaborative approaches, such as 'talking circles', 'communities of practice' and broader acts of public participation. (For examples, refer to Aquash, 2013; Macfarlane & Cartmel, 2012; McCotter, 2001; Taylor, 2013; Umbreit, 2003; Warner & Grint, 2006; and refer back to Step 2 in Chapter 4.)

Acting as a sensitive pedagogue can reflect the statement: 'Pedagogy is the vision and approach that unpacks the opportunity for teacher and child alike to participate in knowledge transformation' (Semann & Soper, 2012, p. 16). This quote reflects the idea of being a 'creator', which is another descriptor to add to your collection of key ECE professional roles – along with team stakeholder (Chapter 4) and policy designer (Chapter 5). Just as the noun phrase 'being a designer' was singled out to imply and represent being more than functional with policy portfolios, 'being a creator' of everything surrounding children's meaningful learning also implies more than just 'doing pedagogy'. Creating pedagogically sound interactions, dialogues, experiences, spaces, curricular maps, teaching ways and documentation cycles are all part of this focus. This pedagogy work reflects the idea that children's learning intertwines with

Part 2 Thinking About Practices as Roles

educators' teaching. The result is that both learning and teaching represent and become:

- Beyond the ordinary
- More relevant and emergent
- Wiser in manner
- Pioneering, imaginative and inventive
- Expanding of people's habits of mind
- More than what seemed like a good thing at the time.

Knowing what ECE pedagogy encompasses

These team actions contribute to and frame children's learning with caring routines. They involve consideration of educators' teaching motives, their styles and relationships, and their thinking about these human features. Such thinking brings a political lens to pedagogy work (Skattebol, 2010), and this means that being a pedagogy creator includes the vital element of interpreting relevant legislation – such as Australia's *NQS* with *Quality Improvement Plans*, the *National Law* and *National Regulations* (ACECQA, 2013a, 2013b; for scholarly examples refer to Brennan & Adamson, 2014; Cartmel, Macfarlane & Casley, 2012; Fenech, Giugni & Bown, 2012; Logan, Sumsion & Press, 2013).

For undertaking this pedagogical role, government documents funnel into the specific curriculum guide *Belonging, Being & Becoming, The Early Years Learning Framework for Australia* (AGDEEWR, 2009). Formally and normatively the *BBB-EYLFA* curriculum document links particularly with *NQS* Quality Areas 1, 2, 3 and 5, but also with all other QAs (Cheeseman, Fenech & Staff at Tigger's Honeypot Childcare Centre, 2012; ECA-ACARA, 2011). For comparison, the New Zealand document *Licensing Criteria for Early Childhood Education and Care Centres 2008 & Early Childhood Education Curriculum Framework* detailed regulatory processes and whole setting requirements along with assessment criteria (NZ Ministry of Education, 2011). It included an overview of the curriculum regulation standard and a brief of the *Te Whāriki* curriculum guide. This guidebook refers to 'service curriculum' rather than 'pedagogy'. It states: 'service curriculum means all the experiences, interactions, activities and events – both direct and indirect, planned and spontaneous – that happen at the service. Teaching practices, including planning, assessment, and evaluation form part of the service curriculum' (NZ Ministry of Education, 2011, p. 7). Beyond such government documents, Sellers (2013) provided examples of *Te Whāriki* in action, and Duhn and Ritchie focused on New Zealand's *Te Whāriki* with a sustainability lens (Duhn, 2012; Duhn, Bachmann & Harris, 2010; Ritchie, 2012, 2013; Ritchie Duhn, Rau & Craw, 2010). In Singapore, parallel pedagogical resources for educators were collected into the toolkit *Nurturing Early Learners* (*NEL*), which included:

Chapter 6 A professional role – a pedagogy creator

- *NEL, A curriculum framework for kindergartens in Singapore* (Ministry of Education Singapore, 2012)
- *NEL, Framework for Mother Tongue Languages* (Ministry of Education Singapore, 2013b)
- *NEL, Educators' Guide: Overview* (Ministry of Education Singapore, 2013a).

Influences on pedagogy

We can begin our exploration of influences on contemporary ECE pedagogy with questions, so we might ask:

- What are the origins of various pedagogical components today?
- Which models and frameworks informed governments when they framed policy and law?
- Which research findings do professionals consult about children, their learning and educators' teaching?
- Which everyday actions do early childhood educators engage in, and why?

Once again, a consideration of origins and backgrounds leads us to a starting point focused on educators' values and beliefs, along with their life experiences and other contextual influences. Working from origins means exploring historical and contemporary ECE theories and philosophies as well as various learning approaches and models.

Foundational premises for pedagogy

Educators can undertake historical work by researching archival documents, interrogating curricular discipline resources and inquiring into professional bodies' archival records. There are many examples of historical people, places and practices that influenced and still inform today's views of young children and their early education (refer back to Chapter 3). Exploring these ideas can enhance and deepen your role as pedagogy creator. This process of guiding and prompting your creativity with pedagogy ought to be open-ended and flexible in order to accommodate individuals' lived experiences. Thus it is suggested that you view components of ECE pedagogy through several 'understanding lenses'. In fact, there are so many options that only a small selection of lenses, or theoretical approaches, are introduced here to help focus your current journey. These focal 'understanding lenses' can assist you with viewing and thinking about:

- Philosophical stances
- Children as engaged citizens
- Human diversity with social justice.

Part 2 Thinking About Practices as Roles

Understanding philosophical stances

The philosophical history of early childhood education is as much about images of children and childhood as it is about their everyday living and learning. The historical roots of ECE usually go back at least a couple of hundred years, with many authors referring to Rousseau's book *Emile* (lived 1712–1778, born Geneva; Rousseau, 1762/2010; Hewes & Leatherman, 2005; Taylor, 2013). Some historical perspectives go back 2000 years to Mentor and mentoring in Greek mythology, particularly Homer's *The Odyssey* (Carruthers, 1993; Mills-Bayne, 2013; Nolan, 2007; Verducci, 2012). More specifically for early childhood education there have been many diversely influential people over the centuries, such as Susan Isaacs and Patty Smith Hill (refer to list below). They had a cumulative effect on our images of young children and the look of early childhood pedagogy, including curricula, resources, spaces, child–adult interactions and relationships, ways of learning and forms of teaching.

The following is a list of key historic professionals who influenced ECE:

- Frederich Froebel (lived 1782–1852, Germany)
- Maria Montessori (lived 1870–1952, Italy)
- Robert Owen (lived 1771–1858, England)
- John Dewey (lived 1859–1952, USA)
- the MacMillan sisters, Rachel and Margaret (lived 1859–1917 & 1860–1931, Scotland and England)
- Caroline Pratt (lived 1867–1954, USA)
- Susan S. Isaacs (lived 1885–1948, England)
- G. Stanley Hall (lived 1844–1924, USA)
- Patty Smith Hill (lived 1868–1946, USA).

Moving forward from these historic people, psychology rather than sociology became a driving force behind education in general, and particularly early childhood education. The major psychological views of child development were disparate and varied from behaviourist to phenomenological (Sellers, 2013; Spodek, 1973). Over time, other ideas and theories were mixed in between to create multiple lenses. Later thinkers and writers also influenced children's lives and early childhood education. A number of these people are noted here:

- Jean Piaget (lived 1896–1980, Switzerland)
- Lev Vygotsky (lived 1896–1934, Russia)
- Carl Rogers (lived 1902–1987, USA)
- Erik Erikson (lived 1902–1994, USA)
- Abraham Maslow (lived 1908–1970, USA)

Chapter 6 A professional role – a pedagogy creator

- Urie Bronfenbrenner (lived 1917–2005, USA)
- Albert Bandura (lived 1925 to present, USA)
- Howard Gardner (lived 1943 to present, USA)

(Further references to these thinkers and writers can be found at: Arthur et al., 2012; Chaille, 2008; Charlesworth, 2014; Edwards, 2009; Fleer, 2010; Goffin, 1994; Hewes & Leatherman, 2005; Page, 2000; Press & Wong, 2013; Sellers, 2013; Spodek, 1973; Ungar, Ghazinour & Richter, 2012; and, refer back to Chapter 3, Step 1.)

Many of the ideas, programs and resources that these famous contributors 'gave' to young children, families and educators are still influential around the world. As a link with the embodiment lens running through this book, it is worth asking: Where is the representative balance of women as key influencers from historical times to contemporary times?

Pause and reflect 6.2

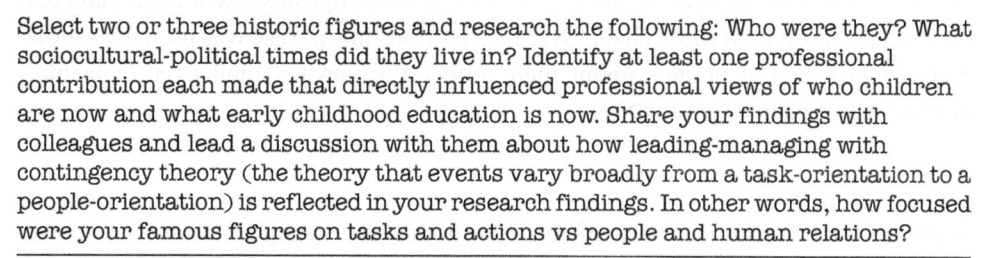

Select two or three historic figures and research the following: Who were they? What sociocultural-political times did they live in? Identify at least one professional contribution each made that directly influenced professional views of who children are now and what early childhood education is now. Share your findings with colleagues and lead a discussion with them about how leading-managing with contingency theory (the theory that events vary broadly from a task-orientation to a people-orientation) is reflected in your research findings. In other words, how focused were your famous figures on tasks and actions vs people and human relations?

More recently, from the mid-to-late 1900s, many contemporary ideas about early childhood pedagogy originated in the USA. Broadly, they represented education as learning and teaching via curricula with a number of theoretically based curricula models. As an example, we can refer to Project Head Start, which began as an eight-week summer experience in 1965. The various American Head Start models included key examples of linking children's interactions, relationships and learning with various theories. The original models represented either, more:

- Behavioural and instructional or structured ideas – the Behavior Analysis Approach, the DARCEE early intervention Program and the Bereiter-Engleman-Becker Program
- Phenomenological and enrichment or more open ideas – The Bank Street Model, The Tucson Early Education Model and the Piagetian Ypsilanti Model – later referred to as High Scope. (For examples, refer to Charlesworth, 2014; Connor, 2008; Goffin, 1994; Hewes & Leatherman, 2005; Hohmann, Banet & Weikart, 1979; Spodek, 1973.)

Part 2 Thinking About Practices as Roles

Some Head Start models helped shape contemporary Australian early childhood education, and they provided a platform for budding ECE researchers in Australia, New Zealand and beyond. These two broadly different theoretical approaches were not part of a continuum. However, over the years the extremes softened and were scholarly subdivided into a larger number of theoretical approaches to early childhood pedagogy. Worldwide, these diversified approaches continue to influence our conceptions and images of children in distinct ways, including our understandings of children's learning. Such influences extended to how educators teach, the spaces and places they arrange and which resources and artefacts are negotiated with children.

Understanding children as engaged citizens

One historical image of young children has been the 'tabula rasa'. This originated from a Roman Latin-writing, wax tablet ('tabula' for table). It was heated and then smoothed or scraped to remove any etchings ('rasa' for scrape away or erase) before being re-used. This early object and related function were later refined as the idea of 'blanked-out', which was an interpretation of 'blank slate', from English slabs of black slate that children wrote on with white chalk. Over the centuries this phrase was used to describe children in terms of notions about their minds and lacking intellectual capacities, particularly at birth (Moore, 2009).

Beyond 'empty'

Many community and professional views of infants and young children have moved beyond the 'empty' or 'erased' image. However, public and professional constructs of 'child as ...' exist, with some still reflecting aspects of *tabula rasa*. A few examples are:

- *Child as ... a threat or monster and embryo adult* (Woodrow, 1999) vs *child as ... strong, capable and resourceful* (Malaguzzi, 1987; Victorian Curriculum and Assessment Authority, 2008, p. 25)
- *Child as ... competent learner, active thinker and involved doer* along with *child as ... active constructor* (Caiman & Lundegard, 2014; Harris & Manatakis, 2013; Stuhmcke, 2012)
- *Child as ... performing curriculum complexly* (Sellers, 2013).

Today's sociocultural-historic concepts of children and childhood, along with findings from recent decades of brain research and neuroscience, are very far removed from children being considered empty vessels and the idea of early education as only pure potentiality for later education (Fleer, 2010; Sellers, 2013). Contemporary ideas about children being actively engaged do inform professionals about how educators work with the young and how they set up places and spaces that they cohabit. One broad concept of children and their development relates to transitions alongside their

Chapter 6 A professional role – a pedagogy creator

participating in the various everyday practices of settings or institutions – the home and the early childhood site.

For example, Fleer (2010) expected ECE professionals to read and re-read both children as learners and themselves as educators to broaden their views of early childhood learning and development. A decade earlier, the concept of dispositions within ECE pedagogy was problematised. Campbell (1999, p. 23) visualised ECE social forces and power through double, 'competing-readings' and called for 'the need to make the political more pedagogical'. Another writer relayed ideas about young children as – becoming children, becoming power-full, becoming curriculum (Sellers, 2013). All these ideas mean that pedagogy creators face relevant yet potentially challenging considerations on a daily basis. From broad and multiple readings about children in context, professionals uncover core concepts about the early childhood years. 'Resilience' and 'agency' are examples of key attributes, and these attributes affect other aspects of a child's whole being.

Resilient children

'Resilience' is a core childhood concept. Being resilient represents children as encompassing certain human qualities or abilities. For example, young children may face challenges in life and deal with everyday difficulties. These personal abilities are associated with having a strengths foundation or more positive approach to life. This can mean being able to 'bounce back' within both near and more distant ecologies or settings (for examples, refer to Linke & Radich, 2010; Ungar, Ghazinour & Richter, 2013). Furthermore, being resilient is a component of children's meaningful sense of overall wellbeing (South Australian Department of Education and Children's Services, 2010).

Agentic children

Agency is another core childhood concept. This quality is associated with confidence or an eagerness to engage in daily life and everyday learning. Young children can be active contributors to surrounding relationships and settings. When children are confident at home and in early childhood settings, they may display curiosity, creativity and persistence (Arthur, 2010). These kinds of dispositions can in turn add to a collection of habits of mind that results in child agency being fuller. Agency is an internal force informed by numerous respectful and attentive human interactions over time (Whitington, 2014). It happens when children engage and connect with others, as they confidently ask or seek or make decisions. Having agency is a sign of being at least partly empowered for a particular circle of relationships within geographic and emotional places. In some contemporary ECE literature, young children are viewed as true 'agents for change' because they are very capable of being active with issues and actually undertaking actions related to such issues. Examples of taking control and participating meaningfully link with Early Childhood Education for Sustainability – ECEfS (Caiman & Lundegard, 2014; Stuhmcke, 2012). These authors acknowledge differing notions of ECE agency and then work from the idea of 'agency as an open-ended, situated and transactional process' (Caiman & Lundegard, 2014, p. 3). This childhood concept of being an agent can be stretched to children being action agents, citizens and rights partakers (Davis, 2014; Hayward, 2012; Hill, McCrea, Emery, Nailon, Davis, Dyment & Getenet, 2014).

The idea of childhood agency again highlights the use of lenses by adults to view children as sociable people rather than objects. Being cherished as an authentic agent is vastly different from being considered a closeted artefact or an empty vessel. The implications of these two views of childhood flow into ways that educators teach and the ways they encourage children's learning. This means that as part of creative pedagogy, we can ask:

- Are young children seen and treated as commodities?
- If so, how, when, where and why? (refer to 'consumption' ideas below)
- What does this mean for leader-managers as pedagogy creators?

Engaging in consumption

Unfortunately today, both education and children seem to be very 'marketised', which means they are active consumers who are consumption-oriented. This situation happens across society in general and within an expanding global and economic rationalist framework. Various forms of mass media actively contribute to all of us being 'remotely controlled' in larger and smaller timeslots and across numerous places. Such 'controls' particularly influence our food choices and dressing styles, with these encompassing young children even though they can be marginal and invisible (for examples, refer to Bayley, 1999; Bone, 2005; Cook, 2012; Duncan & Bartle, 2014; McCrea, 2006). In fact, everyday life is generally saturated with consumerist temptations and much of this media influence has embodiment angles (Australian Ethical, 2014; Probyn, 2003; Sturken & Cartwright, 2009). These temptations contribute to the idea that everyday life and individuals are less agentic with more economics that are firmly set in the political correctness of everyday life (Trentmann, 2012).

More specifically, early childhood settings filled with children and educators continue to deal with corporatisation and privatisation (Press & Woodrow, 2005). Particularly during the 1990s, business-oriented practices of marketing, privatising and corporatising influenced the Australian early childhood education field and contributed to certain contemporary images of children. Such practices also influenced children's daily living and community learning spaces. It is important to consider how these realities can run counter to educational concerns for social justice and 'common good' within children's services. Sites can be more business-oriented with attention to

Chapter 6 A professional role – a pedagogy creator

financial interests and parental-work mandates, rather than more community-centred with children's educational aims as the focus. However, rather than accept a dichotomy of business structure vs a totally different ECE administration, we can be part of reconceptualising and sensitively blending these influences for the best (refer to being a rights advocate, Chapter 7). Think about how and when you and colleagues might intertwine the business world and the ECE world. How might they be combined at times to help us better serve children, pedagogical interests, staff positioning and local communities (Press & Woodrow, 2005)?

Finally, both children's resilience and their agency relate to human rights at personal, beyond personal and international levels (Davis, 2014). This means that it is important to pause here and re-position these childhood concepts within an eco-caring frame of 'rights with responsibilities'.

Pause and reflect 6.3

Again, this is a timely place to consider the lenses that relate to children being engaged. Think about how much ECE settings as a collective organisational field contribute to children being engaged vs being objects. Share ideas with colleagues and particularly identify: How, as a leader-manager acting in the role of pedagogy creator, you might support and guide other educators during their investigations of 'child as engaged'. How might a sustainable way lens assist you? What influence might the idea of 'rights with community responsibilities' have on your brainstorming with others?

Understanding our diversity and social justice

Here we move beyond the child as an individual to explore the emotional, relational and political contexts or geographies of ECE. There are many instances where young children may encounter justice during their everyday lives. By stepping backwards before moving forward, you will understand how contemporary views of children have changed in terms of more wisely recognising family diversity and adhering to fairness with justice for everyone.

Cultural responsiveness

One important childhood concept is being culturally responsive. This concept can be gazed at and framed as a leading-managing challenge for all educators as they collectively struggle with the question: How do we reflect, plan and implement learning and curricula for culturally responsive pedagogy? This idea of creating pedagogy steeped with cultural responsiveness is relevant and valuable for all children, regardless of their membership within a sociopolitically dominant group or various non-dominant groups (Chen, Nimmo & Fraser, 2009).

For educators to become culturally responsive and to meaningfully enact this ideal, they ought to acknowledge their own feelings of agency and empowerment. This means seeking deep understandings of oneself and one's related beliefs. Here you might refer back to ideas in the first couple of chapters for support. Having such understandings can strengthen professionals' pedagogical confidence and their creativity, as they establish learning features, such as: indoor and outdoor culturally safe environments; sensitive adult–child interactions; and relevant and authentic educational resources.

Responsive resources

Chen, Nimmo and Fraser (2009) sketched an intentional and systematic anti-bias journey founded in educators' reflective self-study 'on action' and 'for action'. To support this reflection, the authors designed a personal anti-bias study guide with options for educators' progressive over-time responses. Possible responses moved from 'not yet: this is new territory for me' to 'the next steps for me: my goal is'. This guide is one example of how a team of early childhood educators might initially reflect on the personal and then share their impressions and meanings for greater individual and collective understandings.

Similarly, Flores, Casebeer and Riojas-Cortez (2011) were concerned about early childhood teachers being 'culturally efficacious'. This term means educators are culturally competent, with positive attitudes, and can implement authentic pedagogy. They initially created a 'culturally responsive ecology' conceptual framework, which became the basis for an Early Childhood Ecology Scale. The framework's dimensions offered guidance for educators to contemplate young children's ways of living and learning and relevant aspects of pedagogy. The intertwined dimensions reflected early education principles and practices with serious attention to cultural linguistic tones. The clarity of this cultural linguistic lens rested with dimensions which encompassed:

- Sociocognitive interactions
- Sociocultural expressions and artefacts
- Socioemotional ways that educators promote respect
- Sociolinguistic promotion of natural language within experiences
- Sociophysical relevant spaces and boundaries (Flores et al., 2011, pp. 270–72).

The framework and Scale could be useful tools for professionals leading-managing the creation of meaningful and just pedagogy. This might also be a time for pausing and returning to MacNaughton and Hughes' (2011) 'A Fairness Alerts Matrix' (discussed also in Chapter 2). There are many resources that can support both a leader-manager and other educators as they jointly engage with sociocultural aspects of being pedagogy creators (for examples refer to Mundine & Giugni, 2006; Richardson, 2011; Summerville & Hokanson, 2013; Wong, 2013). More specifically there are perpetual

Chapter 6 A professional role – a pedagogy creator

issues such as children's involvement with various community celebrations (Dau & Jones, 2004). Beyond Australia, Singapore's *Nurturing Early Learners, Framework for Mother Tongue Languages* is another relevant resource (Ministry of Education Singapore, 2013b). As a synthesis task, you might contrast ideas from these authors and then form a unique pedagogical approach for viewing ECE diversity and social justice (refer back to Chapter 2, Step 1).

The essence of understandings

For a final example of 'understanding lenses', professionals can consider children's sustainable learning. This is highlighted here to further encourage you to build upon the 'embracing sustainability' thread that weaves through this book. Overall as a synthesis, it is important to emphasise that there are other 'understanding lenses' worthy of educators' consideration. Such further investigations have particular value because our current focus is on being a pedagogy creator as a key leading-managing role. After reviewing the Feature professional reflection: Jan's story, below, with various pedagogical lenses, note which understandings she focused on and speculate about why these might be so important for her as a pedagogical leader-manager.

Feature professional reflection: Jan's story

When I consider my personal philosophy, I reflect on how to incorporate the importance of children. The foundation of my philosophy is valuing relationships that are respectful and nurturing, accompanied by a broad awareness of child development. The importance of the here-and-now for a young child combined with opportunities for the tomorrows of a child's life also guide my practice. At our centre, consideration is given to our educators' personal philosophies and the centre philosophy, and a balance is sought to bring all of these together.

Our everyday moments with children are what make up our program and practice. While consideration is given to these moments as they are lived, we continually reflect on the importance of these routine and spontaneous moments. We ponder how they support our children's learning and becoming. One way we do this is to provoke children's deeper thinking and ask them questions. The idea is that we are helping them to develop their own philosophies. For example, we asked: 'What do you want to: see happen; learn about; engage in at the centre?' We also explore these questions in combination with what their roles and responsibilities are in the centre. We found that when we unpacked the children's philosophical statements, they wanted the following:

- to play (being)
- to have friends and develop safe relationships (belonging), and
- to learn and explore (becoming).

Part 2 Thinking About Practices as Roles

We then looked for families' contributions and responses. We asked parents: 'What do you value for your child?' Families' views were also unpacked. Their desires and aims were clustered into a few key pedagogical experiences for the children:
- learning (becoming)
- developing social skills (belonging)
- having a safe environment (being), and
- feeling happiness (being).

A provocation: *In paragraph one, Jan revealed some of her pedagogical values about young children's everyday experiences in their regional early childhood setting. Think about and brainstorm with colleagues: How might you as a leader-manager go about engaging a team of educators in discussions about children's learning desires and those that parents identify?*

Pause and reflect 6.4

At this ending point for Step 1, reflect on: What do you believe your first two or three priorities would be when you take on this leading-managing role of pedagogy creator? You might start this thinking by asking yourself questions based on ideas presented above. For example, ponder the 'understanding lenses' and identify two or more beyond these.

As an act of leading-managing via this pedagogy creator role, select one sociocultural-historic event that influenced conceptions of childhood and early learning and then explore contemporary political actions that still reflect this vision.

Step 2: Which responsibilities help frame children's learning?

In line with Australian policies and publications, there are broad community 'desires' for young children to develop senses of *being, becoming and belonging* (AGDEEWR, 2010, 2009, nd; Elliott, 2014a; Lee, 2012). There are community and professional ideas about children's growth, their well-being and educational 'outcomes'. These are framed in terms of supporting young children now and into their future lives. In a nutshell, an idealistic expectation is that children are or will be confident, considerate and capable, and will love their learning. Such community desires lead us to broad questions:

- How is children's learning framed at a broad government perspective?
- How is learning framed within the leading-managing of whole ECE settings?

The above questions raise additional ones:

- Who will do this pedagogy work?
- What is it that educators will do each day, and each week?

Chapter 6 A professional role – a pedagogy creator

Relevant responses might include ideas about how positional and situational leader-mangers, educational leaders and others act as pedagogy creators. It is envisioned here that professional pedagogy actions relate to caring with routines as well as learning with curricula.

Responsibility for caring with everyday routines

Acts of caring for others are essential components of every early childhood setting. Additionally, eco-caring is closely linked with common routines that happen across indoor and outdoor spaces. Together these ideas reinforce the importance of context and a sense of place for both adults and children. As explored in Chapter 3, early childhood settings include physical spaces, emotional places and geographic and interpersonal climates. And so, we can ask: What is the caring that happens in these places?

Caring not only encompasses duty of care (refer to Step 3 in Chapter 4) but also many other connected and complex considerations (Collins & Ting, 2014). In fact, caring is much more when intertwined within the leading-managing role of pedagogy creator. Caring extends to how and why routines are planned, organised and monitored, including reconsideration of adult–child relationships and child learning engagement. Here controversial issues arise for educators to negotiate. For example, how much planning, what is planned and how are things organised? This means that adults are not the only ones attending to daily life routines in early childhood settings. Rather, there is authentic educational involvement of young children; the young are contributors who help and engage by 'pitching in' (Littledyke & McCrea, 2009; Rogoff, 2003).

Caring crossroads

Caring intersects with what we may consider 'adult routines', such as basic health, safety and nutrition. You might like to think of this as an intersection or crossroads on your professional path. It is important to look both ways and proceed with caution. This caution reflects the importance of noting that these adult routines can be adjusted so that children are directly involved in 'carings', as these 'routines' expand into: personal and collective well-being; safety with full emotional security; and cycles-of-food learning (McCrea, 2014). This means that many everyday routines contribute to children's co-learning with educators. Such an approach engages children in everyday responsibilities, while they are strengthening their capabilities, confidence and agency as setting-citizens. This approach creates another balancing act for staff as pedagogy creators, and it raises the questions:

- When will children be encouraged to contribute?
- How will discussions and negotiations happen with children?
- What 'caring routines' or parts of them might children engage with?
- What self-help abilities will children be practising and developing?
- Why are such engagements worthwhile and important?

Part 2 Thinking About Practices as Roles

This is where pedagogical leading-managing happens, as a leader and other staff jointly think about these questions, create others and make professional decisions. One useful framework for educators is *Reflect, Respect, Relate*. This approach intertwines four adult–child variables, and these are:

- Relationships
- Active learning environments
- Well-being of children
- Children's involvement (South Australian Department of Education and Children's Services, 2010).

For early childhood settings to function effectively, many routines are identified and completed, with this happening across broader sociopolitical surroundings. In Australia, one starting point for identifying essential routines is the *National Quality Standard* (ACECQA, 2013a), with educators having foundational guidance from professional resources such as the *ECA Code of Ethics* (ECA, 2006) and others. As expected, an approach touched with sustainability, including eco-responsibility for routines, is encouraged here; and so, you are referred back to:

- *National Quality Standard*, 'Standard 3.3: The service takes an active role in caring for its environment and contributes to a sustainable future'
- *ECO SMART* ... (Gaul, Nippard, & Watson, 2012).

The usual routines that leader-managers will have responsibility for are listed below; however, other team members may also take responsibility for one or more of these routines:

- Supporting children's total health and well-being
- Illness and injury; risks of abuse or neglect
- Encouraging rest, relaxation and sleep
- Undertaking safe hygiene and cleaning practices
- Facilitating regular, relevant physical activity
- Promoting and/or providing nutritious foods and breastfeeding
- Ensuring appropriate supervision both indoors and outdoors
- Planning for emergencies
- Maintaining buildings, yards and furnishings.

Note that each of these routines is composed of several tasks and practices, and each links with one or more standard policies found across the early childhood education field (refer back to Chapter 5). (Key references: Click & Karkos, 2011; Daly, Byers & Taylor, 2004; Duncan & Bartle, 2014; Freeman, Decker & Decker, 2013; Hearron &

Hildebrand, 2007; Sims & Hutchins, 2011; online resources at ResponseAbility: www.responseability.org.)

Pause and reflect 6.5
Young children's well-being and their meaningful involvement are relevant aspects of pedagogy; and, these have particular relevance when educators intertwine caring with routines. Consider how you might work with colleagues to jointly create a list of authentic routines as components of children's learning. Design two or three mentoring strategies for using with colleagues. How could you lead this brainstorming about what is in or out and why?

Financing

One major component of planning and organising whole-setting routines involves a financial lens. This is where leading-managing considerations move to encompassing a blend of pedagogical ideas with financial considerations of purchasing or not. Related professional questions include: 'What is supply and what is demand or wants for us? What is to be purchased? What is to be re-used? What is to be borrowed? What will we share?' These intersects include everyday routines, children's engagement and being more ethically responsible for the world, with each changing the other. The idea of 'collaborative consumption' is a key approach for such considerations (Australian Ethical, 2014). The boundaries of budgets, the politics of funding and doing ethical accounting are all aspects of 'pedagogy with purchasing or not'. Furthermore, finances intertwine across whole early childhood settings and influence every area and event within – thus money does matter! This also means that finances and budgeting are serious tasks within all the facets of ECE leading, managing and administering (for examples, refer to Bruno, 2009; Freeman, Decker & Decker, 2013; Waniganayake et al., 2012).

Responsibility for children's learning

Children's learning and their meaningful curricula are inseparable. This means that taking responsibility for planning curriculum is another vital aspect of professionals' pedagogy creator role. It is also important to note that adults' 'personal/professional baggage' influences the shaping of children's learning experiences alongside defining their teaching approaches. For example, educators' 'baggage' contains a personal and professional union of beliefs, lived experiences and previous education (refer back to Chapter 3, Step 1, for types of services and varying furnishings and resources). The context for pedagogical leading-managing highlights an educational leader working closely with others. For an Australian example refer to *NQS*, QA7 – 'Element 7.1.4: Provision is made to ensure a suitably qualified and experienced educator or co-ordinator leads the development of the curriculum and ensures the establishment of clear goals and expectations for teaching and learning'. Consider the Professional reflection: Lisa's story, from the lens of her as an educational leader in action.

Professional reflection: Lisa's story

The cargo net: reflections on teaching. At the kindergarten where I teach, we have a cargo net for the children to climb on. Watching children approach the net always intrigues me. Some forthrightly attack the net vertically, trying to get to the top quickly. Others climb horizontally along the net. Some gingerly place their feet on the rope, as if unsure of the rope's strength or their own. Others begin to climb one way, and then change direction. Some follow another's lead, waiting until another child or adult guides their steps. Some enjoy manoeuvring their arms and legs into the sections of the net so it supports them as they swing on it.

For me, teaching is like climbing a cargo net. Sometimes I go steadfastly. Now and then, I retrace my steps or change direction. Often I feel like I am waiting for another, as I seek insights from further reading or collaborative reflections. The patient guidance from those higher up on the net inspires me. Many times I am 'egged on' from below. Every so often, I climb down exhausted and rest, returning to the net with renewed strength and vigour.

A provocation: Even though this story about Lisa's teacher-feelings is quite brief, it offers insights into her pedagogical disposition. Lisa with her cargo net has educational moments of: personal confidence, reflection and reconsideration, some doubt, seeking others, changing, inspiration, depending on others, feeling overwhelmed. At this point on your professional journey, what metaphor would you select to openly, honestly reveal your level of confidence for creating learning opportunities with young children?

Crucial curricula

There are many ways to support children's learning within early childhood settings. A few examples set the scene for the kinds of thinking and deciding that leader-managers along with colleagues encounter as they collectively take on a creator of curriculum role (for detailed examples, refer to Anning, Cullen & Fleer, 2008; Arthur, et al., 2012; McLachlan, Fleer & Edwards, 2013; Sciarra et al., 2013; Sims & Hutchins, 2011). One of the most accepted educational approaches is child-centred with hands-on play and learning. Children share ideas and resources while learning cooperatively. Settings are filled with open-ended learning materials that children engage with and manipulate based on their interests. Children's interactions and thoughts emerge from themselves, others and artefacts (refer to Jones & Nimmo, 1994; Sellers, 2013).

Chapter 6 A professional role – a pedagogy creator

Pause and reflect 6.6

What other philosophically informed principles and approaches contribute to everyday curriculum programs for young children? If you were an educational leader, what resources would you gather for leading a brainstorming session with a staff team? Respond to this question in terms of your topic being: 'Reflect and compare current curriculum ideas with potential approaches'.

This curriculum section of your professional path could be relatively straight and clear, but it may well be littered with some bumps of complexity. Clarity reflects early childhood curricula being integrated and so disciplines are interconnected. Complexity reflects learners interacting within various sociopolitical contexts. Thus, curricula features along your path exemplify children's learning as experiential and intertwined, rather than content knowledge being artificially separated or isolated one from another. Such linking of disciplines resembles criss-crossing webs more than individual threads. Similarly, Sellers (2013) contested and reconceived young children's curriculum by using rhizomes from nature (underground plant stems) and a mapping milieu. This criss-cross webbing included a number of learnings and knowledges. As an example, sustainability concepts can support each learning or knowledge area, particularly when educators have philosophical foundations that include 'green lens' values. Common intertwined learning disciplines or areas cover:

- The sciences and mathematics
- Languages, literature and literacies with some ICT (information, communications technology)
- All the arts – music, painting and drawing, drama
- Well-being, safety and security, health
- Food and meals
- Sustainable nature study with gardening
- Physical actions and activities, including fundamental movements.

Children enact these broad disciplines through their: relationships with peers and adults; play and learning resources or artefacts; and active use of geographic spaces. Educational artefacts and incidents are very diverse, for example:

- Sand and water with props
- Musical instruments
- Yoga and meditation
- Wooden blocks with natural manipulative items

Part 2 Thinking About Practices as Roles

- Storybooks and other literature
- Wooden puzzles and pieces of wood
- Nature study with care of plants and animals
- Gardening beds and containers.

Beyond physical items, indoor and outdoor environments have been referred to as the 'third teacher' (refer to Chapter 3). Just like with routines, your leading-managing role spans selecting and purchasing resources as curriculum items. Decisions about resources may or may not reflect a 'green lens'. However, you are encouraged to lead, manage and administer children's curricula with acts that resist and counter contemporary hyper-consumption. Pause here on your journey to consider the following:

- In what ways might early childhood settings reduce consumption of 'toys', while engaging more in making-do, recycling and re-using?
- What might you and colleagues gather to establish artefact treasures and collections in natural fibre baskets, wooden boxes, timber cabinets?
- How would you use this approach to further encourage children's curiosity?
- How might this collections approach extend educators' weaving of learning webs for and with children?

Pause and reflect 6.7

Review the last few pages and pull out your eco-caring compass. Consider with colleagues all the ways that you could take account of your beliefs about both 'rosy' embodiment and 'green' sustainability as you plan and create curricula with young children. Incorporate ideas about: When and why you would contribute and share intentionally with children; and when as educator you would be silent and wait for children's ideas and interests to emerge.

Step 3: Who is involved in children's learning?

It is obvious that the leading-managing role of pedagogy creator embraces thinking about who is involved in children's learning. There are consequential questions of how, when and where. In fact, there are numerous people involved in children's learning, including the children as active contributing partners. Let's consider how this involvement is defined, planned for and undertaken. It seems that leader-managers with staff teams ought to approach their pedagogy work with aspirations, and these will be shaped by awareness of diversity and recognition of complexity inside early childhood settings and places beyond-the-fence.

Chapter 6 A professional role – a pedagogy creator

Children's involvement

Earlier in the chapter, we explored how young children learn and how they engage with their surroundings. Thus, children's contributions, their agency and voices have much currency. This is especially so in terms of societies' complexities which include power, participation and nurturing children's leadership (Caiman & Lundegard, 2014; Mevawalla, 2013; Sullivan, 2010). Some of these ideas are reflected in the Australian *National Quality Standard*, particularly 'QA5: Relationships with children'. Children involved in their own learning are supported when educational contexts facilitate experiential and emergent approaches. Additionally, following on from the diversity and social justice understanding lens in Step 1, the involvement of all children is vital. In Australia, this means that Indigenous children deserve unique considerations.

Educators' involvement

It goes without saying that educators are deeply involved in young children's learning. However, there are many ways that educators might undertake this role. Some educators interact and cooperate fully with children; others are committed but interact with more distance. Within these two images of educators we can consider and observe others engaging in all kinds of ways with children. The wide variety of reasonable and acceptable forms of being an educator reflects back to peoples' dispositions, values and understandings about children and childhood (Macfarlane & Cartmel, 2012; Nuttall, 2003; refer back to Chapter 2). This variety also reflects the act of educators questioning their images and knowledges of themselves as adults working with young children. Thus, there are questions such as:

- What is an educator?
- Who is an educator?
- What is a teacher?
- What does an educator do?
- What constitutes leading-managing educational enterprises for pedagogical purposes?

Additionally, educator-work with young children is probably influenced by ideas such as 'women's business' (Sims & Hutchins, 2011) and by predominant views of children's development (McLachlan, Fleer & Edwards, 2013). Being an educator who is a pedagogy creator is another pressure; however, this can also lead to opportunities. While taking on a leader of education role may weigh on one, this act can also open up options for greater contributing with others and empowering all.

Looking in a mirror at one's self and reflecting on one's beliefs and actions form important ways of better understanding who one is and how one interacts with children (Cartmel, Macfarlane & Casley, 2012; Hallet, 2014; Woodrow, 2014; refer back to

Part 2 Thinking About Practices as Roles

Chapter 1). Using diaries, journals and portfolios can be valuable for self-study, as educators document their ideas, record events that have occurred and note self-questions and personal musings (Friedman, 2012; Nolan & Reynolds, 2008). At times the leading-managing role of pedagogy creator revolves around mentoring, guiding and sometimes supervising others. These actions can help with balancing the values and practices of people with the places where they work. Think about these actions as you read the Professional reflection: Lavinia's story, below.

Professional reflection: Lavinia's story

Managing children in the early years requires professional, academic, and motherly skills to assist in the everyday running of an infant centre. It was way back in 1987 to early 1989 that I was assigned to head a small rural remote community class of children on an outer island of Fiji, where the boat would come once a month to bring supplies. Well, this was not an issue as we were continually flooded with whatever natural and organic edibles that were around. Though money was of essence and rare, it was saved ... smile! We used and consumed what nature had for us. My classroom was a Fijian bure (a traditional Fijian house) sitting beside the seashore. So one can imagine the type of environment we had – exposed to the sand, sea breeze and all the natural playthings that were around and still untouched by so-called 'development'.

I was in charge of grades K, one and two, in a multi-grade situation that is still prevalent in most Fiji Island schools. My task was enormous as I was the only staff in charge of fifteen children, ranging in age from three to seven years. I saw my position as a leader, a manager and an administrator. And most importantly being a facilitator of children's learning across the three grades. Looking back, it seems to me that having a teaching qualification was not enough. I had to have the right personal and professional skills to interact effectively with the fifteen children under my care.

Being the sole pedagogical manager of the three grades was challenging, so I had to look seriously at other ways of getting assistance. The only way was engaging the community in my work. Consultation with the village community proved prolific. Families were very willing to come on board and support any worthy cause for the sake of their children's education. Rostered parents as learning facilitators were established, carefully followed and monitored. Grandparents were rostered for storytelling times and traditional skill activities such as weaving and making lovo (the traditional Fijian way of baking using hot stones; this is synonymous with a Maori hangi in New Zealand). The whole village became engaged in the education programme. It was terrific to see the support. I felt like going the extra mile for this work. I could feel their feelings and they could feel mine.

As the educational leader of the bure space and place, mentoring was part and parcel of the everyday learning and teaching programme, as parent helpers engaged with children. 'Difficult staff' or 'difficult parents' had no place in this education centre, as the village chief

Chapter 6 A professional role – a pedagogy creator

was around as an exemplary supporter. He represented a cooperative or collective protocol that everyone listened to and obeyed politely. The 'village rights' were exercised within a community where only the chief's voice was heard. The interactions I had through engaging with this community provided a two-way scenario. We each learned from the other – adults and children. And as I look back, I now believe that my pedagogical leadership experience was built upon this traditional and customary relationship. Even now, I sincerely thank the chief and the village community for contributing to such an experience in my early professional career.

A provocation: Refer back to Step 4 in Chapter 1, 'What is leading with managing?' Particularly review the ideas about divisions of 'labour' and 'authority'. What 'labour' did Lavinia as teacher share with others? Who was the educational 'authority' shared with? How might 'labour' and 'authority' divisions be defined and shared in a typical Australian children's centre today – preschool, kindergarten, child care centre? Ask staff in early childhood settings for their views on these two ideas.

Family and community involvement

Working in meaningful ways with parents and extended families is essential business for all early childhood educators (Cartmel, Macfarlane & Casley, 2012; Goodfellow, 2009). Across the early childhood field, parents are often recognised as their children's first teachers; however, there are also examples of an opposing position (Whitsel & Lapham, 2014). Parents are serious role models of many aspects of everyday life. Similarly, there is a long history of parents having informal, direct and even formal engagement with children and their learning within early childhood settings. Some of this volunteering as teacher aides and visiting educators has become more limited as both mothers and fathers work full-time, and often long hours, most days of the week. As families become more culturally and economically diverse, their desires for their children, as well as their abilities or time to actively participate in ECE pedagogy, will continue to change. One Australian example of linking with families to support their understandings of contemporary ECE pedagogy happened in 2013, when the *BBB, EYLFA* booklet became readily available in ten community languages with online versions.

The leading-managing role of pedagogy creator takes on a special visionary and re-visioning lens when educators and parents work together for children's learning. In fact, educator–parent interactions might be enhanced if 'Circles of Change' (CoC) framed their discussions (Macfarlane & Cartmel, 2012). The CoC model involves participants in a deep reflective process of deconstructing, confronting, theorising and thinking otherwise. It also involves using body resources – our senses, memories and feelings (link with our embodiment thread). Similarly, as early childhood leader-managers and other staff members work outside, beyond-the-fence, tools like CoC,

Part 2 Thinking About Practices as Roles

along with leadership of learning cultures (Hallet, 2014), can help with informing and guiding the broader public about children's learning. Such approaches assist with advocating for community members' potential involvement inside early childhood settings.

Conclusion

Your travels through this child-focused chapter encompassed lots of walking with much thinking. You may have even done some wandering like spiritual pilgrims of old, particularly because we have only 'glimpses' of the moment (refer to the quote at the start of this chapter). Historic pilgrims were on personal journeys to particular places as they searched for meaning. If this pilgrim metaphor is applied to ECE, you will continue to explore the creator of pedagogy role as you travel and look through lenses for important childhood concepts. It will be essential that you remain alert during these wanderings because images of the child, childhood and children's learning will continue to change. Such ongoing adjustments might represent the uneven edges of this pedagogical stretch of roadway. This means that your leading-managing role of pedagogy creator involves ongoing advocacy for what to keep and protect and what changes to embrace. In Chapter 7, ideas about being an advocate will assist you with keeping and changing.

Dear Nadine

The recent National requirement to nominate an educational leader in early childhood settings adds a particular urgency to this chapter. For some, the role will be additional to other positional leadership roles they have fulfilled in their setting (group leader, director). The journey and content Steps that are introduced here will complement how readers may have already been working with others, planning and reflecting on children's learning. This chapter prioritises the need for inclusion at all levels – especially finding ways for educational leaders to work with and alongside educators from diverse personal and professional backgrounds.

Some educators, especially graduates with four-year early childhood degrees, who may have been employed to fulfil the educational leadership role, can set their compasses and use the references to historical and current ECE philosophical underpinnings, models, theories and research to guide their way. My feeling is that what such graduates bring to the setting (whether or not they are appointed as the educational leader) is their curriculum content knowledge. They will also have been exposed to theories and research on pedagogy, environments and reflexivity. They can use each of these knowledges to leverage collaborative decision-making, while also acknowledging and learning from the experienced wisdom of other educators. The first challenge will be to identify particular content from their studies that can add ideas and strategies, and that they are comfortable sharing with other educators and

Chapter 6 A professional role – a pedagogy creator

parents. A second challenge will be to share these ideas in ways that build relationships and generate professional dialogue and collective decision-making.

This chapter's focus on pedagogy and pedagogue relates well to the descriptors of pedagogical leadership in the *Educators' Guide to the Early Years Learning Framework* CD (which uses descriptors such as: model professional and ethical practice; mentor others; commit to ongoing professional learning and inquiry; build partnerships with colleagues, families, schools, community workers and allied health professionals to promote the best learning opportunities for all children; act as advocates). The aspects of leading-managing discussed throughout this chapter will, I think, support educational leaders to develop other educators' capacities to adopt the five pedagogical leadership skills noted above. My own research into the development of pedagogical leadership bears this out, especially in terms of the educational leader role of leading and managing relevant professional learning.

The chapter includes many 'big ideas' that are worth grappling with. The most transcending for me is the idea of knowledge transformation. My belief is that this is what pedagogical change is all about. In some ways all the previous chapters have been leading to this point. Knowledge is transformed when we begin to look at what we do differently. The notion introduced in this chapter of curriculum as political activity is an idea worth pursuing. It will take courage, but can be achieved when educational leaders adopt what this chapter describes as a 'cultural responsiveness' lens for curriculum decision-making. This chapter offers diverse opportunities for reflexivity, such as the ones I have described. It could easily be re-visited by readers from time to time – especially if they are appointed as educational leaders of settings.

Regards,
Di

Pause and reflect 6.8

Which idea in this chapter most influenced your current beliefs, and why? Record your personal feelings, inspirations and professional thoughts in your 'journal'.

Chapter 7

A professional role – a rights advocate

A non-violent revolution is not a program of seizure of power. It is a program of transformation of relationships, ending in a peaceful transfer of power.

Mohandas K. Gandhi (2007, p. 40)

Broad concepts

In this chapter, your professional path moves on to what some would consider the edges of an early childhood education roadway, or maybe even a sidetrack. Being an advocate may be viewed as taking on a trailblazer mantle; this is a person who marks out a route through what is seen as wilderness. Such a trail could involve sharp hairpin turns as the contour of the land is followed. Clearing a trail and going around these bends may reward you with new vistas of the ECE profession and field. This trailblazer metaphor can be applied across ECE, where it relates to the intrigue of politics and forces of power at all layers of government and in the corporate world. Here, you will be thinking about the following Steps:

- What are the leading and managing facets of a rights advocate role?
- Which responsibilities link with professional vision and moral higher ground?

Chapter 7 A professional role – a rights advocate

Pause and reflect 7.1
Before progressing, think about: 'What are my understandings and beliefs about the above questions?' After considering each of the above questions, create an entry in your 'My professional leading-managing journal' by jotting down a couple of learning aims for your engaging with this chapter.

Step 1: What are the leading and managing facets of a rights advocate role?

This leader-manager role relates to and focuses on advocating within early childhood settings and often beyond them. We will investigate examples of positional leaders as well as situational or distributing leaders attending to both human and Earth rights (link back to rights and fairness in other chapters). In this chapter advocacy is acknowledged as one challenging component of a professional journey through the ECE field.

An advocate

Within the ECE context, it is worth noting that there are those who might describe being an advocate as an idealised or romanticised form of leadership. Such a position includes consideration of advocacy as being beyond the scope of management responsibilities. The first view could mean that leading-managing is idealised to such a point that it is seen as over-emotional, nostalgic or starry-eyed (Knight, 2010). For an example, Alvesson and Spicer (2011, p. 19) identified key challenges within historic and current perspectives of leadership theory, and their third scoping issue was: 'ideas that emphasize the importance of morality, involvement and authenticity in leadership are typically too romantic ... They often speak more clearly to our ideological presuppositions than what leaders actually do.' Hopefully this is not the view your reach during your explorations of leading-managing via advocacy.

'First thing'

We begin by asking: What is a rights advocate? When and where does one, on behalf of others and with others, take on this vital yet political role? One initial idea related to these questions is the proposition that 'rights with advocacy' ought to be 'the first and last thing' that we do as ECE professionals. This is because the here-and-now with children today is the central proposition and purpose of early childhood education and our related profession. This living and learning as education must be authentic, sensitive and relevant for young children. When educators undertake meaningful interactions with young children, this represents an in-the-moment display of advocacy.

Part 2 Thinking About Practices as Roles

Another way of viewing this idea is that in educators' work their voices are vital tools of interaction. Such sharing via voice turns educators' words into a form of advocacy. However, there will be a particular challenge here if educators' work practices are limited or unprofessional; and, such poor role modelling ought not be taken as examples of meaningful advocacy. This is because many professionals would not believe in and therefore could not support such workplace actions. Therefore, questionable actions ought not surface or be displayed inside a setting or in the public eye. With professional work representing voices, and often voices that are heard in public, it is important that educators reflect carefully and think meaningfully about embodiment. That is, what am I saying with my workplace-body?

In essence it appears to be logical that professionals are not 'out there' doing political advocacy, if they haven't been advocating right now in everyday ways at 'home' for themselves and with children, colleagues and families. As discussed before, this everyday advocacy encompasses people, places and practices. Such advocating requires people's time and shared spaces. At the setting level, advocacy happens among educators along with positional or situational leader-managers; and such team-negotiated sharing ought to reduce chances of unrealistic romanticism (Meindl, Ehrlich & Dukerich, 1985). For example, a team of staff might advocate to parents for their support that more outside learning time happens every day for the under-twos.

'Last thing'

An alternate view of advocacy focuses on this role being the 'last thing' that professionals might do. In fact, many working in the ECE field may believe that being a rights advocate is distant, scary, or even unrealistic. This 'last thing' approach is realistic because a large part of true advocacy happens 'out there' in the wider world with beyond-the-fence communities. Being 'out there' is a public and usually quite political position. Additionally, there is the potential that people might have more to lose by becoming public figures, and one consequence of this could mean that leader-managers are positioned as 'tall poppies' (Moore, 2010, pp. 167–9). Despite this, taking giant steps into the wider world for advocacy has broader and deeper aspects than undertaking these steps just within early childhood settings.

'Leading advocacy' happens in various socioemotional ways and eventually extends everywhere (Bruno, 2009; Rodd, 2013; Waniganayake et al., 2012). Both internal and wider world advocacy could be less scary, dangerous and difficult, if practices such as establishing a critical mass, engaging in some passive resistance, and encouraging a deeper and wider ripple effect were collectively embraced as a professional platform. This might be another pausing point for revisiting the personal and professional balancing log considered in Chapter 1 (view Figure 1.1). As you do this, think about all the kinds or types of professionalism that leader-managers engage in and then represent these on a log from one end to the other. How dangerous might each type be inside settings and outside?

Vision and morality facets

This rights advocate role involves revealing professional vision and standing for a moral higher ground. For our work here, a vision can be held in one's mind and also recorded for sharing and referring to. It is a response to questions like:

- Where are we going?
- Where do we want to be?
- What imaginings of the present and the future am I passionate about? Why?

Vision work within advocacy often focuses on children and it reflects the theoretical stances of educators and educational sites. In essence, advocacy is about understanding the real world of ECE and positively working towards balancing everyday professional actions with particular professional ideals. Such ideals encompass both inspirations and aspirations. As an example, ponder the Professional reflection: Dianne's story, below, about the role of spirituality in ECE.

Professional reflection: Dianne's story

Lens on spirituality

Contexts. In the two centres that I worked, being part of the spiritual community opened doors to acceptance and belonging within that community. Both centres had a top-down management style, which was linked to the history and culture of each community. Exclusion from or inclusion in these communities manifested subtly at times and quite obviously at other times. The organisations were influenced by individual members' concepts of leadership.

Spirituality. Although I found Aboriginal spirituality intriguing, it remained an element of division between community members and myself as a non-Aboriginal person. Spirituality in community appeared to me to be deeply elemental and strongly binding of family and community through links with country and language. It seemed to me that spirituality was exclusive to members of the group but differed from kin group to kin group and from individual to individual. Yet, there was also encompassing spirituality enfolding Aboriginality as a whole. If my colleagues, friends or community members shared cultural knowledge with me I felt very privileged. In the Aboriginal community, knowledge was traditionally transferred verbally from Elder to child or children learned from watching and copying adult actions.

In the Steiner/Waldorf centre, each member of the community was encouraged and supported to self-direct their personal spiritual journey. Although the philosophy seemed structured and constant, the individual teacher was the driver of their personal spiritual journey, whereas it seemed that in the Aboriginal centre, kin group spirituality was paramount. In both centres and for both communities, spirituality was important – it bound members together, it identified members, it created inclusion and exclusion from the group.

Views of children. The Aboriginal family view of the child seemed to be 'agentic'. Independent from a young age, the children care for younger siblings and family members and have more freedom and responsibility than many children outside Aboriginal communities. Children are seen as competent but not as little adults. Children are children and childhood has value in itself. Communications between adults and children were usually very natural and positive. Often teaching was by example and in voices that were quiet but clear.

The child in the Steiner centre was viewed as 'the innocent child'. Childhood had relevance in its own right, but children were considered to be 'still becoming' earthy beings. Until they turned seven, the child was not considered a cerebral, reasoning being. It seemed that children were enveloped in a protective blanket within a natural organic environment; this pedagogy was underpinned by natural rhythms of seasons and movements of the Earth. Communication between adults and children was gently direct, with teachers being considered the holders of knowledge and children learning by example and demonstration.

A provocation: In this professional reflection, Dianne shared professional impressions and experiences from her work in two unique preschools – one Aboriginal focused and the other Steiner based. How might you use Dianne's impressions as a springboard for identifying your own professional stance about images of young children and thus how interactions happen with them? How would your stance then inform your professional vision for young children and the ECE profession? Also, link back to the 'understanding lenses' in Step 1 of Chapter 6.

In a kindred way, the idea of moral higher ground is challenging for professionals to describe and others to understand and enact. There are elements of integrity, respect and ethical advantage. However, it is important to clarify that the facets, purposes and intent here are not related to special deserving or snobbery. Essential workplace morality is displayed when team members act as true professionals with personal agency. Additionally, both social professionalism and service professionalism link with ongoing guidance from one or more codes of ethics (Barblett, Hydon & Kennedy, 2008; ECA, 2006; Fasoli & Woodrow, 1991; Katz and Ward, 1993; Stonehouse, 1991). Both visioning and morality feature in Step 2.

Doing advocacy

With the above as background, advocacy can be viewed as actions related to embracing the rights that ground a profession and professionals. Our focus includes understanding rights, caring about justice, and having feelings for voice, but it goes further. The vital extension here is action – that is, doing and acting 'for rights' and 'for personal agency'. This focus also comprises reasonable community responsibility, extended cooperation and common good sentiments. Professional understanding with purposeful actions happens in a 'present' temporal space, rather than being idealised somewhere in the potential or future.

Feature professional reflection: Jan's story

Human advocacy. In the scheme of things I am a small drop in the ocean of the early childhood education field, though every drop makes a small ripple and creates change. As an advocate for the rights of children, families and educators in our centre, and then for our community, I believe we can make impacts through thoughtful collaborative partnerships. When creating collaborative partnerships with families and community, I firstly consider, 'How are we seen?' – that is, the centre and the children within the community. What is our visibility? I then ponder, 'How can we teach our children their role in the community and help them learn about reciprocal relationships and caring for others?' These kinds of advocating are done in many ways as we encourage children and families to take on the role of looking after others outside our centre and within our community.

One way we do this is to 'be' in the community. We regularly share celebrations with the residents of our local retirement home. We invite them into the centre where children learn to host and care for others during 'The biggest morning tea'. The moments we capture in our souls, of our children and elderly together, could bring tears to the hardest hearts. They often bring tears to the residents' eyes. Our children spend the week before the event cooking and preparing for the residents and on the day they are considerate, kind hosts, while interacting, offering hugs and accepting many kisses. We also visit the retirement village for Mother's Day, Father's Day and Christmas to share these celebrations. Once again children prepare for the day with baked goods and their own special gifts for our elders.

Eco-advocacy. Advocating can also be done with an environmental perspective. We look globally and share our eco-caring focus with children and families. Together, we also consider ways they can support sustainability practices. The children have not only become adept at recycling at our service, but they are sharing their knowledge and thus impacting on their own families' recycling habits at home.

In summary, our centre's collaborative relationships are defined as creating a sense of belonging for all our stakeholders as we continue to build respectful, supportive interactions. These relationships reflect the views and beliefs of others as we work together for the benefit and growth of children.

A provocation: Jan's story includes lots about people but also caring for the more-than-human. Think about how Jan's examples of working with people, particularly elders, and for the Earth could form a learning story and be turned into an information display for other early childhood settings. Take the position that other settings are just beginning to look at ideas around human rights, Earth rights and advocacy for both. Share your initial display ideas with colleagues, gather their extensions and then document strategies, resources and layouts.

Part 2 Thinking About Practices as Roles

Pause and reflect 7.2

Think about how you might encourage and challenge colleagues to be personally 'inspired' to act in the 'best interests' of young children. Also, consider how you might mentor team members through a process of identifying individual and collective 'aspirations' for ECE beyond one's own workplace. As leader-manager, what script would you prepare for saying and doing this mentoring? For example, consider ways of brainstorming with your workplace team. You might explore the questions: What does the UN international children's 'right to education' mean in Australia? What is early childhood education, if you were defining it in about twenty-five words? Also, prepare sample notes that you could use at a community meeting about young children in the neighbourhood.

Step 2: Which responsibilities link with professional vision and moral higher ground?

This role of advocate truly reflects being professionally responsible in special ways. Thus, considering this role might indicate a re-identification of oneself in terms of advocating:

- Who am I?
- Who do I want to be, professionally?
- What kinds of advocacy am I capable of and confident with?

Such reflection turns us back to ideas in Chapter 1. And thus, think about what images you might see if you peered into a professional mirror:

- What do these images mean about me being an advocate?
- Why are these the images that appear for me?
- Which ECE values do my images link with?

This imaging of a different ECE agenda and ECE world is possible for everyone. Taking professional responsibility for advocacy starts with one's self and extends beyond.

A rights basis

If professionals and ECE settings are to establish a rights core, what leader-manager images and qualities are essential? A rights foundation indicates the centrality of respect and dignity within all relationships. Furthermore, ideas around privilege and rules may well inform aspects of a rights advocate role.

Chapter 7 A professional role – a rights advocate

Different educators and situational leader-managers might work within ECE sites or outside, and some may advocate in both locations. In essence, various responsibilities that compose being an advocate originate from rights. You might refer to the United Nations' Human Rights website and then move to the child focus for an international ECE perspective (UNICEF & Bernard van Leer Foundation, 2006). Within Australia, re-exploring whose rights are represented in the *ECA Code of Ethics* (ECA, 2006) is a relevant engagement for individuals and teams (Davis, 2014).

Leading-managing with an advocacy lens does broaden one's role and how it is undertaken. This means that a rights advocate has particular responsibilities; which may include being:

- A legal eagle
- An activist
- A social justice upholder
- A media-watcher.

These responsibilities can be centralised but at certain times they might also be shared around a team. For a practical team approach, advocating with others, including children, could happen by acknowledging and celebrating Human Rights Day on 10 December each year; this date represents the 1948 adoption of the Universal Declaration of Human Rights. Working together to outline advocacy responsibilities is vital. This identification of potential ideas helps everyone, young and older, move forward to relevant visionary and morally high actions (also refer back to Paula Jorde Bloom's leader-manager roles in the Foreword).

Change, futures and advocating

Near and distant changes are major influences on professionals, including their acting as rights advocates. Such change can be so dynamic that looking for examples might mean that everyday ECE events are distorted for individuals, and this situation may well result in distinct advocacy responses at the time. Thus, to be effective with one's advocacy, there is a balancing act that begins with self but has a public face. Such actions reflect one's vision and standing with moral higher ground. Thinking about immediate and longer-term change alongside possible futures for the early childhood education field represents taking on an agent-of-change responsibility. This means that ECE leader-managers have to cope with changing events and altering contexts while they engage in rights advocacy work. Dianne's story, below, has elements of context, change and advocacy.

Professional reflection: Dianne's story

Journey of advocacy

An outsider. Being an outsider may sound negative, but in fact it can be an opportunity to learn something new and to become something new. In other words it is a chance to grow, to expand understandings and to create new thinking, new attitudes, new ways of being and doing. I like to keep an open mind and heart so that there is room for what is new to me. I am not a reactionary person; in fact I like to think things through before I respond or act. At times, this causes difficulties because many folk would prefer an immediate response. What can I say? – 'Let me think about that and I'll get back to you.'

I was obviously an outsider or 'other' person at the preschool. I did not share culture or background with anyone; had not been to school with staff or community members; none of my children had grown up in the community; I was not introduced to the community by Elders or any members. I was a 'blow in' with a completely different frame of reference about what was most important in an Aboriginal preschool. It seemed that consultation and transparency were not a priority. This leadership/management approach could probably be linked to the community's responses to government colonialist and integration policies and procedures, as well as some ongoing government and community attitudes. There were signs of anger, lateral violence, resistance to 'white fella ways', and there was persistence in holding onto a communal separateness. These were constants within the setting, and I tried to navigate them by listening, learning, using gentle persistence and developing understandings from within and beyond the community.

The setting. The two large rooms were airy and full of light. The routine was adaptable, as were the staff, and this afforded us opportunities of changing the day when we thought it was helpful. For example, if the children were very unsettled we just moved outside, ate our meals there and when ready we came back inside. At other times the two rooms worked together as one, opening to the outside play area as a choice. In this way, stress was reduced and joy and happiness increased. There was also a Safe Place. This was where a child wanting be alone could enjoy some quiet time. The space was created from a lawn mower box fitted with a rug, pillow and curtain. Additionally there was a small selection of sensory toys for the Safe Place. If someone was in the Safe Place, that quiet time was respected without disruption.

Kindling culture. Through working at the preschool, I came to believe that a standardised set of outcomes for early childhood pedagogy was impractical and unfair. Pedagogy needs to reflect family history, culture and experience for it to be real to children and make sense. I had to learn about what was important to this community, and my best teachers were colleagues, families and the children. Although I studied Aboriginal Education, it was through the generosity of my colleagues and some families that I gained a more acute understanding of the children. An example of the failure of standardisation was expectations about developing language and effective communication. Most of the children at the preschool spoke a soft Aboriginal English and had excellent communication skills in that dialect. I found that when I used a combination of Aboriginal Dialect and Standard English, the children were relaxed and

Chapter 7 A professional role – a rights advocate

attentive. But my use of Dialect was seen as insulting by some adults and my use of Standard English could be too. I often explained that I was not denigrating the Aboriginal Dialect but was attempting to bridge both dialects. This was because both Aboriginal English and Standard English are means of communicating, and children need both in their lives, now and into the future.

Diversifying pedagogy. Talking about talking can be good fun, and this encourages meta-cognition about how language works. Discussing vocabulary and meanings, such as 'That's deadly', and exploring phonemic awareness, such as 'the written word house starts with h', do not denigrate home language. They open doors to clearer understanding of a second dialect or language. For some adults in the community, this concept was not acceptable. They felt this was an assimilative approach to children's education and care. Their true feelings meant that children's ways of speaking ought to be left to families. Also, many of the children suffered from hearing loss, which affected language development, communicating, listening, learning and at times their social/emotional growth. Thus, a Community Health speech therapist visited regularly and worked with the children. We implemented a sensory integration programme that children really enjoyed. We found that if children worked through this programme just before a group-time, they settled, listened, understood and participated more readily.

I was free to develop learning programmes in my own way. I felt that a version of Italy's Reggio Approach best suited the children's experiences and learning styles. However, I always had in the back of my mind the 'oral tradition way' of passing on knowledge by rote. The children, educators and sometimes families worked together on projects: questioning, learning, researching, testing, documenting, making mistakes, laughing and trying again. A transformative pedagogy represented my advocacy for young children and their learning. This approach was about empowering children to critically examine our society and to develop communication techniques and strategies for working towards changes in our society. Overall, I found every day working with these Aboriginal children an absolute joy.

A provocation: If you were Dianne, which rights advocacy issue would be most important to you for acting in the best interests of children? Why? Remember, she was an Australian Celt in an Aboriginal-focused early childhood setting, and the newest early childhood educator. How and when would you raise this 'best interests' issue and others with colleagues?

Advocacy responsibilities within settings

Within early childhood settings, advocacy happens particularly on behalf of young children and in quite direct ways. Of course, children's rights have already been touched on in other chapters. However, there is a difference here, because in this chapter leader-managers are positioned to actively engage in any number of advocacy acts and do so with children's rights in mind.

Similarly, advocacy for educators is important and can be a timely role depending on the complexity of settings, the broader context and various sociocultural matters. With a rights orientation, staffing issues might include: working hours, insurance, annual leave and holidays, workers compensation, and preventative well-being programmes. All these are relevant aspects of advocacy for adults. Consideration of these kinds of workplace issues means that staff advocacy campaigns take place beyond-the-fence (link back to staff in Chapter 4). As a counter to ongoing health and sickness costs within services and across society in general, there has been a broader Australian turn that provides work-based well-being programs. Thus, some workers have access to massages, exercise sessions, food awareness events, health education services and even yoga (Sinclair, 2007).

More advocacy

Beyond children and staff, there are parents and families that may be supported in their everyday lives when ECE leader-managers advocate and brokerage on their behalf. In Australia, the *NQS* Quality Area 6: 'Collaborative partnerships with families and communities' incorporates a few standards and a number of elements that can form a basic advocacy platform for leader-managers to move forward with staff teams (ACECQA, 2013a). To gain a broader picture of advocacy for the early childhood education field, this is a timely place to pause and view examples from other countries around the world. Your professional path considerations might focus on investigating:

- How do various governments view families?
- What are early childhood educators' perspectives of families?
- What do countries' policies include about parental roles, their responsibilities and family rights, for example in the USA, the UK, Europe, South America and Africa?
- How much do countries refer to or reflect the United Nations' positions on the child, education and families? What about going beyond these to an expanded rights framework (Davis, 2014)?

Visioning

In Step 1 of this chapter, the idea of a professional vision being a common aspect of leading was introduced. We might ask: Is it common, and if so what do visions look like? How are they created? It is important to have a vision and to guide and lead others to create a joint vision for a whole setting. This responsibility may be supported and accomplished in various ways. For example, a team-based interaction for creating and sharing a vision might happen as educators engage in professional storytelling and story writing. Such a thinking and writing process does take time, and so will defining a vision with any professional documentation. Professionals can also identify relevant aspirations from other sources and various worldly experiences. Both inspirations and aspirations form a basis for professionals' work as they move back and forth from a precautionary stance and protecting wise practices to also embracing meaningful new practices. This movement also includes a temporal element – from the past, to now and for the future. As a way of doing such advocacy, visioning can include and be displayed in a number of ways, such as:

- Building a principled foundation
- Displaying hope
- Using a democratic voice
- Acting as a pace-setter
- Operating with respect
- Behaving meaningfully
- Doing reflective mentoring
- Being authentically proactive
- Sitting still, openly and silently
- Being rebelliously and ordinarily spiritual
- Practising sociocultural justice
- Fostering optimism
- Utilising eco-caring lenses
- Desiring a peaceful future.

(See: Bruno, 2009; Carroll, 2007; Chen, Nimmo & Fraser, 2009; Cook & Rouse, 2014; Costa & Kallick, 2008; Davis, 2008; Davis et al., 2009; Elliott, 2014a; Fenech, Giugni & Bown, 2012; Noddings, 2007; Nolan, 2007; Page, 2000; Pramling Samuelsson & Wagner, 2012; Ritchie, 2012; Sinclair, 2007; Waniganayake et al., 2012.)

Advocacy responsibilities beyond-the-fence

Networking, brokering with the wider community and acting with global awareness begin within ECE settings. Each of these actions can be operationalised by using a project approach with adults and establishing a management lifecycle process. For example, after engaging with nitty-gritty tasks at a setting level, a team can then turn and go further afield with an advocacy lens guiding them. Engagement tasks could include:

- Scoping and timing an event using a project format
- Planning quality management with consideration of risks
- Considering resources procurement alongside cost management
- Attending to broad human resources issues (Chapter 4)
- Implementing communications management processes (Chapter 2).

Part 2 Thinking About Practices as Roles

Ensuring that settings are clear about their key internal processes, their various external commitments and their collective values can help facilitate a staff team's movement towards wider world advocacy.

Advocacy attributes

Being a leader-manager who advocates and champions the case of young children represents 'going public'. This action includes working to change and improve the professional and social image of staff and children. It involves a number of background professional attributes and leading-managing abilities. Professionals ought to possess:

- Pedagogical and political knowledges
- Effective communication patterns
- Relevant dispositional styles
- Solid but sensitive planning competences.

With such attributes in hand, mobilising a 'beyond' vision (Fenech, Giugni & Bown, 2012) and 'doing' as political activism (Sumsion, 2006) mean professionals are taking a stand 'out there'. Such championing raises further professional issues, such as: What kind of stand? When to take a stand? Who will I stand with, and why? As a broad response to these questions, it is proposed that ECE professionals, including both situational and positional leader-managers, embrace a moral higher ground position.

Being moral

Taking or holding a moral higher ground represents a person's values, strengths, integrity and 'fairness' (MacNaughton & Hughes, 2011; Nolan, 2007; Rodd, 2013; refer back to 'A Fairness Alerts Matrix' in Chapter 2). As an example, reframing conceptions of caring to include elements of caring about, taking care of, care giving and care receiving can support leader-managers' professional actions and interactions (Woodrow & Busch, 2008). This is particularly true when the reframing is founded on moral higher ground ideas. A similar framework moves the ethic of care to what has been called 'humanistic love'. This love involves care, responsibility, respect and knowledge. These four elements relate to ECE leader-manager advocacy, with leaders acting as: moral agent, community builder and democratic leader (Ehrich & Knight, 1998). Think about how this frame might help you as a moral advocate actually undertake this role beyond-the-fence of early childhood settings (return to Chapter 1, Step 3, 'Pause and reflect 1.7', and review the examples below). You might do this by:

- Acting ethically with staff and families
- Establishing a professional ethos
- Pioneering a service mantra and stewardship for and with others
- Being a children's champion

Chapter 7 A professional role – a rights advocate

- Engaging humbly in circumstances
- Having courageousness
- Portraying honesty with sincerity
- Acting in harmony with others
- Exemplifying active democratic citizenship
- Living with genuineness of spirit
- Displaying compassion with integrity
- Proclaiming a less judgemental stance
- Researching future options and supports
- Nurturing tolerance with wisdom
- Persevering with optimism
- Using creative artistry with wisdom (refer to Goodfellow's encouragements in Step 3 of Chapter 1).

(See: Cameron, 2012; Ebbeck & Waniganayake, 2003; Goodfellow, 2001; Hallet, 2014; Rodd, 2013; Sara, 2009.)

The Professional reflection: Lavinia's story, below, contains dilemmas and aspects of advocacy with professional vision and moral higher ground.

Professional reflection: Lavinia's story

As Coordinator of Early Childhood at the University of the South Pacific, one of the professional roles and very challenging tasks that I do is advocacy for children and the rights stipulated in the United Nations *Convention on the Rights of the Child* (*CRoC*). However, the *CRoC* in the face of the Pacific people is totally new, and I recall one of the community elders in Fiji saying, 'What is *CRoC*? What other rights are you talking about here? Our children do have rights, but these rights are closely guided by elders to show them the correct right'. In fact, most Pacific people say that *CRoC* has gone against the traditional ways of children's rights in our own Pacific way. And this is one of the many changes that has tended to universalise people. For many this has been hard to accept, as people have different epistemologies that we value and vice versa. As I advocated from a professional viewpoint, I can say that children's rights in international terms have been utterly rejected by some who viewed the *CRoC* concepts as weird. This idea touched the raw nerves of adult decisions, and their actions have been tested.

In my role, I often explained succinctly to elders in the Pacific communities how to work around the *CRoC*, as I believed that when explained correctly to children and communities, it would be well accepted. I agree with Freeman (1996, p. 70) that 'Rights are entitlements, valuable commodities' which we 'do not have to grovel or beg to get'. I know that in Fiji and

Part 2 Thinking About Practices as Roles

in most of the Pacific Island States, children's rights have not received widespread public or political support. Therefore, as I went on duty-tours to the smaller Pacific Island States, I made it my core business to first of all create a positive interactive relationship with stakeholders and share views of how to go forward with the *CRoC*. As I look back at my professional role – as a rights advocate – I was basically ensuring good relationships with people at local, national and the upper national levels. While in some situations the indigenous people still remain silent, this says a lot as silence has both 'yes' and 'no' aspects. While I kept insisting on the importance of children being recognised in our individual communities, I also advocated the *CRoC* path to academics and professionals working on children's issues. The *CRoC* is the way forward if we want our children to live a life worthy of being a child and excel into the future. As professionals working with children, we have an important role in advocating for them by taking a proactive approach towards recognising the rights of all children and responding by trying to change systems, policies and individuals.

In summary, I believe that as a professional working for the well-being of and a good future for our children in the Pacific, child advocacy is vital. We need to aggressively advocate for raising the status of children, increasing their self-determination. Such actions include responsiveness and accountability by institutions affecting them. Professionals should be educating government and local agencies about the *Convention*. It can provide a common basis for understanding, and a framework for planning and operating services for children. Child advocacy is not about undermining the role of parents, families or teachers; nor is it about denying children their childhood – it is all about supporting our children for a better tomorrow.

A provocation: *Lavinia's work with many is an example of the widespread parameters that advocacy can involve – community elders, families, professionals, government officials. Think about how, as an Australian ECE leader-manager, you might introduce the International CRoC document to a new group of parents as their children are enrolling in your early childhood setting. What would your opening statement be?*

Advocacy everywhere

The responsibilities of a rights advocate can be very broad, as indicated earlier in the lists regarding 'visioning' and 'moral positioning'. Some of these actions are easier to embrace, while others take more courage and support. There are possible competing or contradictory ways of advocating for the whole early childhood education field, and everyone touched by such actions. In fact, some writers make a distinction between being an advocate and being an activist or activist professional (Ebbeck & Waniganayake, 2003; Waniganayake et al., 2012; Woodrow & Busch, 2008). Returning to earlier professional ideas, it seems obvious that team work and a collaborative ambiance are vital for educators personally and so that they can support each other professionally and as advocates.

Chapter 7 A professional role – a rights advocate

Pause and reflect 7.3

A rights advocate takes on responsibilities both within ECE settings and in the broader community. Two key ways of leading-managing for advocacy were highlighted in this second Step – visioning for today and into the future, and being moral. Work with some colleagues to identify examples of: a visioning process for a new early childhood setting; and how to act morally during a challenging encounter with a local community group.

Conclusion

In this chapter you explored what it might be like to take on a rights advocate role, especially from the position of leading-managing across the early childhood education field. Aspects of advocacy and ways of enacting it were considered, with a focus on creating a professional vision and establishing one's moral higher ground. Some professional issues and challenges linked with being an advocate for rights were highlighted during this journey.

Additionally, this point could be an ending for you. However, you are encouraged to continue your professional thinking, acting, thinking again and then reflecting, and to use documentary story writing. In the context of keeping a professional journal, writing is a sensible and meaningful way of exploring yourself and others. Your thinking and reflecting to this point represent time spent travelling through this book. This place and point in time may be another beginning for you as various career options and paths surface and are revealed for you.

Dear Nadine

This chapter brings us full circle. In this most important chapter, readers are asked to think yet again about 'Where are we going?' 'Where do we want to be?' and 'What imaginings of the present and the future am I passionate about?' By looking inwards and answering these questions honestly, we are able to take up the challenge and act authentically on behalf of children, families and the profession. I have recently been introduced to constructs about 'advocating with and alongside' rather than advocating 'for or on behalf of'. I think this is a more empowered way to consider advocacy. What do readers think?

Our work with the community beyond-the-fence is a growing area of interest and research, especially in terms of social, economic, environmental and political sustainability. Recent action on 'collective impact' has seen a range of organisations act together to improve outcomes for children. Kania and Kramer (2011) coined this concept in the *Stanford Social Innovation Review*. Happily there is often a focus on children's early years; and so, leaders of early childhood organisations and individual services can and do play a significant role in a 'collective impact' model. Just like the change strategies outlined in many of the chapters

Part 2 Thinking About Practices as Roles

throughout this book, the key conditions for collective impact relate to having a common agenda and a shared understanding of what needs to be addressed. There is also the question of how this might be done, for example by: collecting data and measuring results regularly for alignment and accountability; having a plan of mutually reinforcing action; and ensuring open and continuous communication to build trust and (a common) motivation. The collective impact model takes a further step of suggesting the establishment of a coordinating 'backbone' organisation.

In any community an early childhood setting can play an important role in collective change activities; and in some small communities ECE sites may take on 'backbone' coordinating responsibilities. I wonder if readers might adopt many of the strategies outlined in this final 'advocacy' chapter and generate mutually reinforcing action with other sectors that hold children's well-being as paramount to their future lives. Reading Dianne's story reminded me of a collective approach to improving children's outcomes and their lives. I think that when we all work to create common respectful understandings then we move forward together as advocates for children's right to belong and to learn.

My overall impression is that this entire book can be called an act of advocacy. It has taken courage to write it in a way that adopts a higher, yet humble, moral ground. Each chapter focuses on the 'hard work' of leading. There is a mix of detailed leadership theory and practice introduced, together with broad insights into conceptualising early childhood leadership to meet current challenges across the early childhood education field. The contributions from Jan and other colleagues provided examples of lived experiences as leaders. In this chapter Jan shows how we can advocate alongside children and in so doing give them agency to advocate for a better future for themselves and others. Simple local acts of kindness are so easy and so important. I think that they help us to gain confidence in our capacity to advocate beyond-the-fence. It takes patience to build strong inclusive relationships within and outside of early childhood settings – Lavinia's story bears this out. I marvel at how leaders like Lavinia are willing to tackle the difficulties they face with compassion for those who do not share their ideals. Here lies true strength and generosity – a key leadership message that readers can take from this book.

I wish the best for those who have journeyed with us, as contributors and readers,

Di

Pause and reflect 7.4

Which idea in this chapter most influenced your current beliefs, and why? Record your personal feelings, inspirations and professional thoughts in your 'journal'.

References

ACECQA. (2013a). *Guide to the National Quality Standard*. Sydney, NSW: ACECQA. Online at: www.acecqa.gov.au.

ACECQA. (2013b). *Guide to Developing a Quality Improvement Plan*. Sydney, NSW: ACECQA. Online at: www.acecqa.gov.au.

ACECQA. (2013c). *Guide to the National Quality Framework*. Sydney, NSW: ACECQA. Online at: www.acecqa.gov.au.

AGDEEWR. (2009). *Belonging, Being & Becoming, The Early Years Learning Framework for Australia*. Barton, ACT: Commonwealth of Australia.

AGDEEWR. (2010). *Educators Belonging, Being & Becoming: Educators' Guide to the Early Years Learning Framework for Australia*. Barton, ACT: Commonwealth of Australia.

AGDEEWR. (nd). *The Early Years Learning Framework in Action: Educators' stories and models for practice*. Barton, ACT: Commonwealth of Australia. Online at: www.education.gov.au/early-years-learning-framework.

Ailwood, J. (Ed.). (2007a). *Early Childhood in Australia: Historical and comparative contexts*. Frenchs Forest, NSW: Pearson Education Australia.

Ailwood, J. (2007b). Introduction. In J. Ailwood (Ed.), *Early Childhood in Australia: Historical and comparative contexts* (pp. vii–xii). Frenchs Forest, NSW: Pearson Education Australia.

Ailwood, J. (2007c). Motherhood, materialism and early childhood education: Some historical connections. In J. Ailwood (Ed.), *Early Childhood in Australia: Historical and comparative contexts* (pp. 51–65). Frenchs Forest, NSW: Pearson Education Australia.

Almers, E. (2013). Pathways to action competence for sustainability – six themes. *The Journal of Environmental Education*, 44(2), 116–27. doi: http://dx.doi.org/10.1080/00958964.2012.719939.

Alvesson, M., & Spicer, A. (2011). Theories of leadership, Chapter 2. In M. Alvesson & A. Spicer (Eds.), *Metaphors We Lead by: Understanding leadership in the real world* (pp. 8–30). Milton Park, ENG: Routledge.

References

Ang, L. (2011). *Early Childhood Education in a Diverse Society: An ethnographic study of preschools in Singapore*. Singapore: Singapore Committee of OMEP. Online at: www.omep-sgp.org/.

Anning, A., Cullen, J., & Fleer, M. (Eds.). (2008). *Early Childhood Education, society and culture*. London, ENG: Sage Publications Ltd.

Aquash, M. (2013). First Nations ways of knowing: The circle of knowledge. *First Nations Perspectives*, 5(1), 25–36. Online at: http://www.mfnerc.org/wp-content/uploads/2013/04/Section2_First-Nations-Ways-of-Knowing-The-Circle-of-Knowledge.pdf.

ARACY. (2013). *The Nest Action Agenda*. Braddon, ACT: ARACY.

Armstrong, H. (2013). Indigenizing the curriculum: The importance of story. *First Nations Perspectives*, 5(1), 37–64. Online at: http://www.mfnerc.org/wp-content/uploads/2013/04/Section3_Indigenizing-the-Curriculum-The-Importance-of-Story.pdf.

Arnold, R. (2005). *Empathic Intelligence: Teaching, learning, relating*. Sydney, NSW: University of New South Wales Press Ltd.

Arthur, L. (2010). The Early Years Learning Framework: Building confident learners. In S. Cheeseman (Ed.), *Research in Practice Series* (Vol. 17 (1)). Deakin West, ACT: ECA, Inc.

Arthur, L., Beecher, B., Death, E., Dockett, S., & Farmer, S. (2012). *Programming & Planning in Early Childhood Settings* (5th ed.). South Melbourne, VIC: Cengage Learning Australia.

Aubrey, C. (2011). *Leading and Managing in the Early Years* (2nd ed.). London, ENG: Sage Publications Ltd.

Australian Ethical. (2014). 2014: The year of collaborative consumption. *Good Money*, Edition 2. Online at: http://www.australianethical.com.au/system/files/documents/Good Money_Final_PDF.pdf, 6–9.

Ball, S. (2003). The teacher's soul and the terrors of performativity. *Journal of Education Policy*, 18(2), 215–28. doi: http://dx.doi.org/10.1080/0268093022000043065.

Ball, S., & Olmedo, A. (2013). Care for the self, resistance and subjectivity under neoliberal governmentalities. *Critical Studies in Education*, 54(1), 85–96. doi: http://dx.doi.org/10/1080/17508487.2013.740678.

Bangamalanha Centre. (2013). *8 Aboriginal Ways of Learning* website *wiki*. Online at: http://www.8ways.wikispaces.com.

Bansal, I., & Hingorani, P. (2013). Mapping emotional competencies of Mahatma Gandhi: A biographical analysis. *Journal of Human Values*, 19(2), 133–45. doi: http://dx.doi.org/10.1177/0971685813492267.

References

Barblett, L., **Hydon, C.**, & **Kennedy, A.** (2008). The Code of Ethics: A guide for everyday practice. In J. Connor (Ed.), *Research in Practice Series* (Vol. 15 (1)). Watson, ACT: ECA, Inc.

Baxter, C., **Gelenter, C.**, **Ryan, P.**, & **Weingarth, L.** (1988). *Keeping on Track: Children's services administration manual*. Sydney, NSW: Community Child Care Co-operative, Ltd (NSW).

Bayley, S. (1999). Food as fashion, Chapter 1. In C. Catterall (Ed.), *Food: Design and culture* (pp. 34–53). London, ENG: Laurence King Publishing.

Biesta, G., & **Tedder, M.** (2007). Agency and learning in the lifecourse: Towards an ecological perspective. *Studies in the Education of Adults*, 39(2), 132–49.

Bin-Sallik, M. (2003). Cultural Safety: Let's name it!. *The Australian Journal of Indigenous Education*, 32, 21–8.

Blanchard, K. & **Hodges, P.** (2003). *The Servant Leader*. Nashville, TEN: Thomas Nelson.

Bloom, P. J. (1988). *A great place to work: Improving conditions for staff in young children's programs*. Washington, DC: NAEYC.

Bloom, P. J. (2005). *Blueprint for Actions: Achieving center-based change through staff development* (2nd ed.). Lake Forest, IL: New Horizons.

Bloom, P. J. (2007). *From the Inside Out: The power of reflection and self-awareness*. Lake Forest, IL: New Horizons.

Bloom, P. J. (2014). *Leadership in Action: How effective administrators get things done* (2nd ed.). Lake Forest, IL: New Horizons.

Bloom, P. J., **Hentschel, A.**, & **Bella, J.** (2010). *A Great Place to Work: Creating a healthy organizational climate*. Lake Forest, IL: New Horizons.

Bloom, P. J., **Hentschel, A.**, & **Bella, J.** (2013). *Inspiring Peak Performance: Competence, commitment, and collaboration*. Lake Forest, IL: New Horizons.

Bloom, P., **Sheerer, M.**, & **Britz, J.** (1991). *Blueprint for Action: Achieving center-based change through staff development*. Mt. Rainier, MD: Gryphone House, Inc.

Bolton, R. (1979). *People Skills: How to assert yourself, listen to others and resolve conflicts*. Englewood Cliffs, NJ: Prentice-Hall.

Bone, J. (2005). Breaking bread: Spirituality, food and early childhood education. *International Journal of Children's Spirituality*, 10(3), 307–17. doi: http://dx.doi.org/10.1080/1364436 0500347607.

Boris-Schacter, S., & **Vonasek, G.** (2009). Dear Gayle, Dear Sheryl: Using e-mail for a principal mentorship. *Phi Delta Kappan*, 90(7), 490–94.

References

Boud, D., & Hager, P. (2012). Re-thinking continuing professional development through changing metaphors and location of professional practices. *Studies in Continuing Education*, 34(1), 17–30. doi: http://dx.doi.org/10.1080/0158037X.2011.608656.

Boyatzis, R., & Akrivou, K. (2006). The ideal self as the driver of intentional change. *Journal of Management Development*, 25(7), 624–42. doi: http://dx.doi.org/10.1108/02621710610678454.

Boyd, W., & Ailwood, J. (2007). Comparing early childhood education and care across Australia, Chapter 6. In J. Ailwood (Ed.), *Early Childhood in Australia: Historical and comparative contexts* (pp. 77–92). Frenchs Forest, NSW: Pearson Education Australia.

Bredekamp, S. (Ed.). (1987). *Accreditation Criteria and Procedures of the National Academy of Early Childhood Programs*. Washington, DC: NAEYC.

Brennan, D., & Adamson, E. (2014). *Financing the Future: An equitable and sustainable approach to early childhood education and care*, SPRC Report 01/14. Sydney, NSW: UNSW. Online at: www.sprc.unsw.edu.au/media/SPRCFile/Financing_the_Future.pdf.

Bronfenbrenner, U. (Ed.). (2005). *Making Human Beings Human: Bioecological perspectives on human development*. Thousand Oaks, CA: Sage Publications, Inc.

Bruno, H. (2009). *Leading on Purpose: Emotionally intelligent early childhood administration*. New York: McGraw-Hill.

Bryant, L., & Gibbs, L. (2013). *A Director's Manual: Managing an early education and care service in NSW*. Marrickville, NSW: Community Child Care Co-operative, Ltd (NSW).

Bryant, L., Semann, A., Slattery, C., Madden, L., & Gibbs, L. (2009). *The Manual: Managing a Children's Service*. Marrickville, NSW: Community Child Care Co-operative, Ltd (NSW). Online at: www.cccnsw.org.au/wp-content/uploads/the-manual-managing-a-children's-service.pdf.

Bush, T. (2011). *Theories of Educational Leadership & Management* (4th ed.). London, ENG: Sage Publications Ltd.

Caiman, C., & Lundegard, I. (2014). Pre-school children's agency in learning for sustainable development. *Environmental Education Research*, 20(4), 437–59. doi: http://dx.doi.org/10/10.1080/13504622.2013.812722.

Cameron, C. (2012). *Leadership as a Call to Service: The lives and works of Teresa of Avila, Catherine of Siena and Therese of Lisieux*. Ballan, VIC: Connor Court Publishing Pty Ltd.

Campbell, S. (1999). Making the political pedagogical in early childhood. *Australian Journal of Early Childhood*, 24(4), 21–6.

References

Cardno, C., & Reynolds, B. (2009). Resolving leadership dilemmas in New Zealand kindergartens: An action research study. *Journal of Educational Administration*, 47(2), 206–26. doi: http://dx.doi.org/10.1108/09578230910941057.

Carroll, M. (2007). *The Mindful Leader: Ten principles for bringing out the best in ourselves and others*. Boston, MA: Trumpeter Books, Shambhala Publications Inc.

Carruthers, J. (1993). The principles and practice of mentoring, Chapter 2. In B. Caldwell & E. Carter (Eds.), *The Return of the Mentor: Strategies for workplace learning* (pp. 9–24). London, ENG: The Falmer Press, Taylor & Francis Group.

Cartmel, J., Macfarlane, K., & Casley, M. (2012). Reflection as a Tool for Quality: Working with the National Quality Standard. In C. Hydon (Ed.), *Research in Practice Series* (Vol. 19 (4)). Deakin West, ACT: ECA, Inc.

Chaille, C. (2008). *Constructivism across the Curriculum in Early Childhood Classrooms: Big ideas as inspiration*. Boston, MA: Pearson Education Inc/Allyn and Bacon.

Chakraborty, D. (2003). Leadership in the East and West: A few examples. *Journal of Human Values*, 9(1), 29–52. doi: http://dx.doi.org/10.1177/097168580300900104.

Charlesworth, R. (2014). *Understanding Child Development* (9th ed.). Belmont, CA: Wadsworth, Cengage Learning.

Cheeseman, S. (2012). *The educational leader*. ECA/National Quality Standard Professional Learning Program. Online at: www.earlychildhoodaustralia.org.au/nqsplp/e-newsletters/newsletters31–35/newsletter-33/:.

Cheeseman, S., Fenech, M., & staff at Tigger's Honeypot Childcare Centre. (2012). The Early Years Learning Framework: Essential reading for the National Quality Standard. In C. Hydon (Ed.), *Research in Practice Series* (Vol. 19 (2)). Deakin West, ACT: ECA, Inc.

Chen, D., Nimmo, J., & Fraser, H. (2009). Becoming a culturally responsive early childhood educator: A tool to support reflection by teachers embarking on the anti-bias journey. *Multicultural Perspectives*, 11(2), 101–6. doi: http://dx.doi.org/10.1080/15210960903028784.

Choi Wa Ho, D. (2011). Identifying leadership roles for quality in early childhood education programmes. *International Journal of Leadership in Education: Theory and Practice*, 14(1), 47–59. doi: http://dx.doi.org/10.1080/13603120903387561.

Cleary, T., trans. (2004). *Zen Lessons: The art of leadership*. Boston, MA: Shambhala Publications Inc.

Click, P., & Karkos, K. (2011). *Administration of Programs for Young Children* (8th ed.). Belmont, CA: Wadsworth Cengage Learning.

References

COAG. (2009). *Regulation Impact Statement for Early Childhood Education and Care Quality Reforms*, COAG Decision RIS. Council of Australian Governments. Online at: www.coag.gov.au/node/202. Retrieved from www.coag.gov.au/meeting_outcomes.

Coleman, M. (2012). Leadership and diversity. *Educational Management Administration & Leadership*, 40(5), 592–609. doi: http://dx.doi.org/10.1177/1741143212451174.

Collins, S., & Ting, H. (2014). The complexity of care. *Complicity: An International Journal of Complexity and Education*, 11(1), 5–19.

Connor, J. (2008). Learnings from High/Scope: Enriching everyday practice. In J. Tangorra (Ed.), *Research in Practice Series* (Vol. 15 (2)). Watson, ACT: ECA, Inc.

Connor, J. (2011). *Understanding cultural competence*. EYLFPLP e-Newsletter, (no. 7). Deakin West, ACT: ECA.

Cook, D. (2012). Children's consumption in history, Chapter 30. In F. Trentmann (Ed.), *The Oxford Handbook of The History of Consumption* (pp. 585–600). Oxford, ENG: Oxford University Press.

Cook, J., & Rouse, L. (2014). *Leadership and Management in the Early Years: A practical guide to building confident leadership skills*. Albert Park, VIC: Teaching Solutions.

Cornelissen, J. (2005). Beyond compare: Metaphor in organization theory. *The Academy of Management Review*, 30(4), 751–64. Stable URL: http://www.jstor.org/stable/20159164.

Cornelissen, J., Oswick, C., Christensen, L., & Phillips, N. (2008). Metaphor in organizational research: Context, modalities and implications for research – introduction. *Organization Studies*, 29(01), 07–22. doi: http://dx.doi.org/10.1177/0170840607086634.

Costa, A., & Kallick, B. (Eds.). (2008). *Learning and Leading with Habits of Mind: 16 essential characteristics for success*. Alexandria, VA: ASDC. Free online at: www.jtbookyard.com/uploads/6/2/9/3/6293106/ebook-_learning_and_leading_with_habits_of_mind_-_16_essential_characteristics_for_success_2008.pdf/.

CREIO. (1998). *Emotional Competence Framework. Consortium for Research on Emotional Intelligence in Organizations*. Retrieved from: www.eiconsortium.org/reports/emotional_competence_framework.html.

Crowther, I. (2011). *Creating Effective Learning Environments* (3rd ed.). Toronto, Ontario: Nelson Education, Ltd.

Cutter-Mackenzie, A., & Edwards, S. (2013). Toward a model of early childhood environmental education: Foregrounding, developing and connecting knowledge through play-based learning. *The Journal of Environmental Education*, 44(3), 195–213. doi: http://dx.doi.org/10.1080/00958964.2012.751892.

References

Dahlberg, G., Moss, P., & Pence, A. (2001). *Beyond Quality in Early Childhood Education and Care: Postmodern perspectives*. Philadelphia, PA: RoutledgeFalmer.

Daly, M., Byers, E., & Taylor, W. (2004). *Early Years Management in Practice*. Oxford, ENG: Heinemann Educational Publishers.

Dau, E., & Jones, K. (2004). Revisiting celebrations with young children. In P. Linke (Ed.), *Research in Practice Series* (Vol. 11 (2)). Watson, ACT: ECA, Inc.

Davis, J. (2008). What might education for sustainability look like in early childhood?: A case for participatory, whole-of-settings approaches. In I. Pramling Samuelsson & Y. Kaga (Eds.), *The Contribution of Early Childhood Education to a Sustainable Society* (pp. 18–24). Paris, Fra: UNESCO.

Davis, J. (Ed.). (2010a). *Young Children and the Environment: Early education for sustainability*. Port Melbourne, VIC: Cambridge University Press.

Davis, J. (2010b). Early childhood education for sustainability: Why it matters, what it is, and how whole centre action research and systems thinking can help. *Journal of Action Research Today in Early Childhood*, Special Issue, 35–44. Singapore Committee of OMEP.

Davis, J. (2014). Examining early childhood education through the lens of education for sustainability, revisioning rights, Chapter 1. In J. Davis & S. Elliott (Eds.), *Research in Early Childhood Education for Sustainability: International perspectives and provocations* (pp. 21–37). Abingdon, ENG: Routledge.

Davis, J., & Elliott, S. (2003). *Early Childhood Environmental Education: Making it mainstream*. Watson, ACT: ECA.

Davis, J., & Elliott, S. (Eds.). (2014). *Research in Early Childhood Education for Sustainability: International perspectives and provocations*. Abingdon, ENG: Routledge.

Davis, J., Engdahl, I., Otieno, L., Pramling Samuelsson, I., Siraj-Blatchford, J., & Vallabh, P. (2009). Early childhood education for sustainability: Recommendations for development. *International Journal of Early Childhood*, 41(2), 113–17.

de Bono, E. (1987). *Six Thinking Hats*. London, ENG: Penguin Books.

Denning, S. (2005). *The Leader's Guide to Storytelling: Mastering the art and discipline of business narrative*. San Francisco, CA: Jossey-Bass.

Dorrat, L. (2011). Westgarth Bush Kindergarten. *Every Child*, 17(4), 6–7.

Dowling, A., & O'Malley, K. (2009). *Preschool Education in Australia*. Policy Brief, December. Online at: http://research.acer.edu.au/policy_briefs/1.

References

Duhn, I. (2012). Making 'place' for ecological sustainability in early childhood education. *Environmental Education Research*, 18(1), 19–29. doi: http://dx.doi.org/10.1080/13504622.2011.572162.

Duhn, I., **Bachmann, M.**, & **Harris, K.** (2010). Becoming ecologically sustainable in early childhood education. *Early Childhood Folio*, 14(1), 2–6.

Duignan, P., & **Macpherson, R.** (1992). A practical theory of educative leadership, Chapter 7. In P. Duignan & R. Macpherson (Eds.), *Educative Leadership: A practical theory for new administrators and managers* (pp. 171–85). London, ENG: The Falmer Press.

Duncan, J., & **Bartle, C.** (2014). Normalising the breast: Early childhood services battling the bottle and the breast. *Contemporary Issues in Early Childhood*, 15(1), 18–28. doi: http://dx.doi.org/10.2304/ciec.2014.15.1.18.

Dunlop, A. (2008). *A Literature Review on Leadership in the Early Years*. Edinburgh, Scot: Learning and Teaching Scotland. Retrieved from: www.educationscotland.gov.uk/pulications/a/leadershippreview.asp.

Eacott, S. (2013). Asking questions of leadership: Using social theory for more than critique. *Leading & Managing*, 19(1), 18–31.

Eaton, D. (2008). One size doesn't fit all – collaborations with parents. In B. Neugebauer (Ed.), *Professionalism: A Beginnings workshop book* (pp. 102–4). Redmond, WA: Exchange Press Inc.

Ebbeck, M., & **Waniganayake, M.** (2003). *Early Childhood Professionals: Leading today and tomorrow*. Chatswood, NSW: MacLennan & Petty, Elsevier Australia.

ECA. (2006). *Early Childhood Australia: Code of Ethics*. Deakin West, ACT. Online at: http://www.earlychildhoodaustralia.org.au/code_of_ethics/early_childhood_australias_code_of_ethics.html: ECA.

ECA. (2012a). *The Leadership Capability Framework for Early Childhood Education and Care and School Age Care: Leadership practices in contexts of education and care, diversities and complexities* (draft document 2012–2013; not publically available). Deakin West, ACT: ECA.

ECA. (2012b). *Respect, Connect, Enact: A reconciliation action plan for Early Childhood Australia 2012–2016*. Deakin West, ACT: ECA; Retrieved from: http://www.earlychildhoodaustralia.org.au/about_us/eca-reconciliation-action-plan.html.

ECA-ACARA. (2011). *Foundations for learning: relationships between the Early Years Learning Framework and the Australian Curriculum*. Canberra, ACT: ECA-ACARA. Online at: http://www.earlychildhoodaustralia.org.au/pdf/ECA_ACARA_Foundations_Paper/ECA_ACARA_Foundations_Paper_FINAL.pdf.

Edwards, S. (2009). *Early Childhood Education and Care: A sociocultural approach*. Castle Hill, NSW: Pademelon Press.

Edwards, S., & **Cutter-Mackenzie, A.** (2011). Environmentalising early childhood education curriculum through pedagogies of play. *Australasian Journal of Early Childhood*, 36(1), 51–9.

Edwards, S., Moore, D., & **Cutter-Mackenzie, A.** (2012). 'It will be a wasteland if we don't recycle': Sustainability and intentional teaching in early childhood. *Every Child*, 18(3), 12–13.

Edwards, R. & **Usher, R.** (2008). *Globalisation & Pedagogy: Space, place and identity* (2nd ed.). Abingdon, ENG: Routledge, Taylor & Francis Group.

Ehrich, L., & **English, F.** (2013). Leadership as dance: A consideration of the applicability of the 'mother' of all arts as the basis for establishing connoisseurship. *International Journal of Leadership in Education: Theory and Practice*, 16(4), 454–81. doi: http://dx.doi.org/10.1080/13603124.2012.696282.

Ehrich, L., & **Knight, J.** (1998). Prefactory notes on a principled human-centred practice. In L. Ehrich & J. Knight (Eds.), *Leadership in Crisis? Restructuring principled practice: Essays on contemporary educational leadership* (pp. 181–9). Flaxton, QLD: Post Pressed.

Eissler, T. (2009). *Montessori Madness!: A parent to parent argument for Montessori education*. Georgetown, TX: Sevenoff Publishing.

Elliott, R. (2005). The Communication Accretion Spiral: A communication process for promoting and sustaining meaningful partnerships between families and early childhood service staff. *Australian Journal of Early Childhood*, 30(2), 49–58.

Elliott, S. (2014a). *Sustainability and the Early Years Learning Framework*. Mt. Victoria, NSW: Pademelon Press.

Elliott, S. (2014b). Sustainability as the norm in early childhood settings. *Every Child*, 20(1), 10–11.

Elliott, S., & **Chancellor, B.** (2013). Bush Kinder Journey: Westgarth Bush Kinder pilot program. *Every Child*, 19(2), 14–15.

Ellis, C., **Adams, T.**, & **Bochner, A.** (2011). Autoethnography: An overview. Forum: *Qualitative Social Research*, 12(1), Art. 10. Online at: www.qualitative-research.net/index.php/fqs/index.

Farrell, A. (2001). Policy research, Chapter 16. In G. MacNaughton, S. Rolfe & I. Siraj-Blatchford (Eds.), *Doing Early Childhood Research: International perspectives on theory and practice* (pp. 240–53). Crows Nest, NSW: Allen & Unwin.

Fasoli, L., & **Woodrow, C.** (1991). *Getting Ethical: A resource book for workshop leaders*. In M. Fleer (Ed.), AECA Resource Booklets (Vol. July 1991 (3)). Watson, ACT: AECA, Inc.

Feez, S. (2010). *Montessori and Early Childhood: A guide for students*. London, ENG: SAGE publications Ltd.

References

Feez, S. (2013). *Montessori: The Australian story*. Sydney, NSW: University of New South Wales Press Ltd.

Feinstein, S., & Kiner, R. (2011). *The Brain and Strengths Based School Leadership*. Thousand Oaks, CA: Corwin, A Sage Company.

Fenech, M., Giugni, M., & Bown, K. (2012). A critical analysis of the National Quality Framework: Mobilising for a vision for children beyond minimum standards. *Australasian Journal of Early Childhood*, 37(4), 5–14.

Feng, L., & Newton, D. (2012). Some implications for moral education of the Confucian principle of harmony: Learning from sustainability education practice in China. *Journal of Moral Education*, 41(3), 341–51. doi: http://dx.doi.org/10.1080/03057240.2012.691633.

Fleer, M. (2010). *Early Learning and Development: Cultural-historical concepts in play*. Port Melbourne, VIC: Cambridge University Press.

Flores, B., Casebeer, C., & Riojas-Cortez, M. (2011). Validation of the Early Childhood Ecology Scale-Revised: A reflective tool for teacher candidates. *Journal of Early Childhood Teacher Education*, 32(3), 266–86.

Fluckiger, B. (2013). Forging partnerships with parents in Indigenous communities. *Reflections* (50), 18–19.

Foster, J. (2009). *Memory: A very short introduction*. Oxford, ENG: Oxford University Press.

Freeman, M. (1996). *Children's rights: A comparative perspective*. Brookfield, VT: Dartmouth Pub. Co.

Freeman, N., Decker, C., & Decker, J. (2013). *Planning and Administering Early Childhood Programs* (10th ed.). Upper Saddle River, NJ: Pearson Education Inc.

Friedman, D. (2012). *Creating and Presenting an Early Childhood Education Portfolio: A reflective approach*. Belmont, CA: Wadsworth, Cengage Learning.

Frost, R. (1920). *'The Road Not Taken' Mountain Interval* (pp. np). New York, NY: Henry Holt & Co.

Gahan, D. (2007). Historical perspectives on kindergarten education in Queensland, Chapter 1. In J. Ailwood (Ed.), *Early Childhood in Australia: Historical and comparative contexts* (pp. 2–17). Frenchs Forest, NSW: Pearson Education Australia.

Gaul, J., Nippard, H., & Watson, D. (2012). *ECO SMART for Early Childhood, a sustainability filter for Quality Improvement Plans*. Sydney, NSW: NSW ECEEN & NSW Office of Environment & Heritage. Retrieved from info (members only) at www.eceen.org.au.

Gerrissen, L., & The Red Thunderbird Agency. (2009). *The change to speak and the art of listening: The story of the Talking Stick*. Stipo Amsterdam. Online at: www.stipo.info/.

References

Gandhi, M. K. (2007). Selected texts. In T. Merton (Ed.), *Gandhi on Non-violence*. New York, NY: New Directions Paperbook.

Gibbs, L. (1999). *Keeping on Track: Children's services administration manual* (4th ed.). Newtown, NSW: Community Child Care Co-operative, Ltd (NSW).

Giovacco-Johnson, T. (2011). Applied ethics as a foundation in early childhood teacher education: Exploring the connections and possibilities. *Early Childhood Education Journal*, 38(6), 449–56.

Goffin, S. (1994). *Curriculum Models and Early Childhood Education: Appraising the relationship*. New York, NY: Merrill, Macmillan College Publishing Company.

Goldberg, N. (2005). *Writing Down the Bones: Freeing the writer within*, Expanded ed. Boston, MA: Shambhala Publications Inc.

Goleman, D. (2004). *Emotional Intelligence: Why it can matter more than IQ*. London, ENG: Bloomsbury.

Goleman, D. (2009). *Ecological Intelligence: Knowing the hidden impacts of what we buy*. Camberwell, VIC: Allen Lane, Penguin Group (Australia).

Goleman, D., Bennett, L., & Barlow, Z. (2012). *Ecoliterate: How educators are cultivating emotional, social and ecological intelligence*. San Francisco, CA: Jossey-Bass.

Goodfellow, J. (2001). Wise practice: The need to move beyond best practice in early childhood education. *Australian Journal of Early Childhood*, 26(1), 1–6.

Goodfellow, J. (2009). The Early Years Learning Framework: Getting started. In J. Connor (Ed.), *Research in Practice Series* (Vol. 16 (4)). Deakin West, ACT: ECA, Inc.

Gordon, M. (2014). Friendship, intimacy and humor. *Educational Philosophy and Theory*, 46(2), 162–74. doi: http://dx.doi.org/10.1080/00131857.2012.721732.

Gowrie Victoria. (2013). *The Legislative Framework for Australian Children's Services – A Victorian Context*. Carlton, VIC: Professional Support Coordinator, Gowrie Victoria. Online at: www.psc@gowrievictoria.org.au.

Grint, K. (2007). Learning to lead: Can Aristotle help us find the road to wisdom? *Leadership*, 3(2), 231–46. doi: http://dx.doi.org/10.1177/1742715007076215.

Grisham, T. (2006). Metaphor, poetry, storytelling and cross-cultural leadership. *Management Decision*, 44(4), 486–503. doi: http://dx.doi.org/10.1108/00251740610663027.

Hallet, E. (2014). *Leadership of Learning in Early Years Practice*. London, ENG: Institute of Education Press.

References

Hallqvist, A., & Hyden, L. (2013). Work transitions as told: A narrative approach to biographical learning. *Studies in Continuing Education*, 35(1), 1–16. doi: http://dx.doi.org/10/1080/0158037X.2012.712037.

Harris, P., & Manatakis, H. (2013). *Children's Voices: A principled framework for children and young people's participation as valued citizens and learners*. Adelaide, SA: Government of South Australia. Online at: http://www.everychild.sa.gov.au/docs/Childrens_Voices_booklet_web.pdf.

Hawley, K. (2012). *Trust: A very short introduction*. Oxford, ENG: Oxford University Press.

Hayward, B. (2012). *Children, Citizenship and Environment: Nurturing a democratic imagination in a changing world*. Abingdon, ENG: Routledge.

Hearron, P., & Hildebrand, V. (2007). *Management of Child Development Centers* (6th ed.). Upper Saddle River, NJ: Pearson Prentice Hall.

Helstad, K., & Moller, J. (2013). Leadership as relational work: Risks and opportunities. *International Journal of Leadership in Education: Theory and Practice*, 16(3), 245–62. doi: http://dx.doi.org/10.1080/13603124.2012.761353.

Heracleous, L., & Jacobs, C. (2008). Understanding organizations through embodied metaphors. *Organization Studies*, 29(01), 45–78. doi: http://dx.doi.org/10.1177/0170840607086637.

Herbert, J. (2013). Interrogating social justice in early years education: How effectively do contemporary policies and practices create equitable learning environments for Indigenous Australian children? *Contemporary Issues in Early Childhood*, 14(4), 300–10. doi: http://dx.doi.org/10.2304/ciec.2013.14.4.300.

Hewes, D., & Leatherman, J. (2005). *An Administrator's Guidebook to Early Care and Education Programs*. Boston, MA: Pearson Education, Inc./Allyn and Bacon.

Hiley, T. (2006). Finding one's voice: The poetry of reflective practice. *Management Decision*, 44(4), 561–74. doi: http://dx.doi.org/10.1108/00251740610663081.

Hill, A., McCrea, N., Emery, S., Nailon, D., Davis, J., Dyment, J., & Getenet, S. (2014). Exploring how adults who work with young children conceptualise sustainability and describe their practice initiatives. *Australasian Journal of Early Childhood*, 39(3), 14–22.

Hohmann, M., Banet, B., & Weikart, D. (1979). *Young Children in Action*. Ypsilanti, MI: The High/Scope Press.

Hung, R. (2008). Educating for and through nature: A Merleau-Pontian Approach. *Studies in Philosophy and Education*, 27(5), 355–67. doi: http://dx.doi.org/10.1007/s11217-007-9059-x.

Hussain, H., Conner, L., & Mayo, E. (2014). Envisioning curriculum as six simultaneities. *Complicity: An International Journal of Complexity and Education*, 11(1), 59–84.

References

International Association for Public Participation Australia (iap2). (nd). *Foundations of public participation*. Wollongong, NSW: International Association for Public Participation Australia. Online at: www.iap2.org.au/resources/iap2s-foundations-of-public-participation.

IARC. (2011). Carcinogenicity of radiofrequency electromagnetic fields. *The Lancet*, 12 (July), 624–6. Online at: www.thelancet.com/oncology.

Irvine, S. (2013). Still valuing play. *Reflections,* August (50), 4–8. Online at: www.gowrie-tas.com.au.

Jacobs, C., Oliver, D., & Heracleous, L. (2013). Diagnosing organizational identity beliefs by eliciting complex, multimodal metaphors. *The Journal of Applied Behavioral Science*, 49(4), 485–507. doi: http://dx.doi.org/10.177/0021886313485999.

Jaskulsky, L., & Besel, R. (2013). Words that (don't) matter: An exploratory study of four climate change names in environmental discourse. *Applied Environmental Education & Communication*, 12(1), 38–45. doi: http://dx.doi.org/10.1080/1533015X.2013.795836.

Jenkins, M. (2010). Ethnographic writing is as good as ten mothers. *Qualitative Inquiry*, 16(2), 83–9. doi: http://dx.doi.org/10.1177/1077800409350700.

Jones, E., & Nimmo, J. (1994). *Emergent Curriculum*. Washington, DC: NAEYC.

Kagan, S., & Kauerz, K. (Eds.). (2012). *Early Childhood Systems: Transforming early learning*. New York, NY: Teachers College Press.

Kagan, S., & Rigby, E. (2003). *Policy Matters: Setting and measuring benchmarks for state policies – Improving the readiness of children for school*. Washington, DC: Center for the Study of Social Policy. Online at: www.aecf.org/KnowledgeCenter/Publications.aspx?pubguid=%7BC3816332-6C40-4372-8B83-FB36A8D2A3D7%7D or http://www.aecf.org/upload/publicationfiles/ch3622h498.pdf.

Kagan, S., Tarrant, K., & Kauerz, K. (2012) Planning an early childhood system, policies and principles matter. Chapter 8. In S. Kagan & K. Kauerz (Eds.), *Early Childhood Systems: Transforming early learning* (pp. 137–154). New York, NY: Teachers College Press.

Kalantzis, M., & Cope, B. (2008). *New Learning: Elements of a science of education*. Port Melbourne, VIC: Cambridge University Press.

Kania, J. & Kramer, M. (2011). Collective impact. *Stanford Social Innovation Review*. Online at: http://www.ssireview.org/articles/entry/collective_impact.

Karliner, J. (2005). *The Little Green Schoolhouse Report: Thinking big about ecological sustainability, children's environmental health and K–12 Education in the USA*. Berkeley, CA: Green School Initiative. Retrieved from: http://www.greenschools.net/downloads/little%20green%20schoolhouse%20report.pdf.

References

Katz, L., & Chard, S. (2000). *Engaging Children's Minds: The project approach* (2nd ed.). Stamford, CT: Ablex Publishing Corp.

Katz, L., & Ward, E. (Eds.). (1993). *Ethical Behavior in Early Childhood Education, Exp. Ed.* Washington, DC: NAEYC.

Kauerz, K., & Kagan, S. (2012). Governance and early childhood systems – different forms, similar goals, Chapter 5. In S. Kagan & K. Kauerz (Eds.), *Early Childhood Systems: Transforming early learning* (pp. 87–103). New York, NY: Teachers College Press.

Kaza, S. (2008). *Mindfully Green: A personal and spiritual guide to whole earth thinking*. Boston, MA: Shambhala Publications, Inc.

Kennedy, A. (2011). Pedagogy matters. *Every Child*, 17(3), 24–5.

Kenny, K., & Euchler, G. (2012). Some good clean fun: Humour, control and subversion in an advertising agency. *Gender, Work and Organization*, 19(3), 303–23.

Kinsella, R. (2008). *Everyday learning about being green*. Everyday Learning Series, Vol. 6, no. 2. Watson, ACT: ECA.

Knight, A. (Ed.). (2010). *Australian Mini Thesaurus*. South Melbourne, VIC: Oxford University Press.

Knight, S. (2011). Forest School as a way of learning in the outdoors in the UK. *International Journal for Cross-Disciplinary Subjects in Education, Special issue*, 1(1), 590–95.

Kolb, D. (2008). Exploring the metaphor of connectivity: Attributes, dimensions and duality. *Organization Studies*, 29(10), 127–44. doi: http://dx.doi.org/10.1177/0170840607084574.

Korff, J. (nd). *Acknowledging Country: Creative Spirits – the art of touching spirit and soul*. Retrieved 17 April 2013, from: www.creativespirits.info/.

Krieg, S., Davis, K., & Smith, K. A. (2014). Exploring the dance of early childhood educational leadership. *Australasian Journal of Early Childhood*, 39(1), 73–80.

Lake, R. (Ed.). (2012). *Dear Nel: Opening the circles of care (Letters to Nel Noddings)*. New York, NY: Teachers College Press.

Leclercq-Vandelannoitte, A. (2011). Organizations as discursive constructions: A Foucauldian approach. *Organizational Studies*, 32(9), 1247–71. doi: http://dx.doi.org/10.1177/0170840611411395.

Lee, C. (2012). 'Stories from the Heart': Connecting children and families with our Earth. In N. McCrea (Ed.), *Research in Practice Series* (Vol. 19 (3)). Deakin West, ACT: ECA, Inc.

Lillard, A. (2005). *Montessori: The science behind the genius*. New York, NY: Oxford University Press, Inc.

References

Lillard, A. (2013). Playful learning and Montessori education. *American Journal of Play*, 5(2), 157–86.

Lindholdt, P. (1999). Writing from a sense of place. *The Journal of Environmental Education*, 30(4), 4–10. doi: http://dx.doi.org/10.1080/00958969909601878.

Lindon, J., & Lindon, L. (2011). *Leadership and Early Years Professionalism*. London, ENG: Hodder Education.

Linke, P., & Radich, J. (2010). Children's Resilience: Working with the Early Years Learning Framework. In J. Connor (Ed.), *Research in Practice Series* (Vol. 17 (4)). Deakin West, ACT: ECA, Inc.

Linstead, S., Marechal, G., & Griffin, R. (2014). Theorizing and researching the dark side of organization. *Organization Studies*, 35(2), 165–88. doi: http://dx.doi.org/10.1177/0170840613515402.

Littledyke, R., & McCrea, N. (2009). Chapter 4, Starting sustainability early: Young children exploring people and places. In M. Littledyke, N. Taylor & C. Eames (Eds.), *Education for Sustainability in the Primary Curriculum: A Guide for Teachers* (pp. 39–56). South Yarra, VIC: Palgrave Macmillan.

Logan, H., Sumsion, J., & Press, F. (2013). The Child Care Act 1972: A critical juncture in Australian ECEC and the emergence of 'quality'. *Australasian Journal of Early Childhood – online annex*, 38(4), 84–91.

Macbeath, J. (2006). Leadership for Learning: A quest for meaning. *Leading & Managing*, 12(2), 1–9.

Macfarlane, K., & Cartmel, J. (2012). Circles of change revisited: Building leadership, scholarship and professional identity in the children's services sector. *Professional Development in Education*, 38(5), 845–61. doi: http://dx.doi.org/10.1080/19415257.2012.680603.

MacNaughton, G., & Hughes, P. (2011). *Parents and Professionals in Early Childhood Settings*. Berkshire, ENG: Open University Press, McGraw-Hill Education.

MacNaughton, G., & Williams, G. (2009). *Techniques for Teaching Young Children: Choices for theory and practice*, (3rd ed.). Frenchs Forest, NSW: Pearson Education Australia.

Malaguzzi, L. (Ed.). (1987). *I Centro Linguaggi dei Bambini: The hundred languages of children*. Reggio Emilia, Italy: Comune di Reggio Emilia, Assessorato all'istruzione.

Markiewicz, A. (2012). Closing the gap through respect, relevance, reciprocity and responsibility: Issues in the evaluation of programs for Indigenous communities in Australia. *Evaluation Journal of Australasia*, 12(1), 19–25.

Marotz, L., & Lawson, A. (2007). *Motivational Leadership in Early Childhood Education*. Clifton Park, NY: Thomson Delmar Learning.

References

Marsh, S., **Waniganayake, M.**, & **Gibson, I.** (2013). Scaffolding leadership learning in school education: Insights from a factor analysis of research conducted in Australian independent schools. *Educational Management Administration & Leadership, online first*, 1–17. doi: http://dx.doi.org/10.1177/1741143213502197.

Martin, K. (2007a). Ma(r)king tracks and reconceptualising Aboriginal early childhood education: An Aboriginal Australian perspective. *Childrenz Issues*, 11(1), 15–20. Online at: http://search.informit.com.au/documentSummary;dn=367385701511095;res=IELNZC>.

Martin, K. (2007b). Here we go 'round the broombie tree: Aboriginal early childhood realities and experiences in early childhood services, Chapter 2. In J. Ailwood (Ed.), *Early Childhood in Australia* (pp. 18–34). Frenchs Forest, NSW: Pearson Education Australia.

Martusewicz, R., **Edmundson, J.**, & **Kahn, R.** (2012). On membership, humility, and pedagogical responsibilities: A correspondence on the work of Wendell Berry. *Mid-Western Educational Researcher*, 25(3, Summer), 44–68. Online at: www.eric.ed.gov/?id=EJ998229.

Maynard, T. (2007). Encounters with Forest School and Foucault: A risky business? *Education 3–13*, 35(4), 379–91.

McCormilla, L. (2012). *How to Develop and Update Policies Successfully (without the stress)*. Malaga, WA Child Australia & Professional Support Coordinators National Alliance. Online at: www.pscalliance.org.au.

McCotter, S. (2001). Collaborative groups as professional development. *Teaching and Teacher Education*, 17, 685–704.

McCoy, A., **Rose, D.**, & **Connolly, M.** (2013). Developing evaluation cultures in human service organisations. *Evaluation Journal of Australasia*, 13(1), 15–20.

McCrea, N. (1989). Regulations: A magic pudding or Swiss cheese? Minimum standards – quality standards. *Australian Journal of Early Childhood*, 14(4), 8–15.

McCrea, N. (2002). Learn leading for authenticity – balancing ideals and realities about leadership. *Child Care Information Exchange*, Sep/Oct(147), 10–14.

McCrea, N. (2006). *Everyday learning about healthy bodies*. Everyday learning series, vol. 4, no. 1. Watson, ACT: ECA.

McCrea, N. (2008). What are your green educational values? Consider: children as veggie gardeners. *Every Child*, 14(4), 6–7.

McCrea, N. (2014). Food first: beginning steps towards children's sustainable education, Chapter 9. In J. Davis (Ed.), *Young Children and the Environment: Early education for sustainability*, (2nd ed.). (pp. 189–210). Port Melbourne, VIC: Cambridge University Press.

References

McCrea, N., & Ehrich, L. (1999). Changing leaders' educational hearts. *Educational Management & Administration*, 27(4), 431–40, 455. doi: http://dx.doi.org/10.1177/0263211X990274009.

McCrea, N. & Littledyke, R. (in press). Young children sampling sustainable learning as 'Healthier me', Chapter 4. In N. Taylor, F. Quinn & C. Eames (Eds.), *Teaching for the future: Education for sustainability in primary schools*. Rotterdam, Netherlands: Sense Publishers.

McCrea, N., & Piscitelli, B. (1989a). *An Issues Paper on Voluntary Accreditation of Early Childhood Programs within Queensland*. Kelvin Grove, QLD: Brisbane College of Advanced Education.

McCrea, N., & Piscitelli, B. (1989b). *Voluntary Accreditation of Early Childhood Programs in Queensland: A report to the Minister for Family Services*. Kelvin Grove, QLD: Brisbane College of Advanced Education.

McCrea, N., & Piscitelli, B. (Eds.). (1991). *Handbook of High Quality Criteria for Early Childhood Programs: A revised field guide for planning and evaluating early childhood environments*. Kelvin Grove, QLD: Queensland University of Technology.

McLachlan, C. (2011). An analysis of New Zealand's changing history, policies and approaches to early childhood education. *Australasian Journal of Early Childhood*, 36(3), 36–44.

McLachlan, C., Fleer, M., & Edwards, S. (2013). *Early Childhood Curriculum: Planning, assessment and implementation* (2nd ed.). Port Melbourne, VIC: Cambridge University Press.

McLuhan, M. (1964). *Understanding Media: The extensions of man*. Cambridge, MA: MIT Press.

McNicol, H., Davis, J., & O'Brien, K. (2011). An ecological footprint for an early learning centre: Identifying opportunities for early childhood sustainability education through interdisciplinary research. *Environmental Education Research*, 17(5), 689–704. doi: http://dx.doi.org/10.1080/14504622.572161.

Meindl, J., Ehrlich, S., & Dukerich, J. (1985). The romance of leadership. *Administrative Science Quarterly*, 30(1), 78–102. Stable URL: http://www.jsotr.org/stable/239813.

Mellor, E. (1990). *Stepping Stones: The development of early childhood services in Australia*. Sydney, NSW: Harcourt, Brace, Jovanovich.

Mevawalla, Z. (2013). The Crucible: Adding complexity to the question of social justice in early childhood development. *Contemporary Issues in Early Childhood*, 14(4), 290–99. doi: http://dx.doi.org/10.2304/ciec.2013.14.4.290.

Miller, M. (2010). Repositioning an ethic of sustainability in early childhood education, with Reconciliation as central, Chapter 6. In J. Davis (Ed.), *Young Children and the Environment, Early Education for Sustainability* (pp. 185–211). Port Melbourne, VIC: Cambridge University Press.

Mills-Bayne, M. (2013). The MENtor program for males in early childhood education. *Every Child*, 19(3), 40–41.

Ministerial Council. (2011). *Education and Care Services National Regulations*. Canberra, ACT: MCEECDYA. Retrieved from NSW Legislation website at: www.acecqa.gov.au/ArticleCategory.aspx?pid=372&gcpid=2.

Ministry of Education Singapore. (2012). *Nurturing Early Learners: A curriculum framework for kindergartens in Singapore*. Singapore: Ministry of Education (MoeS). Online at: www.moe.gov.sg/education/preschool.

Ministry of Education Singapore. (2013a). *Nurturing Early Learners, Educators' Guide: Overview*. Singapore: Ministry of Education (MoeS). Online at: www.moe.gov.sg/education/preschool.

Ministry of Education Singapore. (2013b). *Nurturing Early Learners, Framework for Mother Tongue Languages*. Singapore: Ministry of Education (MoeS). Online at: www.moe.gov.sg/education/preschool.

Mitchell, C., & Weber, S. (1999). *Reinventing Ourselves as Teachers: Beyond nostalgia*. London, ENG: RoutledgeFalmer.

Mitchell, M. (2014). *What Does the Children's Rights Report 2013 Say? Child-friendly version*. Australian Human Rights Commission. Online at: www.humanrights.gov.au/publications/what-does-children-s-rights-report-2013-say.

Moore, B. (2010). *What's Their Story?: A history of Australian words*. South Melbourne, VIC: Oxford University Press Australia & New Zealand.

Moore, B. (Ed.) (2009). *Australian Concise Oxford Dictionary* (5th ed.). South Melbourne, VIC: Oxford University Press.

Morgan, G. (2006). *Images of Organization*, (updated ed.). Thousand Oaks, CA: Sage Publications, Inc.

Mundine, K., & Giugni, M. (2006). Diversity and Difference: Lighting the spirit of identity. In L. Fasoli (Ed.), *Research in Practice Series* (Vol. 13 (3)). Watson, ACT: ECA, Inc.

Murray, C., Crooke, M., & O'Doherty, A. (2006). *Diversity and equality guidelines for childcare providers, national childcare strategy 2006–2010*. Dublin, IRE: OMC/DCYA. Online at: www.dcya.gov.ie/documents/childcare/diversity_and_equality.pdf.

NAEYC. (1991). *Accreditation Criteria & Procedures of the National Academy of Early Childhood Programs* (revised ed.). Washington, DC: NAEYC.

NAEYC. (1998). *Accreditation Criteria & Procedures of the National Association for the Education of Young Children* (1998 ed.) Washington, DC: NAEYC.

References

NAEYC. (2007). *NAEYC Early Childhood Program Standards and Accreditation Criteria: The Mark of Quality in Early Childhood Education*. Washington, DC: NAEYC.

NAEYC. (2010). Let's celebrate! 25 years of NAEYC accreditation of programs for young children. *Young Children*, 65(6, Nov), 82–5.

Noddings, N. (2003). *Happiness and Education*. New York, NY: Cambridge University Press.

Noddings, N. (2006). *Critical Lessons: What our schools should teach*. New York, NY: Cambridge University Press.

Noddings, N. (2007). Teaching themes of care. *Character*, XIV(2), 1–5.

Noddings, N. (2012). The caring relation in teaching. *Oxford Review of Education*, 38(6), 771–81. doi: http://dx.doi.org/10.1080/03054985.2012.745047.

Nolan, A., & Reynolds, B. (2008). Portfolios: Documenting a journey. In J. Krabman (Ed.), *Research in Practice Series* (Vol. 15 (4)). Watson, ACT: ECA, Inc.

Nolan, M. (2007). *Mentor Coaching and Leadership in Early Care and Education*. Clifton Park, NY: Thomson, Delmar Learning.

NSW Department of Local Government. (2007). *Engaging with local Aboriginal communities: A resource kit for local governments in NSW*. Sydney, NSW: NSW Dep of Local Government. Retrieved from: www.dlg.nsw.gov.au.

Nuttall, J. (2003). Influences on the co-construction of the teacher role in early childhood curriculum: Some examples from a New Zealand childcare centre. *International Journal of Early Years Education*, 11(1), 23–31. doi: http://dx.doi.org/10.1080/0966976032000066064.

NZ Ministry of Education. (1996). *Te Whāriki, He Whāriki Matauranga mo ngo Mokopuna o Aotearoa, Early Childhood Curriculum*. Wellington, NZ: Ministry of Education. Online at: http://www.educate.ece.govt.nz.

NZ Ministry of Education. (2011). *Licensing Criteria for Early Childhood Education and Care Centres 2008 & Early Childhood Education Curriculum Framework*. Wellington, NZ: New Zealand Government. Online at: www.lead.ece.govt.nz.

OECD (2001). *Starting Strong I – Early Childhood Education and Care*. Online at: www.oecd.org/edu/earlychildhood.

OECD (2006). *Starting Strong II – Early Childhood Education and Care*. Online at: www.oecd.org/edu/earlychildhood.

Page, J. (2000). *Reframing the Early Childhood Curriculum: Educational imperatives for the future*. London, ENG: RoutledgeFalmer.

References

Pittinsky, T. (2005). *Allophilia and Intergroup Leadership.* John F. Kennedy School of Government Faculty Research Working Papers Series; RWP05-038. Cambridge, MA: Harvard University. Retrieved from: http://research.hks.harvard.edu/publications/working-papers/faculty_name.aspx?&PersonId=169.

Pramling Samuelsson, I., & Wagner, J. (2012). Open appeal to local, national, regional and global leaders to secure the world's future: Prioritize early childhood development, education, and care. *International Journal of Early Childhood*, 44(3), 341–6. doi: http://dx.doi.org/10.1007/s13158-012-0071-0.

Pratt, R. (2010). Practical possibilities and pedagogical approaches for early childhood education for sustainability, Chapter 4. In J. Davis (Ed.), *Young Children and the Environment: Early education for sustainability* (pp. 104–53). Port Melbourne, VIC: Cambridge University Press.

Press, F., & Wong, S. (2013). *A Voice for Young Children: 75 years of Early Childhood Australia.* Deakin West, ACT: ECA.

Press, F., & Woodrow, C. (2005). Commodification, corporatisation and children's spaces. *Australian Journal of Education*, 49(3), 278–91.

Prince, L. (2005). Eating the menu rather than the dinner: Tao and leadership. *Leadership*, 1(1), 105–26. doi: http://dx.doi.org/10.1177/1742715005049355.

Prior, J., & Gerard, M. (2007). *Family Involvement in Early Childhood Education: Research into practice.* Clifton Park, NY: Thomson Delmar Learning.

Probyn, E. (2003). Eating into ethics: Passion, food and journalism, Chapter 7. In C. Lumby & E. Probyn (Eds.), *Remote Control: New media, new ethics* (pp. 107–132). Cambridge, ENG: Cambridge University Press.

Pullen, A., & Simpson, R. (2009). Managing difference in feminized work: Men, otherness and social practice. *Human Relations*, 62(4), 561–87. doi: http://dx.doi.org/10.1177/0018726708101989.

Pye, A. (2005). Leadership and organizing: Sensemaking in action. *Leadership*, 1(1), 31–50. doi: http://dx.doi.org/10.1177/1742715005049349.

QDETE. (2013). *Foundations for Success guideline for extending and enriching learning for Aboriginal and Torres Strait Islander children in the Kindergarten year.* Brisbane, QLD: Queensland Government. Retrieved from: http://deta.qld.gov.au/indigenous/services/foundations.html.

Rafanello, D. (2006). Publish your writing: Sharing your ideas with the early childhood community. *Child Care Information Exchange, Nov/Dec(184)*, 68–71.

Rao, S. (comp./ed.) (2002). *Zen Heart, Zen Mind: The teachings of Zen master Ama Samy.* Chennai, India: Cre-A.

Richardson, C. (2011). Respecting diversity: Articulating early childhood practice. In J. Connor (Ed.), *Research in Practice Series* (Vol. 18 (1)). Deakin West, ACT: ECA, Inc.

Riojas-Cortez, M., & Flores, B. (2009). Supporting preschoolers' social development in school through funds of knowledge. *Journal of Early Childhood Research*, 7(2), 185–99. doi: http://ecr.sagepub.com/content/7/2/185.

Ritchie, J. (2012). Titiro Whakamuri, Hoki Whakamue: Respectful integration of Maori perspectives within early childhood environmental education. *Canadian Journal of Environmental Education*, 17, 62–79.

Ritchie, J. (2013). Sustainability and relationality within early childhood care and education settings in Aotearoa New Zealand. *International Journal of Early Childhood*, 45(3), 307–26. doi: http://dx.doi.org/10.1007/s13158-013-0079-0.

Ritchie, J., Duhn, I., Rau, C., & Craw, J. (2010). *Titiro Whakamuri, Hoki Whakamua. We are the future, the present and the past: Caring for self, others and the environment in early years' teaching and learning*. Wellington, NZ: New Zealand Council for Educational Research (NZCER). Online at: www.tlri.org.nz.

Rivalland, C. (2007). When are beliefs just 'the tip of the iceberg'? Exploring early childhood professionals' beliefs and practices about teaching and learning. *Australian Journal of Early Childhood*, 32(1), 30–37.

Roberts, J. (1997). *Maybanke Anderson: Sex, suffrage & social reform*, (2nd ed.). Avalon, NSW: Ruskin Rowe Press.

Roberts, L., Dutton, J., Spreitzer, G., Heaphy, E., & Quinn, R. (2005). Composing the reflected best-self portrait: Building pathways for becoming extraordinary in work organizations. *The Academy of Management Review*, 30(4), 712–36. Stable URL: http://www.jstor.org/stable/20159164.

Robertson, J. (2013). Learning leadership. *Leading & Managing*, 19(2), 54–69.

Rodd, J. (2013). *Leadership in Early Childhood: The pathway to professionalism* (4th ed.). Crows Nest, NSW: Allen & Unwin.

Rogoff, B. (2003). *The Cultural Nature of Human Development*. Oxford, ENG: Oxford University Press.

Rousseau, J. (1762/2010). *Emile*. La Vergne, TN: Book Jungle.

Running Wolf, P., & Rickard, J. (2003). Talking circles: A Native American approach to experiential learning. *Journal of Multicultural Counseling and Development*, 31(1), 39–43.

Sakellari, M., & Skanavis, C. (2013). Environmental behavior and gender: An emerging area of concern for environmental education research. *Applied Environmental Education & Communication*, 12(2), 77–87. doi: http://dx.doi.org/10.1080/1533015X.2013.820633.

References

Sandberg, A., & Arlemalm-Hagser, E. (2011). The Swedish National Curriculum: Play and learning with fundamental values in focus. *Australasian Journal of Early Childhood*, 36(1), 44–50.

Sara, H. (2009). Optimistic carers and children: Pathways to confidence and wellbeing. In M. Young (Ed.), *Research in Practice Series* (Vol. 16 (3)). Deakin West, ACT: ECA, Inc.

Schein, E. (1990). Organizational Culture. *American Psychologist*, 45(2), 109–19.

Schein, E. (1992). Coming to a new awareness of organizational culture, Chapter 14. In G. Salaman (Ed.), *Human Resource Strategies* (pp. 237–53). London, ENG: The Open University & Sage Publications.

Schein, E. (2010). *Organizational Culture and Leadership* (4th ed.). [e-book]. San Francisco, CA: Jossey-Bass.

Sciarra, D., Dorsey, A., Lynch, E., & Adams, S. (2013). *Developing and Administering a Child Care and Education Program*, (8th ed.). Belmont, CA: Wadsworth/Cengage Learning.

Sellers, M. (2013). *Young Children Becoming Curriculum: Deleuze, Te Whariki and curricular understandings*. Milton Park, ENG: Routledge.

Semann, A., & Soper, R. (2012). Pedagogical leadership: Exploring new terrain and provocations. *Reflections*, Winter (47), 16–17.

Sergiovanni, T. (1992). *Moral Leadership: Getting to the heart of school improvement*. San Francisco, CA: Jossey-Bass Inc Publishers.

Shell, B. (nd). *A look at Waldorf and Montessori education in the early childhood programs*. Online at: www.whywaldorfworks.org/02_W-Education/documents/ALookatWaldorfandMontessori.pdf.

Sims, M. (2011a). *Social Inclusion and the Early Years Learning Framework: A way of working*. Castle Hill, NSW: Pademelon Press.

Sims, M. (2011b). *Early childhood and education services for Indigenous children prior to starting school, Resource sheet no. 7*. Canberra: Australian Institute of Health and Welfare and Australian Institute of Family Studies. Retrieved from: www.aihw.gov.au/uploadedFiles/ClosingTheGap/Content/Publications/2011/ctgc-rs07.pdf.

Sims, M., & Hutchins, T. (2011). *Program Planning for Infants and Toddlers: In search of relationships* (2nd ed.). Castle Hill, NSW: Pademelon Press.

Sinclair, A. (2007). *Leadership for the Disillusioned: Moving beyond myths and heroes to leading that liberates*. Crows Nest, NSW: Allen & Unwin.

Sinclair, A. (2010). Placing self: How might we place ourselves in leadership studies differently? *Leadership*, 6(4), 447–60. doi: http://dx.doi.org/10.1177/1742715010379312.

References

Skattebol, J. (2010). Affect: A tool to support pedagogical change. *Discourse: Studies in the Cultural Politics of Education*, 31(1), 75–91. doi: http://dx.doi.org/10.1080/01596300903465435.

SNAICC. (2013). Building stronger communities: Aboriginal and Torres Strait Islander early learning spaces. *Every Child*, 19(2), 10–11.

South Australian Department of Education and Children's Services. (2010). *Assessing for Learning and Development in the Early Years using Observation Scales: Reflect, respect, relate*. Hindmarsh, SA: DECS Publishing.

Spicer, A., & Alvesson, M. (2011). Metaphors for leadership, Chapter 3. In M. Alvesson & A. Spicer (Eds.), *Metaphors We Lead By: Understanding leadership in the real world* (pp. 31–50). Milton Park, ENG: Routledge.

Spodek, B. (1973). *Early Childhood Education*. Englewood Cliffs, NJ: Prentice-Hall, Inc.

Stanger, N. (2011). Moving "eco" back into socio-ecological models: A proposal to reorient ecological literacy into human development models and school systems. *Human Ecology Review*, 18(2), 167–73.

Stober, S., Brown, T., & Cullen, S. (2013). *Nature-centered Leadership: An aspirational narrative*. Champaign, IL: Common Ground Publishing, LLC.

Stonehouse, A. (1991). Our Code of Ethics at Work. In M. Fleer (Ed.), *AECA Resource Booklets* (Vol. May 1991 (2)). Watson, ACT: AECA, Inc.

Stuhmcke, S. (2012). *Children as change agents for sustainabilty: An action research case study in a kindergarten*. (Professional Doctorate), Queensland University of Technology, Kelvin Grove, Brisbane, QLD. (ePrints ID code 61005).

Sturken, M., & Cartwright, L. (2009). *Practices of Looking: An introduction to visual culture*, (2nd ed.). New York, NY: Oxford University Press.

Sullivan, D. (2010). *Learning to lead: Effective leadership skills for teachers of young children*, (2nd ed.). St Paul, MN: Redleaf Press.

Sumsion, J., (2006). From Whitlam to economic rationalism and beyond: A conceptual framework for political activism in children's services. *Australian Journal of Early Childhood*, 31(1), 1–9.

Sumsion, J., Barnes, S., Cheeseman, S., Harrison, L., Kennedy, A. & Stonehouse, A. (2009). Insider perspectives on developing 'Belonging, Being and Becoming: The Early Years Learning Framework for Australia'. *Australasian Journal of Early Childhood*, 34(4), 4–13.

Summerville, J., & Hokanson, J. (2013). *Cultural Perspectives on Learning: Building the foundations for working with Aboriginal & Torres Strait Islander children and families*. Darwin,

References

NT: Shift Consulting Group Pty Ltd. Online at: http://www.childaustralia.org.au/Resources/Cultural-Perspectives-on-Learning.aspx.

Sveningsson, S., & Larsson, M. (2006). Fantasies of Leadership: Identity work. *Leadership*, 2(2), 203–24. doi: http://dx.doi.org/10.1177/1742715006062935.

Swick, K., & Williams, R. (2006). An analysis of Bronfenbrenner's bio-ecological perspective for early childhood educators: Implications for working with families experiencing stress. *Early Childhood Education Journal*, 33(5), 371–8. doi: http://dx.doi.org/10.1007/s10643-006-0078-y.

Talan, T. N., & Bloom, P. J. (2011). *The Program Administration Scale: Measuring early childhood leadership and management* (2nd ed.). New York, NY: Teacher's College Press.

Tayler, C. (2007). Comparative education – studying early childhood education and care, Chapter 5. In J. Ailwood (Ed.), *Early Childhood in Australia: Historical and comparative contexts* (pp. 68–76). Frenchs Forest, NSW: Pearson Education Australia.

Taylor, A. (2013). *Reconfiguring the Natures of Childhood*. Milton Park, ENG: Routledge, Taylor & Francis Group.

Tickner, J., Raffensperger, C., & Myers, N. (nd). *The Precautionary Principle in Action: A handbook*. Windsor, ND: Science and Environmental Health Network. Online at: www.environmentalcommons.org/precaution-handbook.pdf.

Tierney, W. (2010). Globalization and life history research: Fragments of a life foretold. *International Journal of Qualitative Studies in Education*, 23(2), 129–46. doi: http://dx.doi.org/10.1080/09518390903120351.

Trentmann, F. (2012). The politics of everyday life, Chapter 27. In F. Trentmann (Ed.), *The Oxford Handbook of The History of Consumption* (pp. 521–47). Oxford, ENG: Oxford University Press.

Umbreit, M. (2003). *Talking Circles*. Regents of the University of Minnesota. Online at: www.cehd.umn.edu/ssw/rip/resources/rj_dialogue_resources/Peacemaking_Healing_Circles/Talking_Circles.pdf.

Ungar, M., Ghazinour, M., & Richter, J. (2013). Annual Research Review: What is resilience within the social ecology of human development? *The Journal of Child Psychology and Psychiatry*, 54(4), 348–66. doi: http://dx.doi.org/10.1111/jcpp.12025.

UNICEF, & Bernard van Leer Foundation. (2006). *A Guide to General Comment 7: 'Implementing Child Rights in Early Childhood'*. The Hague: Bernard van Leer Foundation. Retrieved from: http://www.unicef.org/earlychildhood/files/Guide_to_GC7.pdf; or http://bernardvanleer.org/a_guide_to_general_comment_7_implementing_child_rights_in_early_childhood; (with background papers): http://www.bernardvanleer.org/English/Home/Other-resources/General-Comment-7/A-guide-to-General-Comment-7-Background-papers.html.

References

Uusiautti, S. (2013). An action-oriented perspective on caring leadership: A qualitative study of higher education administrators' positive leadership experiences. *International Journal of Leadership in Education: Theory and Practice*, 16(4), 482–96. doi: http://dx.doi.org/10.1080/13603124.2013.770077.

Vegas, E., & Santibanez, L. (2010). *The Promise of Early Childhood Development in Latin America and the Caribbean*. Washington, DC: The World Bank. Online at: http://siteresources.worldbank.org/EDUCATION/Resources/278200-1099079877269/547664-1099079922573/ECD_LAC.pdf.

Verducci, S. (2012). Theory in practice: Nel Nodding's mentoring. In R. Lake (Ed.), *Dear Nel: Opening the circles of care (letters to Nel Noddings)* (pp. 125–9). New York, NY: Teachers College Press.

Victorian Curriculum and Assessment Authority. (2008). *Analysis of Curriculum/Learning Frameworks for the Early Years (Birth to Age 8)*. East Melbourne, VIC: VCAA. Online at: http://docs.education.gov.au/system/files/doc/other/analysis_of_curriculumlearning_frameworks_for_the_early_years_birth_to_age_8.pdf.

Wangmann, J. (1991). *Accreditation of Early Childhood Services in Australia*. Canberra, ACT: Child Care Division, Commonwealth of Australia.

Waniganayake, M., Cheeseman, S., Fenech, M., Hadley, F., & Shepherd, S. (2012). *Leadership: Contexts and complexities in early childhood education*. South Melbourne, VIC: Oxford University Press Australia & New Zealand.

Warner, L., & Grint, K. (2006). American Indian ways of leading and knowing. *Leadership*, 2(2), 225–44. doi: http://dx.doi.org/10.1177/1742715006062936.

Waters, J. (2007). *Sowing Seeds of Peace: Australia and the World Organisation for Early Childhood Education*. Melbourne, VIC: OMEP Australia.

Wenger-Trayner, E., & Wenger-Trayner, B. (nd). *Leadership groups, distributed leadership in social learning*. Online at: http://wenger-trayner.com/blog/leadership-groups-for-social-learning.

Whitington, V. (2014). Agency in the early years. In P. Linke (Ed.), *Everyday Learning Series*, (Vol. 12 (1)). Deakin West, ACT: ECA, Inc.

Whitsel, M., & Lapham, K. (2014). Increasing programme effectiveness through parent empowerment: The Getting Ready for School project in Tajikistan. *International Journal of Early Years Education*, 22(1), 105–16. doi: http://dx.doi.org/10.1080/09669760.2013.809658.

WHO. (2011). *Press Release No. 208: IARC classifies radiofrequency electromagnetic fields as possibly carcinogenic to humans*. Online at: http://www.iarc.fr/en/media-centre/pr/2011/pdfs/pr208_E.pdf.

References

Widger, S., & Schofield, A. (2012). Interaction or interruption?: Five child-centred philosophical perspectives. *Australasian Journal of Early Childhood*, 37(4), 29–32.

Wielkiewicz, R., & Stelzner, S. (2005). An ecological perspective on leadership theory, research, and practice. *Review of General Psychology*, 9(4), 326–41. doi: http://dx.doi.org/10.1037/1089-2680.9.4.326.

Wilson, G. (1998). *Complete book of fishing knots and rigs*. Bayswater, VIC: Australian Fishing Network.

Wong, K. (2001). Chinese culture and leadership. *International Journal of Leadership in Education: Theory and Practice*, 4(4), 309–19. doi: http://dx.doi.org/10.1080/13603120110077990.

Wong, S. (2013). A 'Humanitarian Idea': Using a historical lens to reflect on social justice in early childhood education and care. *Contemporary Issues in Early Childhood*, 14(4), 311–23. doi: http://dx.doi.org/10.2304/ciec.2013.14.4.311.

Wong, S., & Turner, K. (2014). Constructions of social inclusion within Australian early childhood education and care policy documents. *Contemporary Issues in Early Childhood*, 15(1), 54–68. doi: http://dx.doi.org/10.2304/ciec.2014.15.1.54.

Woodrow, C. (1999). Revisiting images of the child in early childhood education: Reflections and considerations. *Australian Journal of Early Childhood*, 24(4), 7–12.

Woodrow, C. (2014). Editorial: Refocusing our attention to children's learning and the complex interplay of context and culture. *International Journal of Early Years Education*, 22(1), 1–3. doi: http://dx.doi.org/10.1080/09669760.2014.902639.

Woodrow, C., & Busch, G. (2008). Repositioning early childhood leadership as action and activism. *European Early Childhood Education Research Journal*, 16(1), 83–93. doi: http://dx.doi.org/10.1080/13502930801897053.

Wooltorton, S., & Bennell, D. (2007). Ecological literacy: Noongar way. *Every Child*, 13(4), 30–31.

Zink, R. (2010). Coming to know oneself through experiential education. *Discourse: Studies in the Cultural Politics of Education*, 31(2), 209–19. doi: http://dx.doi.org/10.1080/01596301003679727.

Index

ability repertoires 85
Aboriginal Dialect 154
Aboriginal peoples
  children, views of 150
  kin group spirituality 149–50
  language, Dialect 154
  ways of learning 23
Aboriginal worldviews 61
Aboriginality 149
accreditation 21
acknowledgement (of cultural identity) 23
action(s) 111, 141
  action competencies 19, 22
  action-oriented leadership/leading-managing 25
  action plans for reconciliation 23, 111
  best practice values and actions 21
  caring actions 26
  multiple staffing actions 85
  professional actions 105
  related to embracing rights 150
  roles with actions – team stakeholders 84
activism 158
  advocacy–activism distinction 160
acts (State) 97
adaptability 93
adult learning 51
adult routines 135
adult–child ratios 86
advocacy 53, 72, 74, 156
  advocacy attributes 158
  advocacy everywhere 160
  advocacy–activism distinction 160
  change, futures and advocating 153
  child advocacy 159
  doing advocacy 150
  eco-advocacy 151
  for educators, importance of 156
  everyday advocacy 148
  leading, internal and wider world advocacy 148
  reflections 151, 154, 159
  responsibilities beyond-the-fence 157–60
  rights advocacy 23
  rights advocates 147
  true advocacy 148
  views – idealised leading-managing 147
affect theories 20
affirming 19
agency 129, 132
allophilia 17
ambience 75
ambiguity 27
analysing 85
andragogy 51
anti-bias 132
Appreciative Inquiry 63
appreciative inquiry assumptions 94
artefacts 139
assessing 85
attitude 17
Australian Association for Environmental Education 72
Australian Children's Education and Care Quality Authority (ACECQA) 58, 69, 86
Australian Research Alliance for Children and Youth (ARACY)
  policy beyond-the-fence 111
  The Nest 111
authority (division of) 25

Index

autobiography 4, 50, 52
autoethnography 52
awareness 10–11
  global awareness, acting with 157
  social awareness 23

baggage 137
becoming (three Bs concept) 14–15, 134
being (three Bs concept) 14–15, 134
  'being' in the community 151
  ways-of-being questions 14
beliefs 15–16, 20, 34–40, 141
  personal–professional belief systems 106
belonging (three Bs concept) 14–15, 39–40, 134
Belonging, Being & Becoming, The Early Years Learning Framework for Australia 53, 88, 121, 124, 143
  practice-principles 62
benchmarks, quality 21
best practice 21
'beyond' vision 158
beyond-the-fence 96, 104
  advocacy responsibilities 157
  beyond-the-fence communities, true advocacy in 148
  beyond-the-fence learning sessions 94
  policy within 111
  professional engagements 71
  settings, contexts surrounding 68–75
  workplaces 68–71
bioecological systems theory 60
'blanked-out' 128
body, the 90
  body language 44
brainstorming 152
branding 49
  see also naming
brokering 157

Bronfenbrenner's bioecological systems theory 60
Bronfenbrenner's nested circles or layers 4, 65, 67, 68, 76, 97
bullying 99
'bush' or 'beach' kindergartens 61
business (local) 73

care/caring 27, 158
  care vs education debate 58
  caring actions 26
  caring crossroads 135
  caring relationships 17
  caring with everyday routines, responsibility for 135
  duty of care 97, 99–100, 135
  eco-caring 2, 4–5, 16–17, 19–20, 24, 28, 101, 131, 135, 140, 151
  ethos/ethic of caring 16–17, 19–20, 158
Centre for the Study of Social Policy (CSSP)
  guiding principles for policy work 112, 113
  resources 113
Child Care Act 1972 (Cwlth) 69
child care centres 59
child-centred educational approach 138
childhood 26
  sociocultural-historic concepts of 128–9
children
  Aboriginal (agentic) family view of 150
  adult–child ratios 86
  agentic children 129
  best interests of 152
  child advocacy 159
  children's learning
    children's involvement 141
    educators' involvement 141
    family and community involvement 143
    involved parties 140

Index

responsibilities framing 134
responsibility for 137
children's memory 11
confident, capable and considerate 134
culturally and linguistically diverse 34
empowering 155
'empty' or 'erased' image of 128
as engaged citizens 128
'the innocent child' 150
managing 142
'marketised' 130
professional and social image 158
relationships with children policies and procedures 109
resilient children 129, 130
rights 34, 93, 159
   children's basic rights, honouring 98
safeguarding identity and privacy 46
sociocultural-historic concepts of 128–9
transition from ECE to school 72
well-being 137
Children's Services Regulations 2009 69
Circles of Change (CoC) 143
clarity 139
class 33
clustered talents 85
coaching 91
code of ethics 96, 153
co-learning 50
collaboration 84
   collaborative consumption 137
   collaborative partnerships 96, 151, 156
   collaborative professional learning 51
   leadership intertwining with collaborative approaches 123
colleagues 48
collective self 24
'common good' features 122, 130
Commonwealth of Australia 69–70

communication
   children's communication, supporting 31
   communication crossroads for leaders-managers 41
   communication rules 35
   communications-focused approach 93
   in different settings via 'languages' 32
   exploring 31–54
   interacting and relating 31
   misunderstandings 32
   oral and written communication 44
      images in 35
      metaphors in 35, 36–40
   with others, essential nature 31, 96
   professional communication 41–54
      with colleagues 48
      with parents 48
   relational communicating 93
   Respectful Communication Policy 41, 108
   sharing for meaning 32
communities, needs of 74
community
   'being' in the community 151
   beyond-the-fence communities, true advocacy in 148
   collaborative partnerships with 156
   community engagement framework 96
   community of practice 51, 94, 95, 106, 107
   involvement in children's learning 143
   multiple community languages 34
   networking and brokering with 157
   spiritual community 149
   women's involvement 58
Community Child Care Association 71
Community Child Care Co-operative 71
competence 19–20
   cultural competence 23, 96
   leading competence 27
   self, capable/competent view of 22

Index

complexity 139
computers 46
confidence 13, 134
confidentiality 99
connectivity 77
consumables 73
consumption 130
   collaborative consumption 137
Convention on the Rights of the Child (CRoC) (1989/1990) 98, 159
coordinators 90
core values 19–20
corporatisation 130
creativity 125
   working creatively 19
criss-crossing webs 139
crucial curricula 138
'culturally responsive ecology' conceptual framework 132
culture
   cultural competence 23, 96
   cultural diversity 23, 32, 34
   cultural East to West frames 26
   cultural identity, acknowledging 23
   cultural responsiveness 131
   culturally efficacious teachers 132
   culturally sensitive resources 23
   'culture' vs 'connectivity' 77
   of early childhood settings 37, 93
   evaluation capacity and culture 76
   grouping by 33
   kindling culture 154
   sociopolitical cultures, policy creation within 104
curriculum 123
   crucial curricula 138
   meaningful curricula 137
   theoretically based curricula models 127

de Bono's *Six Thinking Hats* 94
decision making 104
Declaration of the Rights of the Child (1959) 98
designated leader-managers *see* positional leader-managers
diaries 142
difference 35
dignity 152
direct control 27
directing 85
directors 90
   perceptions 90
dispositions 26–7, 93
   'dispositional silhouette' 26
diversity 58
   cultural and linguistic diversity 23, 32, 34
   diversity and equality guidelines 112–13
   of early childhood settings 32, 57–67
   of services 59
   understanding 131
'do no harm' principle 20, 94, 99–100, 122
   see also harm; 'precautionary' principle
documenting/documents 41
   reading 46
doing 14
   as political activism 158
double writing 45
'dressing' 12–13, 17–18
   're-dressing' and 18
duty of care 97, 99–100, 135

Early Childhood Australia (ECA) 72
   ECA Code of Ethics 41, 96, 136, 153
   Getting up to speed – Digital business kit for Early Childhood 73
   policy beyond-the-fence 111

Index

reconciliation action plan 111
Respect, Connect, Enact – A reconciliation action plan for Early Childhood Australia 2012–2016 23
Early Childhood Ecology Scale 132
Early Childhood Education (ECE)
  advocacy – real world of ECE 149
  Digital business kit 86
  ECE Educate site 112, 113
  historical roots 126
  reflections 112, 113, 149
early childhood education and care (ECEC) 57
Early Childhood Education for Sustainability (ECEfS) 64, 130
early childhood professionals *see* professionals
early childhood settings *see* settings
early learning centres 59–60
Early Years Learning Framework for Australia, The, 'three Bs' focus 14–15
Earth 5, 24, 147, 150, 151
eco-advocacy 151
eco-caring 2, 3, 4, 5, 16–17, 19–20, 24, 28, 101, 135, 140, 151
ecophilia 16–17
educare 58
education
  Australian States provision 69
  broader education links 72
  care vs education debate 58
  child-centred educational approach 138
  educational artefacts and incidents 139
  'marketised' 130
  psychology vs sociology 126
  reflection – *Reflections on teaching* 138

Education and Care Services National Law and Regulations 62, 86, 89
educators 89
  cultural responsiveness, agency and empowerment 132
  educational leaders 89
  everyday workplace rights of 97
  parents–educators partnership 96
  pedagogues 123
ego 22
8 Aboriginal Ways of Learning 14, 23, 95
e-interactive tools 47
electronic tools 46
embodiment 4, 14–15, 17, 18, 20, 34, 35, 36, 38, 44, 47, 50, 54, 58, 67, 92, 105, 127, 130, 140, 143, 148
  body language aspect 44
  embodied self 24
Emotional Competence Framework 19
emotions 13, 19–21, 76
  emotional intelligence 16–17, 20, 23
  leading advocacy, socioemotional ways of 148
empathic intelligence 19–20
empathy 19–20, 39
  empathic intelligence 19–20
empowerment 35, 65, 132, 155
  reflection – *Empowering relationships* 66
'empty' or 'erased' image 128
engagement 19–20, 72, 128
  advocacy engagement tasks 157
  community engagement framework 96
  engaging in consumption 130
  gentle engagement vs direct control 27
  as policy designer 111
  professional engagements 71
  with theoretical/professional frameworks 106
enthusiasm 19–20

Index

environment
  environmental and situational analysis 63
  Environmental Education in Early Childhood (Victoria) 72
  indoor and outdoor environments 140
  'third teacher' 140
equality 112
essentialising 33
ethics 16–17, 19–20, 158
  ethical advantage 150
  strong work ethic 93
ethnicity 33
ethos/ethic of caring 16–17, 19–20, 35, 158
evaluation
  evaluating (three-layer administrative process component) 85
  evaluation capacity and culture 76
  of interactions and relationships 33
expertise 19–20

facilities 86
Fairness Alerts Matrix 33, 132, 158
faith 19–20
familiarity 13–14
families
  collaborative partnerships with 156
  cultural safety for all 23
  culturally and linguistically diverse 23, 34
  family knowing, knowing families 32
  family newsletters, double writing in 45
  family practice 33
  in a global world 32
  involvement in children's learning 143
  meeting and greeting 33
  reflection – *A family workplace* 78
  sociocultural backgrounds 33
  support for 110
feelings 13, 20, 37, 76, 93
  thinking–feeling dynamic 19–20
  see also ambience

finances/financing 86, 137
followers 25
forest kindergartens 59–62
four Es 19–20
Four Rs framework 111
furnishings 61
  individualisation to reflect values/aims 63
  indoor/outdoor furnishings 63

Gandhi 52, 93, 146
Gardner's intelligence theory 94
gender 14–15, 26, 35, 50, 90
  enthusiasm and 20
  grouping by 33
  see also embodiment
global world 32
governing (long-term) policies 105
government
  Australian government funding types 59
  links (beyond-the-fence) 68–70
  changeability – political and economic reasons 104
  Commonwealth of Australia 69–70
  documents regarding reconciliation 23
  government accreditation systems 21
  government influence, words/phrases links with 34–40
  other governments and organisations 70
  policy 'normative angle' relation to systems 108
governmentality concept 113
grouping 33
groups
  leadership 'community of practice' groups 94, 95
  positive intergroup attitudes, allophilia and 17
guiding 142

Index

habits
　habits of mind 93, 94, 129
　unfair habits 33
hands-on play/learning 138
harassment 99
harm 20, 94, 99–100, 122
health and safety policies and procedures 97, 109
homogenising 33
human advocacy 151
Human Rights Day 153
humanistic love 158
humanity 31
humour, sense of 93

ideals 103
ideas
　policy designing process 103
　receiving ideas 41
identity
　identity tools 14–15
　　'*Your identity map*' [questionnaire] 14
　identity work
　　acknowledging cultural identity 23
　　identifying one's identity 22
　leader identity in terms of place 22
　personal identity 11–17
　professional identity 17–24
　　changeability notion 22
　protecting identity and privacy 46
　self-identity 52
imagery 39
image(s) 32, 35
　'empty' or 'erased' image 128
　professional and social image 158
incidents (educational) 139
inclusion 111
Indigenous Acknowledgement of Country 23

Indigenous peoples
　acknowledgement
　　of country 23
　　of cultural identity 23
　child and family resources 23
　individual 24
　focus on 12
infancy 31
　mother tongue 32
infantile amnesia 11
influence 67
insurance 86
integrity 93, 150
intelligence
　emotional intelligence 16–17, 20, 23
　empathic intelligence 19–20
　Gardner's theory of nine types of intelligence 94
interaction 141
　communication, interacting and relating 31
　e-interactive tools 47
　evaluating and monitoring 33
　human interaction 65, 77
　leadership intertwining with collaborative approaches 123
　leadership/leaders nature and 24
　of people within settings 65
　process with many 'Cs' 106
　relationships–interactions intertwining with settings 76
　respectful of sociocultural backgrounds 33
　sensitive interaction 25
　voices – vital interaction tools 148
internet research 46
interpersonal confidence 13

Index

journals 142
journey metaphors 2–7, 9, 17, 21, 24, 27–31, 35, 39, 46, 53–6, 60, 65, 83–4, 100, 102, 112, 114, 118, 132, 138, 144, 147, 149, 161, 162

kindergartens 59–60
  'bush' or 'beach' kindergartens 61
  forest kindergartens 59, 61, 62
kindling culture 154
knowing 14
knowledge 158
Knowledge Circle 95

labels 49–50
labour (division of) 25
Lady Gowrie Centres 71
landscapes 60
  influences on 60
language
  Aboriginal Dialect 154
  additional languages, acknowledging 32
  Australian Society for Indigenous Languages 34
  body language 44
  communications via 'languages' 32
  family newsletters, two languages in 45
  grouping by 33
  home language 155
  humanity, centrality to 31
  meta-cognition about workings of 155
  mother tongue 31, 32
  multiple community languages, resources and documents 34
  Standard English 154
laws 97
leadership
  action-oriented 25
  clusters of metaphors relating to styles 38
  complex and ever-changing nature 24–5
  cross-cultural leadership, use of metaphors within 39
  doing with organising 27
  leadership 'community of practice' groups 94
  'leadership for learning' (LfL) 94
  leadership intertwining with collaborative approaches 123
  likened to a form of fantasy 22
  nature-centred leadership stance 97
  practical theory of educative leadership framework 106
  of self and with others 22
  Western leadership 28
  Western vs Eastern leadership 28
leader-managers
  ability repertoires 85
  aspects 21
  communication crossroads 41
  educational leaders 89
  identity
    identifying 22
    relationships, freeing oneself within 22
    in terms of place 22
  leaders
    followers and 25
    leader shaping 26
  leadership likened to a form of fantasy 22
  'micro-landscape' leader-managers 65
  positional and situational leader-managers 20, 23, 26, 41, 46, 51–4, 84, 86, 90, 98, 103, 123
  sensitivity to others' values 106
  positioning as 'tall poppies' 148
  positions held and sociocultural context expectations 26
  professionalism, engagement in 148
  qualities – rights basis 152

Index

reading and writing via computers 46–7
'relational carers' vs 'virtue carers' 17
sensitive and relevant settings 72
support for 85
sustainability and 72
'troubling' 28
leading-managing
  action-oriented 25
  beyond-staffing responsibilities 92
  comfortable relationships 32
  complex and ever-changing nature 24–5
  crucial nature 123
  dispositions 26
    potential influences 26
  with habits of mind characteristics 94
  historical and customary appointments 90
  idealisation of 147
  leader-managers
    leader shaping/manager support 26
    responsibility parameters 34
  leading competence 27
  leading for learning, learning for leading 94
  leading with managing, definition 24
  leading-managing facets
    for pedagogy creators 121
    for policy designers 103
    for rights advocates 147
    for team stakeholders 84–92
  managing children 142
  reflection – *Leading and policies* 110–11
  relational work 25
  respectful 33
  styles 26–7
    potential influences 26
learning
  adult learning 51
  beyond-the-fence learning sessions 94
  children's involvement 141
  co-learning 50
  The Early Years Learning Framework for Australia 14–15
  educator's involvement 141
  8 Aboriginal Ways of Learning 14, 23
  family and community involvement 143
  hands-on play/learning 138
  'leadership for learning' (LfL) 94
  leading for learning, learning for leading 94
  learning programmes 155
  lifelong learning 48, 51
  professional learning 88
  responsibilities framing children's learning 134
  theoretical learnings 26
legal requirements (Australian) 86
legislation 97
lifelong learning 48, 51
see also narrative
linguistics
  linguistic descriptors 106
  linguistic diversity 32, 34
  'linguistic turn' ideas and models 77
listening 41
  diligent listening 44

machine technologies 49
macro-links 72
'marketised' 130
Maslow's Hierarchy of Needs 93
meaning
  making meaning 19–20
    adding clarity – metaphors 36
  meaningful curricula 137
  meaningful policy topics and themes 103

Index

meaning (cont.)
  personal meaning 50
  sharing for 32
  topophilia meanings 77
media
  mass media 130
  media sources 49
memory
  children's memory 11
  memory work 10–11
  reflection – *A moment of memories* 15–16
mentoring 50, 65, 91, 142
messages 32
  conveying messages 41–54
  medium is the message 49
  mixed messages 44
  sharing messages 41
  tone of 35
  see also communication
meta-cognition 155
metaphors 32, 36–40, 112
  clusters of metaphors
    regarding early childhood settings 37
    regarding preferred leadership styles 38
  cross-cultural leadership, use within 39
  'dance' metaphor for leadership 28
  forms of 35
  Images of Organization [book] 36
  journey metaphors 39
  metaphorical mirrors 18, 19
  of organisational life 36
  organisational metaphors 77
  reflection – *Metaphor use* 39
  storytelling, metaphors and poetry links 39, 52
  thinking, influence on 36
micro-links 71

mirrors (metaphorical) 18, 19, 50, 141
misconduct 99
misunderstandings 32
Model of Communication Accretion Spiral 96
monitoring
  interactions and relationships 33
  POM approach 26
Montessori, Maria 61
morality
  being moral 158
  essential workplace morality 150
  moral higher ground 21, 108, 150, 153, 158
    responsibilities linked with 152
  rights advocate role, vision and morality facets 149
mother tongue 31
  acknowledging 32
motivation 93

naming 49–50
  naming places 57
narrative
  personal narrative 48
  storylines 13
  value of 50
National Childcare Accreditation Council 69–70, 115
National Law (NL)/National Regulations 69, 86, 108, 110, 112, 113, 124
  children's basic rights, honouring 98
  'responsible persons' positions 89
National Quality Agenda 69
National Quality Framework 58, 69, 88, 110
  BBB, The Early Years Learning Framework for Australia 88

Index

National Quality Standard (NQS) 62, 86, 88, 108, 112, 113, 136
   collaborative partnerships with families/communities 156
   Guide to the National Quality Standard 53, 62, 87
   pedagogy definition 122
   policy requirements 105, 108
   QIAS, replacement of 70
   'Quality Areas' 86
   reflection – *Leading and policies* 110–11
needs 17
   of centres 73
   of communities 74
   of culturally and linguistically diverse families/children 34
   Maslow's Hierarchy of Needs 93
   see also motivation
negotiation 65
Nest, The [plan] 111
   operating 'commitment' principles 112
nested circles 65, 76
networking 157
New South Wales Early Childhood Environmental Education Network 72
New Zealand Ministry of Education 112, 113
Nurturing Early Learners (*NEL*) 124, 133

openness 93
operating (short-term) policies 105
operating (three-layer administrative process component) 85
organisations 70
   beyond-the-fence organisations 111–15
   communications-focused approach within 93
   descriptions of 36
   'embodied realism view' 77
   human interaction 77
   multiple organisational phenomena 76
   organisational climate 75
   organisational life, metaphors of 36
   organisational structure 76
   what constitutes an organisation 75
   organisational metaphors 77
   setting ambience 75
   workplaces as organisations 76
organising 85
POM approach 26
othering 33
others 96, 154
   faith in 19–20
   getting along with 65
   leadership with others 22
   liking others – allophilia 17
   understanding 52
   working with 19–20
out of school hours programs (OOSH) 69
outsiders 154

parents 96
   as everyday partners (with educators) 96
   professional communication with 48
   staff acceptance of 33
   as team stakeholders 96
participation 123
   levels 97
partnerships 151, 156
   parents–educators partnership 96
pedagogues 123, 124
   sensitive pedagogues 123

Index

pedagogy 154
  diversifying 155
  early contemporary ideas regarding 127
  ECE pedagogy 124
    dispositions within 129
  foundational premises for 125
  influences on 125
  language of 122
  meaning of 122
  pedagogical ECEfS features 64
  pedagogical philosophy, policy and 106
  pedagogical stances, words/phrases links with 34–40
  'pedagogy' definitions 121
  prompting with creativity 125
  viewing with 'understanding lenses' 125
pedagogy creators 121
  leading and managing facets 121
    knowing what ECE pedagogy encompasses 124
people
  collection of people – team 84
  contemplating workplaces 57–79
  exploring communication 31–54
  human features 26
  naming people 49–50
  people's positions 88–92
    position descriptions 89
  relational qualities/attributes 19–20
  self-discovery and 13–14
  within settings 65
    roles 65
  settings influence people; people influence settings 67
  team players 84
  thinkers and writers 126
  understanding self 10–28
personal beliefs 34–40

personal identity (self) 11–17, 24
  balancing self 11–12
  dressing oneself 12–13
  emotional intelligence 16–17
  exploring self 13–16
personal strengths 13
'personal/professional baggage' 137
philosophy
  collaborative philosophical statement 106
  pedagogical philosophy 106
  philosophical stances, understanding 126
  philosophy phrases 107
  policy basis 106
  reflection – *Personal philosophy* 133
  settings and 61
  whole setting philosophy 106
phrases 34–40
place(s) 86, 110
  contemplating workplaces 57–79
  exploring communication 31–54
  in-house rules regarding 99–100
  naming places 57
  self-discovery and 13–14
  sense of place 17
  site/place identification, names and 58
  sociopolitical places, policy creation within 104
  types of places 59–60
  understanding self 10–28
planning (three-layer administrative process component) 85
Planning, Organising and Monitoring (POM) approach 26
play 138
poetry 39, 52
policy
  appearance 115

Index

in-context, sensitive and meaningful topics/themes 103
creation 115
   within socio-political cultures and places 104
definitions 103
designing process 103
designing/reconsidering 108
   guidance 108
for early childhood settings 108
governing (long-term) policies 105
health and safety policies and procedures 109
linguistic descriptors 106
nature
   temporally bound 104
   value-laden 104
nomenclature 112
operating (short-term) policies 105
within organisations beyond-the-fence 111
philosophical basis 106
policies, reasons for need 108
policy making 85
policy portfolios 114
   commonality 108
   reflecting a unique belief approach 106
   relevant 105
purposes 105
recurring cycle of professional attention 116
relationships with children policies and procedures 109
Respectful Communication Policy 41, 108
reviewing for content relevance 115
service management policies and procedures 109
staffing policies and procedures 109
templates 115
themes, issues and variations 108
what a policy is and is not 103
writing policies 116
written structure 117
see also decision making
policy designers 103
   engagement – policy critiques 111
   leading-managing facets 103
policy work
   altering climate 104
   caring for and about 116
   community of practice formation 106, 107
   Europe – diversity and equity guidelines 112
   guiding principles (CSSP) 112, 113
   Keeping on Track folder 115
   'lead-plan-organise-monitor' tasks 116
   local and beyond-the-fence policy work 104, 111
   reasons for conducting 105
   taking responsibility for 116
politics
   political activism, 'doing' as 158
   political ideas, words/phrases links with 34–40
   political self 24
   sociopolitical cultures 104
portfolios 142
positional leader-managers 20, 23, 26, 84, 90, 103, 106, 123
   challenges 98
   communication and 41
   foundational practices 86
   reading and 46
   storytelling 51
positions
   educators 89

Index

positions (cont.)
  position descriptions 89
    review 89
  'responsible persons' positions 89
power 35, 39
  power relationships 35
  words, power and complexity of 34–40
practical theory of educative leadership model 106
practice(s)
  community of practice 51, 94, 95, 106, 107
  ECEfS daily practices 64
  everyday practice 103
  foundational practices 86
  NQR guidance 110
  operating policies covering everyday procedural practice 105
  reflective practice 52
  as roles 84–100, 103, 121, 147–61
'precautionary' principle 20, 46, 99–100, 112, 113, 122
  see also 'do no harm' principle; harm
preschools 59–60
principles
  basic values and principles 20, 112, 113
  'do no harm' principle 20
  Nests' operating 'commitment' principles 112
  from professional affiliations 108
privacy 99
  protecting identity and privacy 46
private self 11–12, 24
  dressing to represent 12–13
privatisation 130
privilege/privileging 33, 39–40, 152
professional communication 41–54

contents 47–50
  beyond the early childhood setting 48
  within an early childhood setting 47–8
  naming people 49–50
  selling the setting 49
forms of 41
professional storytelling and story writing 50
professional guidance (double view) 62
professional identity (self) 17–24
  clothing the professional 12–13, 17–18
  'dispositional silhouette' 26
  identity work 22
  inventing/crafting with less ego 22
  multi-lens approach 22
  values and beliefs aspect 20
  working life 19–20
professionalism 150
professionals
  attributes, skills, knowledge and dispositions 22
  change, futures and advocating 153
  clothing the professional 12–13, 17–18
  exchangeable and overlapping roles 27
  focus 27
  key historic professionals influencing ECE 126
  non-career-staging, levels of 27
  personal qualities, habits of mind, attributes 26
  professional actions, policy purpose and 105
  professional and social image 158
  professional disposition 26
  professional identity 17–24
  role-relationships angle 65
  supporting children's communication 31

Index

Project Head Start 127
psychology 126
public self 24

Quality Improvement and Accreditation System (QIAS) 69–70
Quality Improvement Plan 62, 124
Queensland Early Childhood Sustainability Network 72
questionnaires/questions 14
    ways-of-being/valuing questions 14

reading 46
    via computers 46
reciprocity 28, 111
reconciliation 23, 111
Reflect, Respect, Relate framework 136
reflection
    professional reflection 52
    reflective practice 52
Reggio Emilia 61
reinvention 18
relating
    communication, interacting and relating 31, 93
    leadership/leaders nature and 24
    relational work 25
    relational communicating 93
    relational qualities/attributes 19–20
    'wise' relational, expert knowledge 21
relationships
    building 73, 110
    caring relationships 17
    centrality of respect and dignity within 152
    empowering 66
    evaluating and monitoring 33
    freeing oneself within 22
    importance of 53

policy contributors, authentic relationships among 103
power relationships 35
relationship management 23
relationships with children policies and procedures 109
relationships–interactions intertwining with settings 76
role-relationships angle 65
relevance 28, 111
'remote controlling' 130
research 46
resilience 129
resources 61, 112, 113
    culturally sensitive resources 23
    individualisation to reflect values/aims 63
    relevant resources 63
    resourcing 72
    responsive resources 132
    service diversity, resources outlining 59
respect 23, 28, 93, 111, 150, 158
    centrality within relationships 152
    for families' sociocultural backgrounds 33
    Respectful Communication Policy 41, 108
    respectful recognition (of cultural identity) 23
Respectful Communication Policy 41, 108
responsibility 28, 34, 98, 111, 158
    beyond-the-fence advocacy responsibilities 157
    for caring with everyday routines 135–7
    key staffing responsibilities 92
    responsibilities framing children's learning 134
    'responsible persons' positions 89
    taking responsibility for policy work 116

Index

rights 98
  everyday workplace rights of educators 97
  of families/children 34, 93, 98
  human rights 97, 153
  policy portfolios and 106
  rights advocacy 23
  rights with advocacy 147
  staff sharing, fit into 97
  UN *CRoC* 159
rights advocates 147
  'first thing' view of 147
  'last thing' view of 148
  responsibilities 153
  role – leading and managing facets 147
  views 147
risk management 97
role-modelling 51
roles
  of people within settings 65
  practices as 84–100, 103, 121, 147
  professional roles 27, 84–100, 103, 121, 147
  role positions 88–92
    position descriptions 89
  role-relationships angle 65
  roles with actions 84
  women's roles, normative sociocultural impression of 58
room-labels 49–50
'ropes and knots' metaphor 39
  privileged viewpoint? 39–40
  'small stuff' and 39
routines 135
  whole-setting routines 137

Rudolf Steiner/Waldorf 61
rules 106, 152
  communication rules 35
  staff sharing, fit into 99–100

safeguarding 46
safety 23
self
  balancing, private and social selves 11–13
  capable/competent view 22
  leadership of 22
  multiple selves 24
  re-identification of (in advocacy terms) 152
  reinvention 18
  self-discovery 13–14
  self-exploration 13–16
    time/timing features 13
  self-knowledge 18
    relevance 10–11
  self–service interplay 93
  understanding 10–28, 52
    dressing oneself 12–13
    leading with managing 24
    personal identity 11–17
    professional identity 17–24
  writing style, 'placing self' in terms of 17, 44
sensemaking 27
sensitivity 23, 25, 72
  leader-managers' sensitivity to others' values 106
  sensitive pedagogues 123
  sensitive policy topics and themes 103
servant characteristics 26
service
  diversity, resources outlining 59

Index

NQR guidance for quality 110
reflection – *Looking outside the service & building relationships* 73
self–service interplay 93
service management policies and procedures 109
types of early childhood education services 59–60
settings 72, 154
  advocacy responsibilities within 155
  beyond-the-fence contexts surrounding 68–75
  diversity of 57–67
    cultural and linguistic diversity of 32
    naming places 57
    types of places 59–60
  division of labour; division of authority 25
  early childhood settings
    beyond 48
    clusters of metaphors regarding 37
    design of 61
    different kinds 60
    policy for 108
  furnishings and resources 61
  in-house rules – spaces and places 99–100
  interpersonal climate/cultural feeling 93
  metaphor clusters regarding 37
  people within 65
    influences and interaction 67
    roles 65
  philosophies and 61
  professional communication in 47
  professional foundations 20
    due to relevant policy portfolios 105
  reality, meeting and greeting families 33
  relationships–interactions intertwining with settings 76
  relevant resources 63
  selling the setting 49
    branding 49
  setting ambience 75
  settings as landscapes 60
  setting's guidelines (beyond Australia) 62
  settings influence people; people influence settings 67
  sites for early childhood education 57
  slowing down pace of 31
  whole settings
    governing policies covering 105
    philosophy, policy and 106
    philosophy, requirement 106
  whole-setting routines 137
  words/phrases links 34–40
sexuality 33
sharing
  for meaning 32
  sharing cultural identity 23
  sharing self-stories 13–14
silencing 33
simultaneities 123
situational leader-managers 20, 23, 26, 90, 103, 106, 123
  communication and 41
  reading and 46
  storytelling 51
situational leadership theories 91
Six Thinking Hats 94
slowing down (everyday life) 31
'small stuff' 39
SNAICC 23
social awareness 23
social inclusion 111
social justice 130
  understanding 131
social self 11–12, 24
  dressing to represent 12–13

Index

socioconstructive theory 51
sociocultural backgrounds 33
sociology 126
spaces 74, 86
  in-house rules regarding 99–100
spirituality 149
  kin group spirituality 150
  self-direction of spiritual journey 149
staff
  acceptance of parents 33
  Australian legal requirements 86
  collection of staff – team 84
  directors and coordinators 90
  educators 89
  foundational practices 86
  key staffing responsibilities – team stakeholders 92
    beyond-staffing responsibilities 92
    parents and others 96
    supporting staff 93
  multiple staffing actions 85
  professional and social image 158
  staff sharing 97–100
  staffing information 89
  staffing issues
    advocacy and 156
    reflection – *Roles and beyond* 87
  staffing policies and procedures 109
staging 27
stakeholders
  meaning 84
  team member = stakeholder? 84
  team stakeholders *see* team stakeholders
Standard English 154
standardisation (failure of) 154
standards 21
stimulus questionnaires 14
stories/storylines 13, 22
  sharing stories 13–14
  story writing 50–1

storytelling 4, 48
  metaphors and poetry links 39, 52
  professional storytelling 50
    kinds 51
    uses 51
strengths 13
  strengths approach 94
struggles 106
  staff sharing, fit into 98
'stuff' [term] 39–40
supervising 85, 142
sustainability 4, 15, 36, 38, 47, 52, 54, 60, 64, 67, 72, 73, 96, 114–15, 122, 124, 131, 133, 136, 139, 140, 161
  action competence for 19–20
  Early Childhood Education for Sustainability 64, 130
  ecophilia 16–17

'tabula rasa' 128
talking 41, 44
  oral communication, metaphors in 35
  talking circles 95
  talking out loud 34
Te Kohanga Reo 61
Te Whāriki curriculum guide 124
team stakeholders 84–100
  key staffing responsibilities 92
  leading and managing facets 84–92
  parents as 96
  people's positions 88–92
  roles
    creation, reformation and display 90
    roles with actions 84
  staff sharing and workplace give-and-take 97–100
  team and stakeholder 84
teams/teamwork 88
  comfortable relationships among 32
  growth and change over time 84

Index

meaning 84
reflection – *Being a team* 90
team member = stakeholder? 84
theoretically based curricula models 127
theoretical/professional frameworks 106
thinking 40
  metaphors, influence of 36
  people and places 10–28, 31–54, 57–79
  philosophical thinking 106
    philosophy phrases 107
  practices as roles 84–100, 103, 121, 147
  Six Thinking Hats 94
  thinkers and writers 126
  thinking tool – Fairness Alerts Matrix 33, 158
  thinking–feeling dynamic 19–20
  understanding self 10–28
'third teachers' 140
three Bs concepts 14–15
three-layer administrative process 85
time-related self-exploration 13
tone 49, 93
  official/informal 35
top-down management style 149
transformation 27, 39
  of ideas and society 103
transparency 58, 62
'troubling' 28
trust 16–17, 19–20, 39, 93

understanding 21
  children as engaged citizens 128
  diversity and social justice 131
  essence of 133
  philosophical stances 126
  professional understandings 36
  self 10–28
  'understanding lenses', viewing pedagogy with 125–33

union worker agreements 97
United Nations (UN) 70
Universal Declaration of Human Rights 97, 153

values 15–16, 20, 108
  basic values and principles 20
  best practice values and actions 21
  core values 19–20
  development 21
  narrative, value of 50
  policy background and 106
  policy designing process 103
valuing 14, 21
  ways-of-valuing questions 14
Victorian Children's Services Act 1996 69
vision 27, 93, 153
  'beyond' vision 158
  professional vision 159
    responsibilities linked to 152
  rights advocate role, vision and morality facets 149
  visionary/re-visioning lens 143
  visioning 156
voice 66, 148

well-being 46, 137
wisdom 94
  'wise' relational, expert knowledge 21
women, impressions of community/home roles 58
words
  as form of advocacy 148
  hows and whys of 34–40
  power and complexity of 34–40
  sharing for meaning 32
  What's Their Story?: A history of Australian words [book] 34
  wise words 32
workforce lifecycle 85

Index

workplaces
　ambiguity in 27
　beyond-the-fence 68–71
　　Australian government links 68–70
　　other governments and organisations 70
　conceptual model of workplace settings 76
　contemplating 57–79
　essential workplace morality 150
　everyday workplace rights 97
　give-and-take, rights, struggles and rules 97–100
　health and safety laws 97
　leading-managing, influence on 25
　meaningful workplaces 93
　as organisations 76
　reflection – *A family workplace* 78
　workplace-body 148

work/working life 19–20
　divisions of labour and authority 25
　Earth, working for 24
　identity work 22
　strong work ethic 93
　working creatively 19
writing 4, 5, 17, 44
　'Dear Nadine' letters 6, 44
　double writing 45
　egalitarian nature 51
　metaphors in 35
　'scripto continua' 117
　thinkers and writers 54, 55, 126
　typical professional writing patterns 45
　via computers 46
　writing style, 'placing self' in terms of 44
　'writing with your ears' 34